THE HABIT CHANGE WORKBOOK

How to Break Bad Habits and Form Good Ones

James Claiborn, Ph.D., ABPP • Cherry Pedrick, R.N.

NEW HARBINGER PUBLICATIONS, INC.

Distributed in the U.S.A. by Publishers Group West; in Canada by Raincoast Books; in Great Britain by Airlift Book Company, Ltd.; in South Africa by Real Books, Ltd.; in Australia by Boobook; and in New Zealand by Tandem Press.

Copyright © 2001 by James Claiborn and Cherry Pedrick
New Harbinger Publications, Inc.
5674 Shattuck Avenue
Oakland, CA 94609

Cover design by Poulson/Gluck Designs
Edited by Karen O'Donnell Stein

Library of Congress Catalog Card Number: 01-132293
ISBN 1-57224-263-9 Paperback

Printed in the United States of America

New Harbinger Publications' Web site address: www.newharbinger.com

03   02   01

10   9   8   7   6   5   4   3   2   1

First printing

The Habit Change Workbook *is dedicated to everyone who is trying to change a problem habit and to the researchers who are increasing our knowledge about habit change.*

Contents

Acknowledgments   ix

Introduction   1
From the Authors 🦋 How This Book Can Help You

Part I
Habits: We All Have Them

1 *Good Habits, Bad Habits*   5
Thinking Habits 🦋 Good, Bad, or Indifferent—How Can We Tell? 🦋 You Are Not
Alone 🦋 Your Story

2 *How Habits Develop*   13
Habit Formation 🦋 Habits Serve a Purpose 🦋 The Role of Reinforcement 🦋 Habits
Can Be Changed

3 *What's Stopping You?*   18
Reasons for Not Changing Now 🦋 What Are Your Reasons for Not Changing Now?

4 *Common Problem Habits*   23
Specific Habits 🦋 More Than Just a Habit

Part II
The Habit Change Program

5 *Assessing Your Habit*   29
Behavioral Momentum 🦋 An Operational Definition of Your Habit 🦋 Triggers 🦋
Consequences 🦋 Record Keeping

6 *Getting Ready to Change*   **43**
Stages of Change 🦋 Change Is a Process 🦋 Where Are You in the Stages of 🦋
Change? 🦋 But I've Tried to Change Before! 🦋 Are You Ready to Change?

7 *Taking the First Steps*   **55**
How Effective Is Habit Reversal? 🦋 Habit Awareness

8 *Relaxation*   **67**
How Does Relaxation Help? 🦋 Relaxation Methods

9 *Changing the Way You Think*   **72**
Cognitive Therapy for Habits 🦋 Questioning Automatic Thoughts

10 *More about Changing Thoughts*   **84**
Facilitating Thoughts 🦋 Thought Distortion 🦋 Harmful Beliefs That Shape Our
Automatic Thoughts

11 *Developing Good Habits*   **97**
Do You Want to Change? 🦋 Record Keeping 🦋 Tips for Developing Habits

12 *Maintaining Your Gains*   **106**
Relapse Prevention 🦋 Absolute Ave. or Habit Change Way?

Part III
Detailed Guidance on Specific Habits

13 *Nervous Habits, Trichotillomania, Skin Picking, and Nail Biting*   **121**
Nervous Habits 🦋 Trichotillomania 🦋 Skin Picking 🦋 Nail Biting 🦋 Your Habit
Change Plan for Nervous Habits, Trichotillomania, Skin Picking, and Nail Biting 🦋
Tips for Changing Nervous Habits 🦋 Tips for Skin Picking and Trichotillomania 🦋
Developing Your Habit Change Plan

14 *Sleeping Habits*   **141**
Causes of Sleep Disturbances 🦋 Personal and Social Consequences 🦋 Treatment
Options 🦋 The Habit Change Plan for Insomnia 🦋 Nightmares

15 *Health and Fitness Habits*   **158**
Our Favorite Bad Health and Fitness Habits 🦋 Your Health and Fitness Plan 🦋
Developing Your Health and Fitness Plan

16 *Relationship Habits*   **172**
Your Relationship Habit Change Plan 🦋 Competing Response Practice 🦋 Rewards

17 *Excessive Spending and Shopping*   **181**
Your Spending Reduction Plan 🦋 Developing Your Spending Reduction Plan 🦋
Shopping and Spending Tips 🦋 More Help

18 *Excessive Leisure Activities*   **195**
What Are You Looking For? ✾ Your Balanced Leisure Activity Plan ✾ Negative Consequences ✾ Developing Your Balanced Leisure Activity Plan ✾ Tips for Balancing Your Leisure Activities

19 *Problem Gambling*   **209**
You're Not Alone ✾ Treatment Options ✾ The Habit Change Plan for Gambling ✾ Faulty Beliefs about Gambling ✾ Changing Faulty Beliefs about Gambling ✾ Developing Your Gambling Cessation Plan

Part IV
Further Help

20 *Family and Group Habit Change*   **229**
The Group Habit Change Program ✾ Children ✾ How Family Members Can Help ✾ What if Your Loved One Doesn't Want to Change?

Resources   **236**
Helpful Books about Change ✾ Organizations of Interest

References   **241**

Acknowledgments

This book and my day-to-day work and life would be impossible without the love and support of my wife, Carolyn. She has put up with all my habits and reluctance to change for more than thirty years. I also need to thank all of those who have taught me about helping people, most especially my patients, as they have taught me the most, and Cherry Pedrick, my coauthor and collaborator, who suggested we write the book and helped me make it happen.

—James M. Claiborn, Ph.D., ABPP

I am grateful to my husband, Jim, and my son, James, for their support and encouragement throughout the process of writing *The Habit Change Workbook*. I thank my aunts, Jeannette DeBel, Sally Shull, and the late Margaret Smith, for teaching me the importance of maintaining good habits that lead to long, healthy lives. Most of all, I thank my God for making it all possible.

—Cherry Pedrick, R.N.

We would both like to thank our excellent editor, Karen O'Donnell Stein, who helped us make the principles of habit change easier to follow, Pat Fanning for encouraging us to pursue this project from the beginning, Lori Poulson for the distinctive and inviting cover design, and all the others at New Harbinger Publications who made this book a reality.

Introduction

What we call the beginning is often the end. And to make an end is to make a beginning. The end is where we start from.

—T. S. Eliot

Habit is habit and not to be flung out of the window by any man, but coaxed downstairs a step at a time.

—Mark Twain

Are your negative habits taking over your life? Have you tried and failed, again and again, to lose weight? Do you struggle with nail biting, skin picking, or perhaps hair pulling? Are poor sleep habits interfering with your sleep? Is gambling ruling your life? Are such habits as tardiness, procrastination, or dishonesty interfering with your relationships? Do you spend hours surfing the Internet, watching TV, playing video games, or shopping? If these habits cause problems in your life, this book is for you! We will provide you the skills necessary for making lifetime habit changes.

From the Authors

James Claiborn, Ph.D., ABPP

I am a psychologist who is interested in how people can change their behavior. When others in school were fascinated by Freud, I was reading about Skinner and behavior modification. I have always been interested in behavioral and cognitive methods for changing behavior. In part, my fascination stems from the fact that these methods are both simple and effective. I earned a Ph.D. in Counseling Psychology in 1978 and have been in practice ever since. Over the years I have treated people with all kinds of problems. Many had habits that were destructive. This book is designed to bring what I have learned in my practice to people who wish to change their negative habits.

Cherry Pedrick, R.N.

When Dr. Claiborn and I first decided to write *The Habit Change Workbook*, my husband said, "I think you're very qualified to write this book. You've had plenty of habits." Did I feel encouraged? Yes! Complimented? No! But in many ways my husband was right. Perhaps more than most people, I am a "creature of habit." I think my habits give my life continuity and security. Some of my habits are helpful, and most are inconsequential—they serve no real purpose, but they aren't harmful. However, I have had habits that interfered with my life. They limited my potential and kept me from achieving my goals. So, for me, coauthoring *The Habit Change Workbook* has been a fulfilling adventure. As a result of working on this project, I am better equipped to tackle those pesky habits and develop more beneficial and rewarding ones.

After twenty years of working as a registered nurse, I made a career change. In 1995, I took up pen and paper, mouse and keyboard, and pursued a writing career. I wrote several articles, and then I teamed up with Bruce M. Hyman, Ph.D., to coauthor *The OCD Workbook*, which was published by New Harbinger Publications in 1999. In addition to my being a "creature of habit," my nursing background has helped me contribute to *The Habit Change Workbook*. It is my hope that my personal experience and health knowledge will help others struggling to change unwanted habits.

How This Book Can Help You

The Habit Change Workbook is not intended as a substitute for medical, psychiatric, or psychological treatment or advice by a qualified health professional. It is intended to help people who would like to change the following types of habits or disorders:

- Nervous habits such as skin picking and nail biting, and disorders such as trichotillomania (hair pulling)

- Habits that lead to sleeping problems, such as insomnia and nightmares

- Habits that can adversely affect health and fitness, such as not exercising enough, eating an unbalanced diet, and avoiding going to the doctor or getting recommended screening tests

- Habits that can adversely affect relationships, such as lying, procrastinating, engaging in perfectionism, interrupting, using profanity, and being tardy

- Excessive leisure activities, such as Internet use, television watching, and video-game playing

- Excessive shopping and spending

- Problem gambling

The Habit Change Workbook is divided into four parts. Part I will help you understand how habits are formed and it will help you begin assessment of the habits in your life.* Part II is the core of the book. We will give you step-by-step instructions to guide you through the Habit Change Program. Throughout the book, but especially in these chapters, you will be asked to answer questions and complete charts. Each step builds on the previous step.

---

* **A Word about Addictions**
    Chapter 4 addresses addiction. The treatment of addictions goes beyond the scope of this book, although *The Habit Change Workbook* can have an important place in an overall treatment plan. If you are addicted to or dependent on alcohol, nicotine, or other chemical substances, the principles here can serve as tools to help you escape your addiction.

Information gathered in the first chapters will be used in subsequent chapters, so be prepared to put pen or pencil to paper and work the program from start to finish. Escaping bothersome habits will be your reward.

Part III provides detailed instructions for eliminating specific habits. You will learn powerful strategies for dealing with a wide range of troublesome habits. Part IV will help you reach out to others as you struggle with changing your habits. Family and friends can play important roles in the process of change. A support group may help you get rid of harmful habits by providing education and helping you feel less alone in your struggle. Finally, we introduce you to resources that can assist you as you work to change your habit.

Your participation in *The Habit Change Workbook* is essential to your success. Forms and charts will help you collect information and understand your habit. You will also see Habit Change Strategies like the one below. These are helpful tips that you can copy and tape on your refrigerator door, keep in your car or purse, or place by your favorite chair. They will remind you of key points of *The Habit Change Workbook* and help you stay focused on your goals.

ꭥꙨ Habit Change Strategy

Fill out the charts and forms you find in *The Habit Change Workbook*. Completing them will be an important part of your habit change program.

We see habit change as a journey. The first step is discovering the habit you want to change. Then you'll learn habit change principles and develop your own plans for change. Turn the page now and begin your habit change journey.

Part I

Habits:
We All Have Them

1

Good Habits, Bad Habits

Vices are sometimes only virtues carried to excess.

—Charles Dickens

Our doubts are traitors, and make us lose the good we oft might win by fearing to attempt.

—William Shakespeare

Let's begin by agreeing on what we mean by a "habit." The term "habit" refers to a broad range of behaviors. *Webster's New World Dictionary* (1991) defines a habit as "a) a thing done often and hence, usually, done easily; practice; custom; b) pattern of action that is acquired and has become so automatic that it is difficult to break."

Isn't it interesting that *Webster's* defines a habit as a pattern of action that is difficult to break? From this definition we can see that habits, no matter what kind, are:

- done often

- acquired

- done automatically

- difficult to break

Thinking Habits

When we think of our habits, our habitual behaviors are what usually come to mind. But we also have habits in our heads, in our minds. When we do routine tasks, we engage in habits. When we think, we are also engaging in habits. If we had to consciously think about each step in our everyday tasks, we would end up being horribly slowed down and inefficient. So we develop automatic thoughts—thinking habits—that help us handle most situations reasonably well.

But what happens when our thinking habits get in the way of our achieving our goals and functioning well? Automatic thoughts can become bad habits just as overt behaviors can become bad habits. The Habit Change Program will help you understand your automatic thoughts and help you change some of your thinking habits.

You will probably find that automatic thoughts contribute to some of your problem behaviors. Take sleeping problems—in chapter 14 you will be examining what you *do* when you go to bed and what you *do* when you can't fall asleep. You will also be looking at how you *think* about sleep and sleep problems. You may discover that your automatic thoughts are interfering with your efforts to get a good night's sleep. Throughout this book you will be asked to consider your thinking patterns as they relate to your habits. As you do this, you will learn to gain more control of your problem habits.

✿ Habit Change Strategy

Begin to listen to your automatic thoughts. Do they interfere with your efforts to change your habits?

Good, Bad, or Indifferent—How Can We Tell?

We all talk about good and bad habits, but do we really know which is which? That may sound like a silly question, but consider a daily activity like brushing your teeth. Your first reaction might be to say, "Everyone knows that's a good habit." In most cases it is a good habit, but there are times when it is not. Carl's dentist told him he was damaging his teeth by overbrushing them. He had learned to brush his teeth when he was a child. Wanting to keep them in good condition until old age, he brushed his teeth for fifteen minutes after every meal; he was also brushing too hard. Carl's dentist taught him the right way to brush his teeth. It took some time, but he changed his toothbrushing habits.

Most habits have both good and bad aspects. Think of these as advantages and disadvantages. *The Habit Change Workbook* will help you decide which habits you want to change. To help you determine if a habit is good, bad, or indifferent, you will be asked to list the advantages and disadvantages of the habit. Once you've determined which of your behaviors are bad habits that need to be changed, you will identify good habits you want to develop. Again, you will list the advantages and disadvantages of the habits you want to develop.

You may decide that some of your "bad" habits are not so bad after all and you'd just as soon keep them. Or, like Carl, you may decide that your bad habits just need to be tweaked a bit to make them good ones. The resulting good habit will be your natural reward for changing your bad habit.

✿ Habit Change Strategy

Don't say good-bye to your habit yet. You might just decide to keep it!

You Are Not Alone

It helps to know that we aren't alone in our struggle to change our habits. We all have repetitive behaviors and thoughts that could be classified as habits, and we all have at least one aspect of our behavior we'd like to change. Some are good habits and some are bad. Now we would like to introduce you to a few people with bad habits. Some of these people may seem quite familiar to you, or you may observe similarities between yourself and one or more of the people described, but (except for Cherry Pedrick) they are actually composites of many people with similar habits. As you work through *The Habit Change Workbook*, you will meet these people again.

Cherry's Story

I was thin until I went to college. I wasn't as active in college as I had been previously, and my diet was more erratic, so I put on a few pounds. After college, I got married and had a child. Over the years, I added a couple of pounds each year. I was able to lose twenty pounds about fifteen years ago, but gradually the weight came back. I gained another thirty pounds, partly as a result of medication side effects. I can't place all the blame on my medicine, though. I think age, apathy, and lack of activity are to blame too. I tried walking, but I got out of the habit in the summer and winter months, when it's too hot or too cold. Sometimes I have a headache or I just don't feel like walking.

It would be nice to lose some weight, but my main goal has been to eat right and exercise. I feel better when I am eating healthy foods and getting adequate exercise, but it's hard to keep healthy habits going.

Carl's Story

You've already met Carl. A perfectionist, he wanted to brush his teeth thoroughly, but he was so thorough in his brushing that he developed a habit of overbrushing his teeth. Carl also had a habit of biting his nails. He wanted all of his nails to be perfectly smooth and even. When he was bored or nervous, his nails would bother him even more. Often, he would find his fingers in his mouth without even knowing how they had gotten there.

Margie's Story

Rough skin and blemishes bothered Margie. When she developed acne as a teenager, skin picking became a problem for her. She couldn't "just leave pimples alone," as her mother would often tell her. Margie spent quite a bit of time, sometimes hours, examining her face in the bathroom mirror and picking at blemishes. When she went out, Margie would wear heavy makeup to cover the effects of her picking. Margie also picked at scabs and scratches on her arms. She felt she couldn't tolerate rough skin. It had to be smoothed out. The scars and discolored areas embarrassed her, so she often wore long sleeves.

Betty's Story

Shopping was Betty's favorite activity. Shopping took her mind off her problems, reducing her anxiety. She also shopped when she was bored or had something to celebrate, and of course she liked to shop for gifts. Betty showed her love by giving gifts. When she shopped for gifts, though, she often found things for herself and for her home too. She especially enjoyed a big sale. When she found a bargain, she'd often buy two, three, or more of an item. Sometimes she paid with cash, but more and more often Betty used credit cards, making it difficult for her to pay the credit card bills each month.

Barbara's Story

Barbara had trouble getting out of bed on time. On the weekends she went to bed late and got up late. During the week she tried to go to bed early, but she tossed and turned.

Barbara was still tired in the morning. After pressing the snooze button several times, she would get up and rush to get ready for work. "I'm a night person," she often said. But her boss would reply that this was no excuse. Barbara didn't want to lose yet another job because of oversleeping. Barbara also had a problem with procrastination and tardiness. She tended to put things off until the last minute. Her work suffered as a result of these habits.

Larry's Story

Larry's problem stemmed from the way he dealt with his terrifying nightmares. Larry would get to bed on time, but he woke up feeling exhausted and stressed many mornings. He had vivid nightmares, which he often remembered the next day. Larry frequently woke up in the night, his heart pounding and feelings of terror jolting through his body. He would sleep fitfully the rest of the night, when he was able to get back to sleep. Sometimes he stayed up until morning. Often, these dreams concerned a traumatic assault he had experienced many years before.

Matthew's Story

Matthew wanted to work on his habit of interrupting people. Social situations made him nervous. He worried that he would dominate the conversation and interrupt people—and he often did both. This habit of interrupting hadn't been a problem for him when he was growing up, because his entire family talked over one another. Interrupting was the rule, rather than the exception. But it became a problem when he entered the workforce. He discovered that interrupting and talking while someone else is speaking are not socially acceptable.

Jeff's Story

Busy and single, Jeff felt that he didn't have time to prepare balanced meals. He grabbed fast food on the way to and from work. He kept snacks in his desk drawer "in case I don't have time for lunch." His kitchen was stocked with sodas, cookies, and chips. Jeff was overweight. His doctor told him to lower his intake of fat because his cholesterol was high. The doctor also gave him a diet plan, but Jeff hadn't been successful in following it. Jeff also had trouble sleeping. He would lie awake in bed for hours before falling asleep. Sometimes he read in bed until early morning.

Amanda's Story

Amanda rarely went out without a hat. When she did go without a hat, her hair always looked perfect. That's because she would wear a wig when she went out in public. Amanda has a disorder called *trichotillomania*. It began when she was about twelve. She described a feeling of tightness or tenseness on her scalp. It seemed to be caused by a particular hair. She would find the hair and pull it, but it never stopped there. More hairs had to be pulled. Sometimes she could pull a few hairs and get relief. Other times, she spent hours searching for the right hair, and then she would position her fingers tightly around it and pull. As a result of her hair pulling, Amanda's hair was patchy and noticeably thinner than it had been when she was a child. She felt embarrassed about her disorder but didn't know how to stop.

Lucy's Story

"It's simply a way to relax. It's my entertainment." This was Lucy's usual response when her sister tried to talk to her about her video-poker and bingo playing. Lucy had started out playing bingo about once a month. She enjoyed the rush she felt when she could yell, "Bingo!" and collect her prize. Then she discovered video poker. As with bingo, she played for entertainment, relaxation, and time away from her worries. Soon bingo and video poker were taking up most of her time when she wasn't working. Bills began mounting, and she found that her gambling was resulting in anxiety rather than peace and relaxation.

Fred's Story

Gambling was a problem for Fred, too. He loved to play cards with his friends. Sometimes he won and sometimes he lost. As time progressed, he lost more often than he won. Fred was also a sports fan. Baseball, basketball, football—he watched them all. He placed bets several times a week. "Sports betting is a game of skill," he would say. When he won, he felt encouraged to bet even larger amounts. Losing was disappointing, but the excitement of winning made up for it.

Just as it did with Lucy, gambling took its toll on Fred's life. His wife and children wondered who would come home each night—the happy, excited Fred or the depressed, angry Fred. He spent their savings on gambling debts, putting the family's financial stability in jeopardy. Fred faced losing his home, his car, and his family.

George's Story

Computers were an important part of George's life. He used a computer for word processing at work, paid his personal bills using software on his home computer, and enjoyed playing computer games. Then he discovered the Internet. He found that for a small price he could play his favorite computer games with other enthusiasts. He even got to know some of the people behind the screen names and conversed via e-mail. George also enjoyed "surfing the Net." There was a vast world of information to be explored. He could spend hours clicking from one Web site to another. He visited message boards and chat rooms and joined e-mail lists.

George realized he had a problem with Internet use when he lost his job. His boss warned him that his Internet use was excessive and interfering with his duties, but George felt that he couldn't stop. George also lost contact with most of his local friends and withdrew from his family. The Internet had become his life.

Your Story

What about you? Complete the Habitual Behaviors and Thoughts questionnaire, below. This will help you begin to see how your habits are affecting your life.

🦋 Habit Change Strategy

Answer all of the questions below as completely and honestly as possible. Your success depends on it.

Habitual Behaviors and Thoughts

Do any of your behaviors or thoughts interfere with your family and/or social life?
Describe the effects.

_____

_____

_____

Do any of your behaviors or thoughts interfere with your ability to do your job?
Describe the effects.

_____

_____

_____

Would you be happier without some of your habitual behaviors or thoughts? In what
way?

_____

_____

_____

Describe how your life would be different without some of the habitual behaviors and
thoughts you have listed above.

_____

_____

_____

_____

George's Habitual Behaviors and Thoughts

Do any of your behaviors or thoughts interfere with your family and/or social life? Describe the effects.

Computer and Internet use have greatly affected my social life. I am out of touch with many of my friends. Some are angry with me because I don't do anything with them. Others have expressed concern. My kids are distant and my wife is often angry with me. Thinking about how to get more computer time contributes to all this.

Do any of your behaviors or thoughts interfere with your ability to do your job? Describe the effects.

I'll say! I lost my job because I was spending more and more time surfing the Net and playing computer games. I tried to hide it, but my boss caught me too many times and he fired me. So now I'm having to look for a new job, but with a less-than-glowing recommendation in hand.

Would you be happier without some of your habitual behaviors or thoughts? In what way?

Of course I would be happier! I have lost all respect for myself. I am ashamed that I lost my job because of this habit. I would be happier if I could hold my head up proudly. I would be happier if I had a job and had better relationships with my family and friends.

Describe how your life would be different without some of the habitual behaviors and thoughts you have listed above.

If I had spent less time on the computer and the Internet, I would not have lost my job. I would not have lost so many friends and damaged my relationship with my children and my wife. I wouldn't be behind on my bills because of not working. I would have a life! But I'm afraid I wouldn't have anything to do in my spare time. I don't have any other enjoyable activities or hobbies. I would feel an emptiness in my life. I wouldn't know what to do when I was worried or bored.

Chart 1b

This is just the beginning of your journey toward habit change. Now that you have described your habits, go on to chapter 2, which will help you understand how habits are formed and what purposes habits serve. Understanding how habits begin will help you understand how they can be changed.

✿ Habit Change Strategy

If we can develop a habit, we can surely change a habit.

2

How Habits Develop

Nothing is stronger than habit.

—Ovid

Man does not simply exist, but always decides what his existence will be, what he will become in the next moment.

—Viktor Frankl

Dr. Claiborn admits that he is not the best typist. When he presses the keys on the keyboard, he expects to see certain letters or words appear on the computer screen. His fingers move rapidly (almost unconsciously) across the keyboard. Something close to what he intends to write usually appears on the screen. But often he must hit the backspace key to correct mistakes he has made. He does this in the same automatic, almost unconscious manner as well.

Habit Formation

Dr. C.'s typing and his use of the backspace key are examples of habits. He does them frequently (at least when he's at the computer). He does them unconsciously or automatically. And he acquired the behaviors through repetition.

Researcher D. J. Hansen and his colleagues define *nervous habits* as persistent and repetitive behaviors that serve no apparent social function (Hansen, Tishelman, Hawkins, and Doepke 1990). Nervous habits can begin as a reaction to a physical injury or psychological trauma. A habit can also begin as a normal behavior that becomes more frequent or becomes altered in its form. When a behavior persists after the original injury or trauma has passed, it takes on an unusual form, and is performed in excess, it is a nervous habit.

Negative behaviors are often inhibited by inconvenience and by the person's social awareness of the behavior's peculiarity. But some apparently neutral behaviors can gradually blend in with normal movements. Escaping our awareness, the behavior becomes almost automatic. A habit is formed. As you can see, lack of awareness builds a habit. But awareness of our habit can help us escape it (Azrin 1973).

You probably don't remember how your habit began. It likely started as an innocent behavior among many behaviors in your daily life. Perhaps it gave you short-term relief from anxiety, stress, or boredom. It helped the first time, so you used the behavior to relieve your anxiety again. Soon, you forgot why you performed the activity in the first place.

Why did you develop your particular habit? Why nail biting and not tapping your toes or overeating? Most likely, it was an accident—you hit upon an activity that made you feel better for a while. Genetic and environmental influences may have also played a part. You learned how to handle stress by watching your parents. Margie's mother picked at the skin around her fingers, while her older brother bit his nails. As a small child, she heard her parents tell her brother, "Just stop that!" She vowed never to bite her nails. But chewing and picking at the cuticles around her fingernails seemed acceptable.

The habits we develop aren't always the same habits our parents modeled for us, however. Cherry saw her parents handle their anxiety and stress by drinking alcohol. Witnessing the dangers of alcoholism, she relieved her anxiety by treating herself to snacks and desserts. The sugar and fat seemed to help, and a habit was born. During stressful times, when good nutrition is especially important for all of us, she relieved her stress by eating doughnuts.

So can we blame our parents? Can we blame our genetics and environment? No. We are responsible for our behaviors. Although we probably didn't make conscious decisions to develop our habits, we can decide to change them.

✿ Habit Change Strategy

You didn't necessarily learn that a particular habit could make you feel better, but you may have learned that a habit could make you feel better.

Habits Serve a Purpose

Habits are the stuff of which most of our days are made. We could not function without habits. When we drive, we use a large number of habits so that we can control our cars and get where we're going. If we had to think consciously and deliberately about every one of these acts we wouldn't be able to drive at all, much less be able to carry on a conversation or listen to the radio. Habits are essential to our functioning and are present in almost every area of our lives. Some habits, however, cause us problems.

The phrase "nervous habit" implies a habit that is performed when a person is nervous or anxious. The results of one study did seem to indicate that habits involving hair and face manipulation are more prevalent in anxiety-provoking conditions. Habits involving object manipulation were more prevalent in boring situations (Woods and Miltenberger 1996).

Researchers offer three possible explanations for the development and maintenance of a nervous habit (Woods, Miltenberger, and Flach 1996):

1. The habit is negatively reinforced (see below) by decreasing tension in the area of the body associated with the habit. To put it simply, the relief of tension or anxiety is the reward for engaging in the habit.

2. The habit serves a self-stimulation function: it reduces boredom.

3. The habit produces a reinforced outcome: for example, even nails as a result of nail biting or smooth skin as a result of skin picking.

The Role of Reinforcement

The temporary reduction in anxiety, tension, or boredom that results from habits serves to reinforce behaviors. This can explain why our habits are more prevalent when we are nervous or bored. Habits may be maintained by automatic negative reinforcement—by reducing tension or anxiety. They may also be maintained by automatic positive reinforcement—by providing sensory stimulation and relieving boredom. In addition, habits may be maintained by social reinforcement.

Reinforcement is critical to learning, change, and habit acquisition. Reinforcement is a term psychologists use to describe any event that increases the probability of the behavior it follows. If someone gives you a reward for doing something, you are more likely to do it again. The reward is the reinforcement. Although this example seems simple, the idea of reinforcement can be much more complex.

Reinforcement can involve presentation or removal of a stimulus or event. Stimulus presentation is called *positive reinforcement*—giving a reward is positive reinforcement. Removal of an unpleasant event is *negative reinforcement*. The fastest way to acquire a habit is to reinforce the behavior every time it occurs.

Going back to Dr. C.'s typing, when he presses a key a letter appears on the computer screen. When he sees that it is the right letter he may have some automatic thoughts. That is what he wanted to happen, and he is pleased. His action has just been positively reinforced. And when Carl responds to an uncomfortable sensation by biting his fingernail, and the result is that the uncomfortable sensation is ended, he has negatively reinforced that habit.

When we receive reinforcement every time we engage in a habit, that behavior is learned quickly. Just as reinforcement plays a part in building a habit, it can be useful in changing a habit. When the reinforcement changes, the behavior we learn changes as well. An important part of changing a habit is to remove the reinforcement.

Let's take another look at the nail-biting example. Suppose that every time Carl felt an unpleasant sensation, biting a fingernail relieved it. Then something happened. It just stopped working. Carl no longer received relief. What would we expect? At first he might actually bite a little more often—after all, it always worked before. But after a while the biting would decrease. Perhaps when the unpleasant sensation occurred again, Carl would bite again, but probably less this time since it no longer provided relief. Over time, the biting would almost disappear. If at the same time another response provided relief from the unpleasant sensation, Carl might start to do that action regularly. This scenario sounds pretty simple, as if it's fairly easy to change habits.

The bad news is that we know it is not easy. If it were that easy there would be no reason for us to write this book, and you would have no trouble changing your habits. Unfortunately, reinforcement can be tricky to deal with. Part of the problem is that reinforcement is not usually very consistent. Let's take a look at gambling. When Fred places a bet, he sometimes wins and gets a powerful reinforcement. However, most of the time Fred's gambling behavior doesn't get reinforced at all. There is an unpredictable relationship between the behavior or habit, placing a bet in this example, and the reinforcement, winning. What would happen if Fred stopped winning entirely? Since Fred's experience has been that he may have spells without winning followed by periods of winning, he would be likely to believe that the reinforcement is right behind the next bet and continue to play. This means that it is going to be much harder for him to get rid of the habit.

As you read on, think about the patterns of reinforcement associated with the habits discussed in this book. In most cases, the reinforcement is not consistent. In addition, the reinforcement usually does not just unexpectedly stop. And if the habit in question continues to provide some relief or pleasure, it is likely to continue to be repeated. This is one of the things that makes habit change difficult. However, armed with the understanding of how we learn, we can set out to change habits and avoid the pitfall of thinking of the endeavor as a "simple change."

Habits Can Be Changed

The Habit Change Program focuses on how to change habits. Since habits are learned, we will use what we know about learning to help us most efficiently learn new habits. Habits are *almost* automatic. Some thoughts do precede our habits. Changing habits will require identifying these thoughts. By definition, habits are acquired through repetition. So if we are going to change habits, or acquire new ones, we will need to do some repetition. If a habit is causing problems, it makes sense, in most cases, to try to learn a new habit that, when practiced, makes it impossible to engage in the old habit (called a *competing response*), whether it is a thinking habit or a behavioral habit. As is discussed below, the Habit Change Program uses proven techniques from the fields of behavior modification, cognitive therapy, and cognitive behavior therapy, which help us understand and change our habits.

Behavior Therapy

Behavior therapy and *behavior modification* are terms that refer to the practice of applying knowledge about how people learn and change to helping people who have behaviors or disorders that interfere with their life. The emphasis is on changing specific problem behaviors, not on changing a person's personality or making them become a different person. The methods used in behavior therapy begin with the identification of the problem or target behavior. It is often useful to think about behaviors as excesses or deficits. A *behavioral excess* is a behavior you do too much, too often, or for too long. On the other hand, a *behavioral deficit* is one that you do too infrequently, too little, or for too little time.

Behavior therapy traces its roots to work on learning in the early to mid-twentieth century, ranging from Ivan Pavlov's work with dogs leading to his development of the concept of the *conditioned reflex*, to B.F. Skinner's work with both animals and people in his studies of human and animal behavior. Skinner studied how reinforcement works, and his ideas have been translated into principles used in school and therapy. Scientists have developed the ideas first learned in the animal laboratory, refining and expanding on them to help people with behavior change.

More recently Nathan Azrin and Gregory Nunn (1973) developed a behavior modification procedure that could be applied to unwanted habits and behavior disorders. Their procedure, called habit reversal, is an important part of what we teach in this book. Researchers have found that habit reversal is an effective tool in treating problems like tics, stuttering, hair pulling, and nail biting. When people are taught habit reversal, they can change habits and maintain the changes for years (Miltenberger, Fuqua, and Woods 1998).

Cognitive Therapy

Aaron T. Beck, M.D., developed *cognitive therapy* in the 1960s. It began as a short-term treatment for depression that focused on solving current problems and modifying dysfunctional thinking and behavior. Since then, Beck and others have adapted cognitive therapy to treat other problems, including generalized anxiety disorder, panic disorder, social phobia, substance abuse, couples' problems, eating disorders, obsessive-compulsive disorder, post-traumatic stress disorder, personality disorders, chronic pain, hypochondriasis, and schizophrenia (Beck 1995). Numerous researchers have also added to Aaron Beck's work. A number of different approaches to cognitive therapy, such as rational emotive therapy (RET), have been developed by Albert Ellis and others.

Cognitive Behavioral Therapy

In recent years most clinicians working with cognitive therapy or behavior therapy have started to call what they do *cognitive behavioral therapy.* This is because they combine traditional ideas from behavioral therapy and newer ideas from cognitive therapy to develop the most effective treatments. The cognitive aspect of this type of therapy is focused on how we think and how that relates to how we feel and behave. Much of the thinking we do is in the form of self-talk. This thinking, or self-talk, can help us change a habit or it can contribute to the problem. This book combines behavioral therapy methods, like habit reversal, with cognitive methods, like keeping track of and changing self-talk, to help you change your habits.

Change is not easy, but having knowledge can ease the process. Habit change may seem unattainable now, but knowledge and application of cognitive behavioral therapy can bring about success. Understanding the process of change is an important part of cognitive behavioral therapy and the habit changing process. Understanding helps relieve some of the fears and doubts that are inevitably linked to change. Chapter 3 will help you recognize these fears and doubts and then examine, confront, and refute them.

3

What's Stopping You?

My evil genius Procrastination has whispered me to tarry
'til a more convenient season.

—Mary Todd Lincoln

Never put off till tomorrow what you can do the day after tomorrow.

—Mark Twain

Habits can interfere with every part of our lives. They can keep us from achieving our goals, damage our self-image, and have devastating effects on our health. At this point, you have only begun to see how habits affect your life. In the next chapters, you will begin to recognize the disadvantages—and the advantages—of keeping your habit or changing it. You will also discover the consequences of changing. Only then will you be ready to make a commitment to change.

⏀ Habit Change Strategy

Fear, doubt, excuses, and denial are like chains that keep you enslaved by your habit. Confronting and dispelling your fear will loosen those chains and help you escape your habit.

Reasons for Not Changing Now

By now, you are probably experiencing many fears and doubts about changing. You may even be tempted to put this book in the back corner of a shelf. But don't do it—not yet anyway. Instead, let's examine some of those fears and doubts.

"My habit's not so bad."

If you truly believed this, you wouldn't be reading this book. Or perhaps you are reading this book only because a relative or friend urged you to read it—they see your habit as a problem, but you don't. The Habit Change Program will help you discover the consequences of your habit. You may decide that your habit isn't a bad habit and does not need to be changed, or you may see that it has negative consequences and does need to be changed. To change or not to change? Examine the facts, then make your decision.

"I've had this habit for years. I can't change."

You weren't able to change in the past. You may have tried several times but you didn't succeed in sticking to your plan. This doesn't mean you can't change now. In the past, you did not have all the tools we describe in this book. In reading this book you will learn the methods and skills you need to change your habit.

When you say you *can't* change, most likely you mean that you *don't want* to change. Most people don't like the idea of changing anything, especially something as personal as a habit. We are comfortable with familiar behaviors. They give us security and a sense of normalcy. However, once change is under way, we usually accept the new behavior; eventually it becomes as comfortable as the old behavior.

"I enjoy my habit. It's fun!"

Some habits are just there. We don't like them or dislike them; they are simply a part of our repertoire of behaviors. Other habits are quite enjoyable and we would truly miss them if they weren't available. But these same habits can also keep us from achieving important goals. Are you trading the fulfillment of your long-term goals and dreams for the present and fleeting rewards of your habit? These temporary rewards may have very permanent negative consequences.

"I am my habit."

No, you're not! You may have identified yourself by your habit for years: "I am a gambler," "I am an insomniac," or "I'm a nail biter, and I always will be." Years of trying and failing to give up your habit can have devastating effects on your self-esteem, so at some point you may have decided to simply accept your habit. But you are not your habit. It is important to separate yourself from your behavior. Try to step back and see your habit for what it is—a behavior you are thinking about changing, not something that defines you.

"Changing is too hard."

Yes, change is difficult. Significant change involves time, effort, and commitment. In most cases it will also mean some discomfort for you and perhaps for those you love. In the next chapters you will decide if the effort is worth the results. Do the advantages of changing your habit outweigh the advantages of keeping your habit? Is changing worth the effort? You don't have to decide now. Consider the facts as you discover them, and then make an informed decision.

"I don't have time to make changes."

We all dedicate our time to the things that are important to us. You've heard the phrase, "Time is money." In a way, it is true—we spend time like we spend money. The payoff or result needs to be worth the time spent to achieve it. But as we said earlier, you don't have to decide yet. Read on and gather the facts, then determine if you are willing to dedicate some time to change. Find out if the payoff will be worth your effort and time.

"This is not the right time to change—maybe later."

There will never be a perfect time to change. You've probably heard the saying, "People only change when they hit rock bottom." But we don't have to wait for a crisis to make changes. In fact, making a change can sometimes prevent a crisis. Don't wait for the perfect circumstances. Life is full of problems and complications. When today's problems straighten out, other problems will provide you with another reason to postpone change.

Even if you do believe the saying about hitting rock bottom, how will you decide where the bottom is? Whenever you decide to change, when you decide that the problem has gone on long enough, that is your rock bottom.

"I'm afraid I'll fail."

What if you try to change and you fail? We believe you won't fail, but what if you do? Think of this as a grand experiment, and you have the research of many others who have conducted similar experiments to draw on. There is no failure or success in an experiment, only results. When we don't get the expected result from one experiment, we can go on to life's next experiment. What's the worst thing that could happen? You might still have the habit, but you will know you tried.

"I can't change my habit as long as the people around me are engaging in the habit."

You can't control the behavior of others, but you can control your behavior. It is true that when others are engaging in a habit you are trying to change in yourself, your temptation may be increased. You may decide to make changes in the time you spend with others and the people you associate with.

Perhaps others will follow your example. You could be a trendsetter! Your shopping friends might join you for lunch instead of going on shopping trips. The success of your fitness plan might inspire your family to take a look at their own habits. But even if those around you continue with their habits, you can choose to change your habit. It's your choice!

"I can't change in my present environment."

Your environment is probably filled with temptations. The Habit Change Program will help you recognize the circumstances that make you more likely to engage in your habit. You can avoid some of these circumstances, but others are unavoidable. You will discover ways to substitute other behaviors for your habit that you can use when you find yourself in a tempting situation. With a little creativity, you can also find ways to change your environment, making it more conducive to your new behaviors—your new lifestyle.

"I don't think I could stand the loss of my habit."

Anxiety, depression, grief, and even anger are normal reactions to loss. And habit changing may involve significant loss. We believe that you can withstand these feelings. Relaxation techniques and coping strategies are built into the program to help you deal with these painful emotions. But what if you can't stand it? What if the anxiety or depression becomes severe and nothing you learn here helps? Even if your worst fears came true, you would still have options. You could resume your habit. You could get further help, perhaps by joining a support group or seeking professional help. Acknowledging your fears will help you face them and help you achieve your goals.

Dr. Claiborn sometimes works with people who have chronic pain. At some point, many will say, "I can't stand the pain!" Dr. Claiborn is likely to gently ask, "What does it mean to not be able to stand something?" We all use that expression, or similar ones, in our everyday speech. But what does it really mean? If we say we can't stand something, do we mean that it is killing us? In fact, we probably *can* stand it, but we don't *like* it.

"I'm already under pressure trying to quit another habit."

This seems to make sense. We've always been told to finish one thing before starting another, right? However, in many cases, this is not only an excuse but also a setup for failure. Your habits may be interconnected. Changing one habit or addiction without changing another could be more difficult than changing both together.

Cherry thought she had a problem with her weight. But hers was actually an overall health problem. Her diet was unhealthy and her exercise was limited to occasional walks. It made sense to change her diet and her exercise level. Instead of joining a weight-loss program, she developed a total health and fitness program. The result? More energy, less depression, better health, and, as an added benefit, modest weight loss.

Fred is another example of a person with multiple habits that were interconnected, however, the dangers were more severe. Although alcoholism was his worst problem, he also had problems with smoking and gambling. Treating the alcoholism first seemed to make sense, but his drinking, smoking, and gambling were interrelated. When he smoked, he craved a drink. When he gambled, he craved a drink. Developing a new lifestyle and changing all of these habits was more successful. Not only did he stop drinking, he also escaped the feeling of being controlled by his addictions and habits.

What Are Your Reasons for Not Changing Now?

What about you? What is holding you back? Perhaps you can relate to one of the reasons listed above. Each of us has our own reasons for not changing now. List your reasons below. Then, under each one, spend some time, as long as needed, to evaluate each reason. Look at evidence that supports or refutes your reasons.

1. _____

_____

_____

2. _____

_____

_____

3. _____

_____

_____

4. _____

   _____

   _____

5. _____

   _____

   _____

6. _____

   _____

   _____

7. _____

   _____

   _____

8. _____

   _____

   _____

9. _____

   _____

   _____

10. _____

    _____

    _____

✸ Habit Change Strategy

Don't let fears and doubts hold you back. Decide now to refute your reasons for not changing.

We hope this exercise has brought you closer to confronting your habits and deciding to change. Don't give up if you don't feel empowered yet, or if you don't see a need to change at this time. We've only begun. Later chapters will help you examine your habits more closely and decide if the disadvantages and consequences of your habit make changing worth the effort. Now, let's look at specific habits covered in *The Habit Change Workbook*.

4

Common Problem
Habits

*Let me tell you the secret that has led to my goal. My strength lies solely in
my tenacity.*

—Louis Pasteur

*All things are possible until they are proved impossible—even the impossible may only
be so, as of now.*

—Pearl S. Buck

From here, we will lead you farther on your habit-changing journey. We will be addressing
various kinds of habits, so each person's path will be somewhat different. Each reader will
walk the same first steps, take a different direction, then meet together to complete the
journey.

We suggest that you first read this chapter and the next two, which will help you define
your habits and get ready for change. Then read the chapter or chapters that best address
your habits. We have divided habits into seven categories, and each category has its own
chapter. We will all meet again in chapters 9 through 12. These chapters deal with confronting
automatic thoughts, maintaining the changes you have made, preventing relapse, and trouble
shooting.

Habit Change Strategy

Think of habit change as a journey. Sometimes exciting, sometimes difficult,
this is a journey with a great reward at the end of the path.

Specific Habits

Below are descriptions of the most common habits people want to change. Does your habit fall into one of these categories?

Skin Picking, Nail Biting, and Trichotillomania

Skin picking and nail biting are sometimes called nervous habits. Other habits also fit into this category: jangling keys, bouncing legs, licking lips, smacking gum, twirling hair, chewing pencils, and so on. Many people have tried to stop these troublesome habits, but they haven't succeeded because they didn't have the information needed to successfully change. We will provide easy-to-understand instructions for changing these habits so that you can succeed.

Trichotillomania is a disorder characterized by repetitive pulling out of one's hair. Once thought to be rare, this disorder is now known to affect approximately 1 to 2 percent of the population. Treatment is available, and while we don't promise a cure, we can help you cope with trichotillomania and control its symptoms.

Sleeping Habits

Millions of Americans have problems with sleep. Insomnia is second only to pain as a complaint people report to their doctor. Some people have trouble getting up in the morning. Others have nightmares or other sleep problems. But many people do not realize that their behaviors may be contributing to their ongoing sleep problems. Changing a few key habits can help you get a good night's sleep.

Health and Fitness Habits

Sometimes it seems as if the entire world is focused on losing weight. While this may be one goal in a fitness program, optimum health and fitness is a more important goal. Often, while individuals are striving to improve overall health and fitness, weight loss is achieved—and maintained. Most of us know what we *should* be doing to promote our health, such as eating a nutritious diet and getting regular exercise, but the problem is carrying out these behaviors. Often we can maintain a health and fitness plan for a short while, but how do we continue the plan over the long term? This will be our focus—developing healthy habits and keeping them throughout your lifetime.

Relationship Problems

Do you tend to exaggerate or embellish the truth—or perhaps even lie? Has procrastination, perfectionism, a tendency to interrupt, or a propensity for swearing harmed your relationships? We will help you examine your relationships for the effects of harmful habits. Changing just a few habits can often transform a relationship.

Excessive Shopping and Spending

Overspending can have devastating effects, not only on the people with the habit but also on their families. But how can we stop spending money? We need to buy food, and certainly no one wants to cancel holiday gift giving. We will help you examine your spending habits so that you can get back on a more reasonable financial track.

Excessive Leisure Activities

Are your leisure habits taking over your life? Do you spend hours watching TV, playing video games, or surfing the Net? We will help you identify your destructive leisure activities and habits. You don't have to give up having fun—instead you can diversify your activities and make habit changes that can lead to a more productive life.

Problem Gambling

Millions of people engage in excessive gambling. It is an insidious habit that is best treated early. Some people will be able to use the Habit Change Program to stop their destructive gambling habits and develop healthy habits. For others, the Habit Change Program will be the starting point. We will refer you to other resources so that you can get support and professional treatment.

More Than Just a Habit

Habit or disorder? Habit or addiction? Does it matter? Yes—disorders and addictions require more involved treatments than those used for habits. The Habit Change Program may be beneficial, but further help will be needed.

Addictions

Habits that involve the use of chemicals go beyond an emotional desire to engage in the habit. The body begins to crave the chemical, to the point of addiction. To help determine whether your habit has developed into an addiction, ask yourself the following questions: Is the ingestion of alcohol, nicotine, or other chemicals a problem for you? Do you simply abuse alcohol, or are you physically dependent on the chemical? Could you quit "cold turkey," or would you need professional help in order to stop?

These issues are beyond the scope of *The Habit Change Workbook*. Stopping the use of alcohol or drugs abruptly can have serious consequences. If chemical dependence may be a problem for you—if you even *suspect* it could be a problem—we urge you to seek professional help now. Talk with your family doctor. If you don't have one, or if you are too embarrassed or afraid to consult your doctor, there are other resources.

The Addiction Workbook, by Patrick Fanning and John T. O'Neill, L.C.D.C. (1996), is an excellent starting place. Their workbook can point you in the right direction and assist you on your journey to recovery. Fanning and O'Neill begin *The Addiction Workbook* with this excellent advice:

> If you are currently very sick, suicidal, suffering acute withdrawal symptoms, or injured, you need more immediate help than a book can provide. Right now, check the "Alcoholism" listing in the *Yellow Pages*. Call the local council on alcohol and drug dependence. Explain your situation, and ask for their recommendation. You can also call Alcoholics Anonymous, and they will send someone to help you through your crisis. (1)

Chronic heavy drinking can cause or aggravate serious medical problems, including liver disease, brain damage, ulcers, hypoglycemia, anemia, convulsions, kidney failure, gout, vitamin deficiencies, high blood pressure, impotence, eating disorders, diabetes, and fetal alcohol syndrome. It can also increase your chances of developing cancer of the liver, stomach, colon, breast, pancreas, lung, or bladder. The physical damage caused by drugs depends on what drugs are used. Drug use can result in problems with the brain, liver, kidneys, heart, lungs, circulation, immune system, and sexual organs.

There is now no doubt that cigarette smoking is harmful to your health. When you smoke, you are inhaling at least forty-three different substances that can cause cancer. Cigarette smoke contains about four thousand chemicals. Cigarette smoking has harmful effects on your circulation, lungs, heart, skin, eyes, teeth, mouth, throat, voice box, and stomach. And it can be harmful to your unborn baby if you are pregnant. Need you any further reason to quit? Quitting smoking is difficult; however, help abounds. There are several ways to go about quitting. Your doctor can help you choose the smoking-cessation program that is best for you.

Once you've started on your recovery journey, the Habit Change Program can help you make lifestyle changes that are essential to addiction recovery. You will find that changing some of your habits will help you quit substance abuse and resist going back to your addiction. Good nutrition, exercise, relaxation, stress reduction, positive thought patterns, spirituality, and improved communication skills contribute to addiction recovery. In addition, you may find that many of the ideas in this book are helpful additions to your treatment for addiction problems. If you seek help from professionals, show them this book and ask them how some of the ideas here might apply to your recovery.

Habit Change Strategy

If your habit involves the use of a chemical, such as alcohol, nicotine, or other durgs, seek professional help first, then use *The Habit Change Workbook* to make overall lifestyle changes that will promote recovery.

Obsessive-Compulsive Disorder

Obsessive-compulsive disorder (OCD) is characterized by compulsions that are distressing, time consuming, or that interfere with relationships, normal routines, or daily functioning. Obsessions are persistent ideas, images, impulses, or thoughts that intrude into a person's thinking and cause distress, anxiety, and worry. Compulsions are repetitive behaviors or mental acts preformed in response to obsessions in an effort to relieve or prevent anxiety or worry. A person with OCD often feels he or she must perform these compulsions in order to prevent or avoid a dreaded event such as illness, death, or perceived misfortune.

The compulsions of OCD have a lot in common with habits. They are done often, they are acquired, and they are difficult to stop. Habits and compulsions are both done in order to relieve anxiety. Like habits, these behaviors are sometimes automatic, although more often they are done with deliberation. So what's the main difference? The biggest difference between habits and compulsions is that, while habits may relieve a generalized feeling of anxiety, OCD behaviors are done to relieve a very specific anxiety from a specific obsession. Another important difference between compulsions and habits is that most habits are in some way pleasurable or satisfying, at least at first. This is not usually true of compulsions, which are typically more associated with anxiety reduction or relief.

The treatment of OCD is similar to the process of habit changing in some ways. The most important difference is the use of exposure and ritual prevention for OCD. The core component of OCD treatment is exposure to the obsessive thoughts and resistance of the urge to perform the ritual.

Trying to push obsessive thoughts out of the mind only makes them stronger—and it makes the urge to perform the compulsion stronger. To better understand this point, let's try an exercise. First, try to think about white bears for three minutes. Take note every time your mind wanders. You can probably do this with only occasional drifting off, and you can probably easily bring yourself back to thinking about white bears. Now try *not* to think about white bears for three minutes. *Whatever you do, don't think about white bears.* Your mind will likely be filled with white bears and the thought will probably be stronger at the end of three minutes than it was at the beginning.

Exposure to the obsessive thoughts of OCD helps because it eventually leads to a decrease in the distress associated with an obsession. Since the compulsion is done to reduce this distress, the need to perform the compulsion also diminishes. Research on OCD shows that exposure works to lessen the obsessions and ritual prevention works to reduce the compulsions.

In contrast, for people without OCD exposure to most habit-related situations would actually increase the desire to engage in the habit. For example, exposure to a dessert table at a party would be a tremendous temptation to a person trying to change eating habits. Exposure to rows of clanging slot machines would be tempting to the problem gambler. Habit changing involves removing temptations from the person's environment. OCD treatment seeks exposure to the temptations (the obsessive thoughts).

Interestingly, many people with OCD are also prone to engaging in habits. For example, people with OCD frequently have problems with skin picking. The Habit Change Program can help people with OCD change their habits, but further help is needed to treat OCD. *The OCD Workbook,* by Bruce Hyman, Ph.D., and Cherry Pedrick is a good resource that can help you begin your education about OCD.

Habit Change Strategy

If you have OCD, the Habit Change Program can help you change your habits, but you'll need to get further help for your OCD.

As you read this chapter, did a particular group of habits match your habitual behaviors and thoughts? The next chapter will help you clearly describe your habit. We'll look at the emotions and situations that trigger your habit and the consequences of your habit.

Part II

The Habit Change
Program

5

Assessing Your Habit

Curious things, habits. People themselves never knew they had them.
—Agatha Christie

Change is not made without inconvenience, even from worse to better.
—Richard Hooker

By now, you probably have in mind a couple of habits you would like to change. This chapter will take you through a series of steps in order to help you define and assess the habit you would most like to change. You'll be asked to answer questions and keep records. It is critical that you actually take out a pen or pencil and write down your answers. You will be tempted to just answer them in your head and not write them down, or you might tell yourself that you will come back to it and do it later. If you are really going to make a change, however, begin now by actively participating in your habit-change process and faithfully completing this workbook. You are going to need to write down your answers.

Behavioral Momentum

Every good salesperson uses a form of *behavioral momentum*. Have you ever noticed that when someone is trying to sell you something they first ask you some questions that lead to "yes" answers? They may say something like, "Wouldn't you like to have bright, shiny teeth?" or "Wouldn't like to be free of debt?" The answer to these questions, of course, is "yes." The salesperson has been taught that getting you to say "yes" at the beginning is likely to lead to your saying "yes" at the critical point of closing the deal. When you start doing something, you are likely to continue.

Unfortunately, the habits that you are trying to change have a lot of behavioral momentum, which is part of the reason they are so difficult to change. Let's face it—we could have written a book containing just one sentence: "Don't Do That." But this wouldn't have helped. We all know there is much more involved in changing a habit than simply stopping. So instead of trying to just stop a habitual behavior, you will need to find a replacement behavior. To find the right replacement, you first need to define your habit.

⚘ Habit Change Strategy

Keep the momentum going. Answer all the questions in this book thoroughly— even if some seem insignificant.

An Operational Definition of Your Habit

An *operational definition* is one that defines the problem in terms that are measurable. After completing this section you will have an operational definition of your habit. One way to understand this is to pretend you must explain your habit to a Martian. Suppose Margie wanted to explain her habit of skin picking. To say, "I pick at my skin" would not clearly define her habit. What parts of her body does she pick at? What provokes or leads up to her skin picking? Does she use tweezers or other instruments to pick at her skin? Are there particular places or situations where Margie is more likely to engage in her habit? All of these questions would help our Martian friend understand Margie's habit.

Make copies of the blank Habit Description chart that follows and complete one form for each habit you are considering changing. Remember—this is only the assessment stage. Only when you have collected all of the information about the habits in question will you decide which ones you want to change. We've provided Margie's Habit Description chart as an example. Answering every question as completely as possible will help you gain the momentum you need to escape your bad habit. So, enough excuses. Pick up the pen or pencil and begin to fill in the answers NOW.

⚘ Habit Change Strategy

Describing your habit will give you valuable information that you can use when you decide whether the habit needs to be changed. It will also give you a starting-point assessment of your habit, so you can later measure your progress.

Habit Description

Describe your habit. _____

_____

_____

When did the habit begin, or when do you first remember doing it? _____

_____

_____

Describe your earliest memory of other people's reactions to your habit. _____

_____

_____

Has the habit changed over time? If so, describe the changes in your habit. _____

_____

_____

How do other people react to your habit now? _____

_____

_____

When do you usually engage in your habitual behavior? Is there a usual time of day?

_____

_____

Do you engage in your habit in a particular place? _____

_____

_____

What else is usually going on when your habit shows up? _____

_____

_____

What effects do other people's reactions have on your habitual behavior? _____

_____

_____

Chart 5a

Margie's Habit Description

Describe your habit. _I pick at the skin on my face. I do this by searching in the mirror for blemishes and imperfections. I dig at the spots with my fingernails._

When did the habit begin, or when do you first remember doing it? _I started at about age thirteen when I first got pimples._

Describe your earliest memory of other people's reactions to your habit. _My mother said, "Just leave it alone!" when I first picked at a pimple. My brother said, "That's disgusting." My friend asked, "What's wrong with your face?"_

Has the habit changed over time? If so, describe the changes in your habit. _I used to pick only at my face, but now I pick at scabs on my arms._

How do other people react to your habit now? _My husband tells me to stop, and my kids give me dirty looks. Sometimes I feel like strangers are staring at my arms._

When do you usually engage in your habitual behavior? Is there a usual time of day? _I usually pick at my face at night before I go to bed or in the morning when I'm getting ready for work. For my arms, there is no particular time of day._

Do you engage in your habit in a particular place? _I usually pick at my face in the bathroom. I pick at my arms anywhere I am alone, often in the car._

What else is usually going on when your habit shows up? _I seem to pick more when I am worried about something or when I'm bored._

What effects do other people's reactions have on your habitual behavior? _I try not to pick at my skin around other people. When they mention the look of my skin I feel embarrassed._

Triggers

You probably experience particular emotions before you engage in your habit. These are *emotional triggers*. The most likely emotional triggers are sadness, anger, fear, stress, and loneliness, but there may be others. You probably have several different emotional triggers. List your emotional triggers in the Habit Triggers worksheet, below.

Certain situations may also trigger your habit. You may have a number of *situational triggers*. It is important to identify as many of them as possible. The worksheet covers some of the questions you have already answered, but filling it in should help you paint a complete picture of your habit. For example, "I only do it at night when my husband is not yet home from work" might be an answer to the question about situational triggers, but it also includes information about the typical time you engage in the habitual behavior.

Think of your situational triggers as high-risk situations. That first cup of coffee in the morning might be a high-risk situation for someone who is trying to quit smoking. As you complete the Habit Triggers worksheet, try to describe as many situational triggers or high-risk situations as you can.

Habit Triggers

What emotions do you usually experience before engaging in your habit? _____

_____

_____

_____

_____

What situations tend to trigger your habit? _____

_____

_____

_____

_____

_____

_____

Chart 5c

Margie's Habit Triggers

What emotions do you usually experience before engaging in your habit? *Most often, I feel worried or nervous. Sometimes I am lonely or bored.*

What situations tend to trigger your habit? *Seeing a pimple or a piece of loose skin. Being in the bathroom, in front of the mirror. Sometimes when I am nervous I find myself scratching my arm or hand.*

Chart 5d

Habit Change Strategy

Just as a log in the middle of a trail puts a hiker at high risk of tripping, triggers put us at high risk of participating in our habits. Take care when you encounter triggers that put your success at risk.

Consequences

Every behavior has consequences. Your habit has consequences. The most significant consequences of your habit are probably the emotional effects. For most people, habits produce a mixture of feelings. You may feel relief or even excitement, and at the same time you may be angry with yourself or feel guilty. It is important to understand these consequences since they are usually part of what keeps a habit going.

Most people think that guilt should motivate a person to stop a habit. Well-meaning family members or friends may have attempted to help you change your habit by trying to make you feel guilty. But this strategy doesn't work. Guilt occurs *after* the undesirable behavior. It is the product of telling yourself, "I shouldn't have done that," or "I should have done that, and I didn't." The result of these negative thoughts is that you feel guilty, but it is too late to change what you feel guilty about.

Worse yet, the guilty feelings may make us more likely to perform the behavior again. There are two reasons for this. First, guilty feelings often lead to our feeling even more helpless. You may end up thinking, "I can't control myself," or "I will never be able to change; I am too weak." With this type of thinking, you are more likely to give up and not even try to change: "I've tried, and I can't control myself, so why bother to try again? It is just going to end in failure and disappointment," you might say to yourself.

Second, guilt doesn't help, because it may actually be an emotional trigger. Think back to what you wrote down as your emotional triggers. If you are more likely to engage in the habit when you are feeling bad and it serves to soothe you, then you are more likely to do it when you are feeling guilty about doing it. It is important to understand this paradoxical cycle. Suppose Ted goes out and has too much to drink. The next day he feels guilty. What can he do to ease his discomfort and perhaps help him forget the things he feels bad about? Well, having a drink might be just the thing. After all, in the past it worked when he was trying not to think about things. The same idea applies to most problem habits. Write a description of the emotional consequences of your habit in the Habit Consequences worksheet, below.

Habit Change Strategy

Guilt doesn't motivate people to change their habits because it encourages feelings that often trigger habits.

It is also important to be aware of the other consequences of your habit, since they often have an impact on what you do and when you do it. Examples of various consequences include criticism from others, scars, debt, being tired or sore, having to wear clothing that hides the effects, and more. After you've listed the emotional and other consequences of your habit, think about how these consequences affect your behavior—do they in turn make your habit worse? Remember Carl, the nail biter? When he bites one nail, it is shorter than the rest, so he feels that he should bite the others. Biting one nail leads to biting all of his nails. Include these types of consequences on your Habit Consequences worksheet.

Habit Consequences

What are the emotional consequences of your habit? _____

_____

_____

What are some other consequences of your habit? _____

_____

_____

Describe how these consequences in turn affect your habit. _____

_____

_____

_____

_____

_____

_____

Chart 5e

Margie's Habit Consequences

What are the emotional consequences of your habit? _When I pick at my face, I feel like I am doing something productive. I feel more relaxed, and I stop worrying about my problems. When I get done, I feel guilty and angry with myself. I feel that I am weak because I can't control myself._

What are some other consequences of your habit? _My face is scarred. Sometimes it is red and it hurts. My arms have scars all over them and they usually have several scabs. People stare at me sometimes, and my friends ask what happened to my arms or my face._

Describe how these consequences in turn affect your habit. _Picking often produces a scab. If the scab has rough edges, I pick it some more, then it bleeds, and I end up with a scar._

Chart 5f

Record Keeping

Now that you have examined the consequences of your habit, you are ready to go on to the next step, discovering when your habit seems to affect your life the most. Your Habit Record will tell you when you had the urge to engage in the habit, whether you engaged in it or not, how long the urge lasted, and the automatic thoughts and emotional reactions you had.

First, let's define _automatic thoughts_. When people are asked what they are thinking while they are doing something familiar or habitual, the usual answer is "Nothing." We are often unaware of what is going on in our minds at these times. When you engage in a complex behavior such as driving your car, you have to be processing a lot of information. Think back to the last time you had to stop at a traffic light. What did you have to do in order to stop? What did you have to think about? You're probably thinking, "I just stopped the car—I didn't have to think about it."

Although you may not realize it, automatic thoughts played a big part in your stopping the car. If the road was familiar, you automatically looked up at the traffic light. Then you had to look and determine which color light was lit. If the red light was lit, you had to recall what you know about red traffic lights. There is nothing magic about red that tells us to stop. It is simply something you learned. Then you had to stop the car. First you needed to remember which pedals to push. You needed to make a number of observations about your car's movement and location in order to stop in the right spot. This involved judging distance, speed, deceleration, road conditions, and more. All of this went on automatically, and at the same time you may have been talking to a passenger, listening to the radio, or reading a bumper sticker.

Being able to quickly process so much information helps to ensure our survival, but when it comes to problem habits, those automatic thoughts can get in the way of change. This is especially true when our automatic thoughts are tied to emotional triggers. So we have to learn what those automatic thoughts are, what emotions are involved, and learn to change our responses. Fortunately, learning to "catch" or become aware of our thoughts is not too difficult. We will discuss how to change your automatic thoughts in a later chapter, but for now, we'll record them.

✖ Habit Change Strategy

Listen carefully to your automatic thoughts. Are they helpful and encouraging? Or harmful and discouraging?

Make a few copies of the Habit Record and the Triggers and Consequences Record forms. Using these forms, keep records of your habit for five to seven days. If the Habit Change Program is going to work for you, completing these records is essential. If you are thinking of changing more than one habit, complete a form for each habit. It is best to concentrate on one or two habits at a time, no more than three. As you choose the habits you will focus on, consider if two or more habits are related. Working on related habits may help you change your most bothersome habit. When you have completed the records for your habit or habits for five to seven days, go on to the next chapter.

Habit Record

Date and Time	Type of Urge	Did You Give In? Duration of Urge	Emotion	Automatic Thoughts

Chart 5k

Margie's Habit Record

Date and Time	Type of Urge	Did You Give In? Duration of Urge	Emotion	Automatic Thoughts
8/1 7:00 A.M.	Pick skin on face	Yes—30 min. ☹	Disgusted with myself and afraid, then relieved	I will just do this to get rid of those spots. Then I will quit. It feels so good to get the junk out of a pimple. I am disgusting and have no self-control. It's over.
8/1 10:00 P.M.	Pick skin on face	No!—20 min. ☺	Anxious at first, then proud	If I do just a little, it won't hurt. Maybe I can put it off this time. Gee, the urge seems to be getting weaker. I can do it! I made it! I didn't pick. I can win.
8/2 9:00 A.M.	Pick a scab on my arm	Yes—5 min. ☹	Nervous as I was driving to a meeting	Oh, I'm picking again. Well, I have to finish now. I need to get that scab smooth.
8/2 10:00 P.M.	Pick skin on face	Yes—20 min. ☹	Disgusted, guilty	This is part of getting ready for bed. There is some loose skin and I need to smooth it. I could just wash my face and put night cream on. That would help. No, I need to get rid of that loose skin.
8/3 7:00 A.M.	Pick skin on face	Yes—4 min. ☹	Guilty, nervous, hurried, then relieved	I'm in a hurry. I got up late and now look at my face. I just have to look OK today. I'll smooth out this one here, then I'll stop. Why couldn't I have stopped? Well, I am in a hurry. I don't have time to worry about it now.
8/3 9:00 P.M.	Pick scab on arm	No!—15 min. ☺	Bored, anxious, proud when I resisted	I won't do it this time. That sore needs to heal. I won't let this habit control me.

Chart 5l

Carl's Habit Record

Date and Time	Type of Urge	Did You Give In? Duration of Urge	Emotion	Automatic Thoughts
8/1 9:00 A.M.	Bite nails	Yes—5 min. ☹	Disgusted with myself, nervous	This nail is rough. I need to smooth it out. No I don't need to. But I want to. I'm disgusting.
8/1 11:00 A.M.	Bite nails	No—15 min. ☺	Proud, but anxious, like something is left undone	Maybe I can do this. Maybe I can quit. I don't know, it is hard.
8/1 4:00 P.M.	Bite nails	Yes—4 min. ☹	Relieved to be doing something with my hands	I knew I couldn't stop. Here I am doing it again. I didn't even know I was doing it. But I am. I could wait until I get home and use a file to smooth out this nail. But I need to have it smooth now.
8/1 7:00 P.M.	Bite nails	No—20 min. ☺	Bored, then anxious when I didn't give in, proud	My finger is in my mouth. No, I won't do it this time. I refuse to give in to this habit.
8/2 10:00 A.M.	Bite nails	No—15 min. ☺	Nervous about meeting, worried	Keep your hands in your lap. Don't even move your hands near your mouth. It's hard. But what will people think if they see me biting my nails? They'll think I'm weak and nervous.
8/2 1:00 P.M.	Bite nails	Yes—5 min. ☹	Relieved meeting is over; deprived because can't do my habit	They're my fingers! I should be able to do what I want with them. It doesn't hurt anyone else. It's not like I'm doing something that will affect others.

Chart 5m

Triggers and Consequences Record

Date and Time	Type of Urge	Emotional Trigger "I felt...."	Situational Trigger "I was...."	Consequence of Action

Chart 5n

Margie's Triggers and Consequences Record

Date and Time	Type of Urge	Emotional Trigger "I felt ..."	Situational Trigger "I was ..."	Consequence of Action
8/1 7:00 A.M.	Pick skin on face	Hurried, nervous, bothered by pimples on face	In the bathroom, getting ready, putting makeup on.	My face doesn't look any better. The pimples are still there.
8/1 10:00 P.M.	Pick skin on face	Anxious, tired	In the bathroom, getting ready for bed. Washing face.	I feel proud that I resisted.
8/2 9:00 A.M.	Pick a scab on my arm	Nervous, bored	In the car, driving to work. One hand free.	The scab just looks worse now and will take even longer to heal.
8/2 10:00 P.M.	Pick skin on face	Tired, worried about something	In the bathroom, getting ready for bed. Noticing some loose skin around a scab.	My face looks worse now, not better.
8/3 7:00 A.M.	Pick skin on face	Hurried	In the bathroom, getting ready for bed. Late for work and in a hurry.	The scab is a bit smoother, but I know it didn't need to be. It's probably irritated.
8/3 9:00 P.M.	Pick a scab on my arm	Bored, anxious, proud when I resisted	In the bathroom, getting ready for bed.	I'm proud that I resisted picking. I feel a bit more confident.

Chart 5o

Carl's Triggers and Consequences Record				
Date and Time	**Type of Urge**	**Emotional Trigger "I felt ..."**	**Situational Trigger "I was ..."**	**Consequence of Action**
8/1 9:00 A.M.	Bite nails	Nervous	Driving to work, one hand free.	I feel ashamed of myself. My nails don't look better, they look worse.
8/1 11:00 A.M.	Bite nails	Bored, a bit nervous	Sitting at my desk, paused a bit to think about a form I was filling out.	I resisted. No nail biting this time!
8/1 4:00 P.M.	Bite nails	Worried, thinking about what I need to do when I get home; mind wandering	Driving home from work. Didn't realize my finger was in my mouth.	Feel guilty. Finally stopped myself, but my nails look even worse now.
8/1 7:00 P.M.	Bite nails	Bored	Watching TV, hands free.	I find my fingers in my mouth, but I don't bite. I caught myself this time.
8/2 10:00 A.M.	Bite nails	Nervous about meeting	Sitting around table at a meeting with my boss and a few of my colleagues.	I keep my hands in my lap and somehow resist biting my nails.
8/2 1:00 P.M.	Bite nails	Anxious, tired	Sitting at my desk. No one is in the room to see me.	I almost attacked my fingers, chewing and biting until they were almost even.

Chart 5p

When you've recorded information about your habit and its triggers and consequences for five to seven days, go on to chapter 6. The information you are keeping will help you decide if you want to change your habits.

6

Getting Ready to Change

You must do the thing you think you cannot do.

      —Eleanor Roosevelt

Results! Why man, I have gotten a lot of results. I know several thousand things that won't work.

      —Thomas Edison

We know that people can and do change. We wrote *The Habit Change Workbook* to help people learn proven techniques to change habits and problem behaviors, either by themselves or with the help of a therapist. James Prochaska, Ph.D., and his colleagues have spent years researching how people change—we change in stages. Dr. Prochaska's model defines these stages and shows that different strategies make sense at different stages (Prochaska, Norcross, and DiClemente 1994).

Stages of Change

Below, we will explain the stages and help you discover which stage you are in. This will help you determine what to do next as you prepare to change. Follow Lucy as she progresses through Prochaska's stages of change.

Precontemplation

People in the *precontemplation stage* do not have an intention to change. Since you are reading this book, you are probably not in this stage (unless you are reading it to help someone else change). In the precontemplation stage people don't see the need to change a habit—or they don't see it as a bad habit in the first place.

Lucy began gambling as a way to relax. She enjoyed playing bingo about once a month. She made friends at the bingo parlor and soon was playing bingo every week. One of her new friends invited her to a local casino where she discovered video poker. It was fun and helped her get away from her problems. Lucy's sister asked her about her gambling, "Do you think you might be spending too much time playing bingo?" "No, it's just entertainment," Lucy politely told her.

If you are reading *The Habit Change Workbook* because you want someone else to change a habit, you need to be aware that the person may be in the precontemplation stage. The easiest way to determine if others are in this stage may be to ask them if they intend to change in the next six months. If the answer is "no," then they are in the precontemplation stage. Sometimes people will come to a therapist while they are in this stage; however, it is usually because someone else is putting pressure on them to change. They may actually change the problem behaviors until the pressure is off, but then they usually slip back to their old ways.

Contemplation

You know you have a problem. You're thinking you really should work on it. You're thinking about changing. This is the *contemplation stage*. Research has shown that people can stay in this stage for years without actually changing (Prochaska, Norcross, and DiClemente 1992). In this stage people are often weighing the pros and cons of the problem and its possible solutions. They are thinking about how much energy it will take for them to change and what benefits the habit has.

Lucy spent more and more time playing bingo. Her gambling trips out of town became more frequent. If she couldn't find someone who was interested in making the trip to the casino with her, she went alone. Even worse, gambling was beginning to affect her finances. Credit card debt was getting to be a problem. She met with a financial counselor, who helped her make out a budget. Gambling money was not in the budget. After the meeting with the counselor she met her friends and played bingo, spending the money she had set aside to buy a birthday gift for her niece.

Lucy's sister asked her how the meeting with the financial counselor went. "She told me to stop gambling and stick to a budget," said Lucy. "I know I shouldn't gamble. I know it's a problem. I'm just not ready to stop yet. If I didn't play bingo, what would I do with myself?"

Preparation

Dr. Claiborn likes to tell the following joke to his patients: "How many psychologists does it take to change a lightbulb? Only one, but the bulb has to be ready to change." In the *preparation stage* people are ready to change and may have made some early efforts to change. If you've read this far, perhaps you are in this stage. You purchased *The Habit Change Workbook* with the intention of changing a problem habit. You've filled out forms and answered questions about your habit. You are collecting information about your habit and getting ready to change.

Not long after the appointment with the financial counselor, Lucy's telephone was disconnected because she hadn't paid the bill. Bingo and video poker were becoming severe problems. She recognized that gambling was interfering with her family life and her financial situation. Lucy called her sister, and together they went back to the financial counselor, who helped her set up a budget and gave her information about Gamblers Anonymous. It was hard, but she began going to Gamblers Anonymous meetings and continued attending twice a week. Most of all, Lucy felt hopeful that she could change.

Action

The *action stage* is the one that commonly comes to mind when people think about change. In this stage, people are doing things that others will recognize as efforts to change. When you are in the action stage you are likely to describe yourself as working hard on the problem and may say things like, "Anyone can talk about changing, but I'm really working on it." A person's work in this stage of change is recognized and often supported or praised by others. Sometimes this is a problem because the work in the earlier and later stages—when you also need support—is ignored.

Lucy kept her monthly appointments with the financial counselor and went to Gamblers Anonymous regularly. She went to church with her sister and found she enjoyed this as much as playing bingo. She met new friends, and she found different activities to do with her old bingo friends. Lucy's sister praised her for staying away from gambling and even took her out to dinner to celebrate her first month "bingofree."

Maintenance

Many people will not understand the *maintenance stage* as an active one, but this final stage is very important in preventing relapse. People with certain habits will stay in the maintenance stage for the rest of their life. In this stage, people need to make changes in long-term patterns in order to stabilize themselves and prevent a return of the problem habit.

Lucy developed new ways of relaxing and enjoying herself, and her sister stuck by her and provided support. Lucy liked the challenge of playing chess and joined a chess club. No betting—she just enjoyed the game. At one point, Lucy thought she could make day trips to the casino with her friends and enjoy shopping while her friends played video poker, then meeting them for lunch. But the temptation was too great. She came home broke and angry with herself. This was a turning point for Lucy—she realized that she would need to fight her gambling problem for the rest of her life.

We know that people don't move through these stages in a straight line. Dr. Prochaska describes the process of change as more of a spiral. Almost everyone has made a New Year's resolution to change a habit, lose weight, or do some kind of self-improvement project, and almost everyone has slipped back at some point. The embarrassment and shame of failure may lead to our moving all the way back from the action stage to the precontemplation stage. Mark Twain said, "To cease smoking is the easiest thing I ever did. I ought to know because I've done it a thousand times." He was probably cycling back and forth through the contemplation, preparation, and action stages.

⚘ Habit Change Strategy

Make moving into the action stage a short-term goal as you work toward reaching your long-term goal of changing your problem habits.

Change Is a Process

Dr. Prochaska and other researchers have described ten processes of change. Studies have found these processes to be important in any effort to change (Prochaska, Norcross, and DiClemente 1994). It is interesting to see how these *processes* of change fit within the *stages* of change.

- **Consciousness raising** involves gaining information about yourself and the habit you are trying to change. Reading this book and doing exercises such as the Habit Description worksheet are ways to raise your consciousness. This process is important in the precontemplation and contemplation stages of change. If you are reading this because you want to help someone else change their habit and they seem to be in one of these two stages, then giving them information, confronting them about the effects of their habit, and pointing out when the habit occurs may be effective forms of consciousness raising.

- **Emotional arousal** is another important process in the precontemplation and contemplation stages. This involves experiencing and expressing feelings about the problem or habit and its possible solutions. Doing this may help you move from the precontemplation to the contemplation and preparation stages.

- **Self-reevaluation** involves assessing how you feel about yourself with respect to your habit. This may include examining your values, identifying what you want to achieve, assessing how the habit fits in your life now, and deciding how you would like things to be in the future. This process takes place in the contemplation and preparation stages. Some of the questions you answer in this book are designed to help you with self-reevaluation.

- **Environmental reevaluation** is the process of evaluating how your problem or habit affects your physical environment. Considering how your habit affects other people, your relationships, and your financial well-being are parts of this process. Like self-reevaluation, this happens in the contemplation and preparation stages.

- **Commitment** is the process of choosing to make a commitment to act and believe in the ability to change. This can take the form of a New Year's-type of resolution or a commitment to change by really applying what you have learned here. This process often takes place in the preparation and action stages.

- **A helping relationship** can be an important part of making a change. Therapists are trained to pay attention to these kinds of relationships, and many types of therapy utilize the helping relationship as a major ingredient in change. If you are trying to change without the help of a therapist, being open with someone you trust and discussing the problem or habit you are trying to change can be helpful. Self-help groups can be important in this process. The helping relationship seems to be most important in the action and maintenance stages.

- **Counterconditioning** is a change process that is likely to be recommended by a behavior therapist, but often people discover it on their own. This involves substituting alternatives for the problem behavior. Using relaxation, meditation, and positive self-statements are examples. The *competing response*, used in *habit reversal* and utilized in the Habit Change Program, is a form of counterconditioning. As you will learn in chapter 7, a competing response is a behavior you will engage in whenever you have an urge to start your habit. It is a behavior that is incompatible with your habit. The use of counterconditioning is most important in the action and maintenance stages.

- **Environment control** involves avoiding or changing the stimuli that elicit the problem behavior. People with problem eating habits are using this method when they get problem foods out of their house. Someone who picks at his or her face may need to stay away from the mirror, and someone with insomnia may need to change what he or she does in bed. Like counterconditioning, this process is used in the action and maintenance stages.

- **Reward**, also called *reinforcement*, is a very powerful tool. You might reward yourself or be rewarded by others for making changes. Reinforcements, or rewards, are effective, whether they come from yourself or from others. This is important to keep in mind if you are trying to get somebody else to change. Reinforcement management is important in the action and maintenance stages.

- **Social liberation** involves efforts to increase alternatives to particular behaviors in society at large. This can include action such as advocating for the rights of others or helping other people battle their habits. Although this is important in some areas of change, it usually doesn't play a major part in changing habits.

Habit Change Strategy

Note that punishment does not appear on the list of change processes. The reason is that punishment does not work well for change. Punishing yourself or others is not likely to lead to effective change; it will only make you discouraged and upset.

Where Are You in the Stages of Change?

Now that we have explained some ideas about change, it is time for you to pick up your pencil again. Let's look at where you are in the stages of change.

What stage of change are you in right now? _____

_____

Now review the change processes described above and list the ones that could best help you, given the stage you are in. _____

_____

_____

If you are in the precontemplation or contemplation stage it may be helpful for you to find someone to talk to about your habit. Try expressing some of your feelings about the habit and about changing your habit. Read the sections in this book about your particular habit. This will help you with the *consciousness-raising* process of change.

But I've Tried to Change Before!

You've probably tried to change your habits before. Let's take a look at what happened then. You can learn from what did and didn't work.

Past Habit-Change Efforts

How many times have you tried to change your habit? _____

When was the first time you tried to change? _____

When was the last time you tried to change? _____

How long did you succeed during your most successful try? _____

_____

How did you feel about changing? _____

_____

_____

_____

How did you feel when you relapsed? _____

_____

_____

_____

What kind of thoughts did you have about relapsing? _____

_____

_____

_____

What happened when you relapsed before? Did a specific event lead to your restarting your habit? _____

_____

_____

_____

_____

Chart 6a

Carl's Past Habit-Change Efforts

How many times have you tried to change your habit? _Too many to count, at least fifty._

When was the first time you tried to change? _When I was seven and my teacher ridiculed me._

When was the last time you tried to change? _Last year, then I gave up._

How long did you succeed during your most successful try? _Five months._

How did you feel about changing? _I felt nervous all the time. I didn't know what to do with my hands. And I felt a loss, kind of depressed and anxious quite often._

How did you feel when you relapsed? _I was disgusted with myself. I was angry, depressed. I still feel ashamed and weak because I can't seem to stop biting my nails._

What kind of thoughts did you have about relapsing? _I am just plain lazy. I can't stop biting my nails. I will never be able to quit. What must people think of me? They probably think I am weak, and I am weak. I should be able to control myself better. Just stop. Anyone should be able to do that. But I can't._

What happened when you relapsed before? Did a specific event lead to your restarting your habit? _I had a really bad day at work. I started biting my nails on the way home. I bit on one nail and it was a bit irregular, so I bit it until it was smooth. Then I bit the rest of the nails to make them even. I blew it! After that, I went back to biting them all the time. I gave up._

Chart 6b

What can we learn from your past efforts to change? If you have tried to change your habits many times before, you may think that yours is a hopeless case and that this book won't make a difference. However, unless you have a working crystal ball, you probably can't really predict the future. Learning from your prior attempts to change can help you do better this time. Later, you will use lessons from your past in your relapse-prevention plan. We will also look at the thoughts you had about yourself when you tried to change and when you relapsed, because these thoughts lead to emotional reactions, such as guilt. As we discussed earlier, guilt actually makes you more likely to return to the problem habit.

Let's take a look at Carl's habit of biting his nails. When Carl was a child, his mother and some of his teachers tried many methods to get him to quit biting his nails. They tried punishment methods, such as taking away his favorite things when he bit his nails. They offered to give him a reward if he could stop for a month. His mother and one teacher used shame as well: the teacher talked about Carl's bad habit in front of the entire class. Carl wanted to disappear that day, but he only bit and chewed more.

As an adult, Carl purchased a bad-tasting substance to paint on his nails, but he got used to the taste. He made New Year's resolutions to quit, but they never lasted long. Many times he would simply find himself biting without knowing how he had started. He went to a hypnotherapist, who told him that he could be cured in a few sessions. Carl didn't find this to be any help either and was not even sure if he had been hypnotized.

Habit Change Strategy

Learn from your past attempts to change. Knowledge will help you be successful this time.

Are You Ready to Change?

Why change now? It may seem like a silly question, but something must be motivating you if you have gotten this far. Stating your reasons for change helps solidify your motivation to change. Sometimes a particular incident or an upcoming event makes people want to change. For example, a person might write, "I have my high-school reunion coming up, and I can't show up looking like this." List some reasons why you want to change now. Include reasons that might not have been true before.

_____

_____

_____

_____

_____

_____

✠ Habit Change Strategy

Why do you want to change *now*? At times when your motivation is at its lowest, review your answers and remind yourself *why* you want to change.

Here's another question that may seem strange: What are the advantages or benefits of keeping your habit? We'll put it another way: What do you get out of this habit? Before you answer, remember that relief from stress or boredom may be considered a benefit. Attention from others, even negative attention or criticism, can be a benefit of your habit.

Fill in the boxes in the Habit Advantages and Disadvantages chart. Then look at your results. Are the advantages of changing and the disadvantages of keeping your habit more important to you than the reasons not to change? If so, you are ready to change your habit. If not, you may not be ready to give up this habit.

Habit Advantages and Disadvantages	
Advantages of Keeping the Habit	**Disadvantages of Keeping the Habit**
Advantages of Changing the Habit	**Disadvantages of Changing the Habit**

Chart 6c

Carl's Habit Advantages and Disadvantages

Advantages of Keeping the Habit	Disadvantages of Keeping the Habit
Biting my nails—it gives me something to do when I am bored or nervous.	My nails always look bad.
	My fingers hurt sometimes—often, really.
	I think people stare at my hands.
	My wife finds it disgusting.
	I am afraid my children will learn to bite their nails.
	I think it makes me look nervous and out of control when I bite my nails.

Advantages of Changing the Habit	Disadvantages of Changing the Habit
I will have nice fingernails.	I won't have anything to do when I am bored or nervous.
My fingers won't hurt.	My nails will be rough and ragged.
People won't stare at my hands.	My nails won't be even.
My wife will show approval and be proud of me.	
I can teach my children not to bite their nails; I can teach them that they can overcome habits and other things in life.	
I won't look so nervous, even if I am nervous.	

Chart 6d

Habit Change Strategy

Make a copy of your Habit Advantages and Disadvantages chart and keep it in a conspicuous place. Review it at times when change seems almost impossible.

If you are in the preparation or action stage, you are in a position to take advantage of the next chapter. It will more fully explain the technique of habit reversal and the competing response, which is one of the counterconditioning methods you can apply as you start to move further into the action stage. Now is the time to make a commitment.

Write here exactly how you want to change. _____

_____

_____

_____

_____

Carl:

Write here exactly how you want to change. *I want to stop biting my fingernails. I want to keep my fingernails neat, not too short or too long. I also want to stop trying to get all my nails completely even.*

     In the classic movie *Harvey*, Jimmy Stewart, in the role of mild-mannered, friendly Elwood P. Dowd, does something very important in the process of changing habits: he commits to a date on which he will accomplish a certain objective. Whenever anyone says something like, "We should get together for dinner," he responds by trying to set a date. Now that you know what you want to change, you need to decide when. As Elwood P. Dowd would say, you need to set a date.

Pick a date when you will start applying the tools in the Habit Change Program to changing your problem habit. Write down the date here. _____

Remember that helping relationships are important. Make a list of people who can provide support as you change your habit. _____

Tell your support persons about your commitment and how they can help. Explain how they can reinforce change. What are some specific things they can do to reinforce your efforts?

_____

_____

_____

_____

Carl:

Pick a date when you will start applying the tools in the Habit Change Program to changing your problem habit. Write down the date here. *Tomorrow—I'm ready to get started!*

Remember that helping relationships are important. Make a list of people who can provide support as you change your habit. *My wife, Linda, my friend and coworker Don, and my brother Jacob*

Tell your support persons about your commitment and how they can help. Explain how they can reinforce change. What are some specific things they can do to reinforce your efforts? *My wife could encourage me to fill out all the charts in the book, praise me when my fingernails start looking better, and say something when she sees me absentmindedly chewing my nails. Don and Jacob can offer praise and nudge me when they see me chewing my nails.*

Habit Change Strategy

Set a date to begin changing your habit. Tell someone about your commitment. This will reinforce your dedication to change.

So far, we've all stayed together on our journey toward habit change. Chapter 7 will send you down your own separate path, specifically designed for your habit.

7

Taking the First Steps

Habit with him was all the test of truth, "It must be right: I've done it from my youth."

—George Crabbe

Habit is overcome by habit.

—Thomas Á Kempis

In the 1970s, psychologists and researchers Nathan Azrin and Gregory Nunn developed the technique called *habit reversal*. It has been used successfully to treat tics, stuttering, and nervous habits. Habit reversal is extremely important in changing nervous habits, such as Carl's problem with nail biting and Margie's skin picking. Studies have also proven it successful in treating trichotillomania.

Habit reversal is effective with nervous habits because they are done automatically. While simple automatic behaviors are not the core component of more complex habits, such as gambling, diet and health-related habits, excessive shopping and spending, and sleep habits, habit-reversal is a useful tool for changing these habits as well. Turn now to the chapter that best describes your habit and read it carefully for specific instructions on how to adapt the Habit Change Program to your habit.

How Effective Is Habit Reversal?

Azrin and Nunn have reported remarkable success with habit reversal. In their studies, after the first day of treatment they reported an average 90 percent reduction of the frequency of the targeted habit. After one week, the habit was reduced by an average of 95 percent, after one month an average of 99 percent, and after six months 99.5 percent. A few people, 10 percent, reported that the habit never returned after they learned habit reversal (Azrin and Nunn 1977). Since Azrin and Nunn first introduced their findings, other researchers have repeatedly proven the effectiveness and long-lasting results of habit reversal in changing a variety of habits (Miltenberger, Fuqua, and Woods 1998).

Well, you may be thinking, that's fine if you have access to a thoroughly trained behavior therapist, right? But you can use these methods to change habits on your own. In 1982, researchers Frankel and Merbaum compared the effects of habit reversal directed by a therapist with habit reversal using a patient-treatment manual. They reported only a modest and insignificant increase in the effectiveness of habit reversal when a therapist was involved (Frankel and Merbaum 1982; Miltenberger, Fuqua, and Woods 1998).

Do the results last? In their original research, Azrin and Nunn reported an average 99.5 percent reduction in habit occurrence at the end of six months. But there were relapses. Over time, many participants found that the habit reappeared for a day or more, especially during stressful periods. The participants dealt with relapse by reviewing and performing the habit-reversal procedures again. Some participants called the counselor, who helped them review the procedures. Fewer than 5 percent of the participants needed a "booster" counseling session. More than 80 percent of the participants did not experience relapse. The habit continued to decrease until it was no longer a problem.

Many people believe that if they stop one bad habit they will just replace it with another bad habit. But what if they replace it with one that makes it impossible to engage in the bad habit? This is the idea behind the competing response, the core of habit reversal procedures. You will select a competing behavior that cannot be done while participating in your habit. To be effective, this behavior must be unobtrusive and easy to accomplish. In time, the habit will loosen its hold on you, and you will also lose the need to perform the competing response.

✣ Habit Change Strategy

Recognize the ways in which you are blending your habits with "normal," everyday behaviors.

Habit Awareness

Habit reversal is made up of several individual steps. The first steps involve habit awareness. Habits generally develop slowly and are often well established before the disadvantages appear. We usually participate in habit behaviors without being aware of what we are doing. Recording the description, consequences, advantages, and disadvantages of your habit have helped you become more aware of your habit, which will help you as you begin the process of changing.

Lack of awareness is one of the reasons habits are so persistent. Your habit may seem to be a part of your very being, and people expect you to continue it. At first, family members and friends may mention your habit and try to get you to stop, but after a while they may become so accustomed to it that they no longer notice it. And social custom usually prevents strangers and new acquaintances from commenting.

Margie went to a therapist seeking help for depression. The therapist couldn't help noticing that Margie also had a skin-picking problem. She obviously picked at her face. She wore long sleeves, but her wrists were revealed and it was evident that she picked there too. He interviewed Margie and discussed her symptoms of depression, but he didn't bring up the skin picking. He waited for her to bring up these symptoms. This is the way most people reacted to Margie—they didn't bring it up. They might have noticed that she picked at her skin, but they averted their eyes and didn't mention it. The response of Margie's therapist and other people in her life is common. They may notice the effects of others' habits, but most people won't comment. The lack of reaction makes it easier for us to ignore the effects of a habit and allow us to continue the behavior without trying to change.

Another factor is the mixing of the habit with "normal" or ordinary behaviors. Skin picking or nail biting may occur while you are talking on the phone, reading, or watching TV.

Excessive shopping commingles with everyday shopping for needed articles. These habitual behaviors tend not to be the focus of attention in these settings, so they blend into the background and may not be noticed. Even when people recognize bad habits, many avoid habit change because they fear that when they give up their habit they will experience a great deal of anxiety. Interestingly, this is usually not the case. When people change a habit they often feel less anxious.

Now we'll begin the steps of the habit-reversal process. For this, you will need to refer to the worksheets you completed in chapters 5 and 6.

Step 1: Keep a Habit Record

Review the Habit Record you completed in chapter 5. You need to be aware of how much you are engaging in your habit so that you can track your progress. In addition, you may have noticed that just keeping the record has brought about some changes in your habit. Because of this, record keeping is important for your becoming aware of where you started and how much you have changed, but it is also helpful because it brings about change.

Step 2: List Advantages and Disadvantages

Review the Habit Advantages and Disadvantages chart in chapter 6. If you haven't completed the chart, do so now. This is an important step that is designed to move you into the action stage of change.

Step 3: Identify Preceding Behaviors

What leads to your habit? You will find the Habit Triggers chart in chapter 5 helpful here. What emotions and situations usually precede your habit? If the habit is hair pulling, a preceding behavior might be running your fingers through your hair. For a skin picker, it might be looking in the mirror and searching for blackheads or feeling for rough spots. Describe this behavior carefully. Write your description here.

_____

_____

_____

_____

Carl:

I seem to bite my nails more when I am nervous or bored or worried about something. I might be watching TV, and when that happens I hardly even know I am doing it. All of a sudden, I'll have my fingers in my mouth. At work I might be nervous about a meeting or a project I'm working on.

Step 4: Describe Your Habit

You will find your Habit Description and Habit Record helpful here. Describe the elements of your habit. For example, Margie describes peering into the mirror and searching for blackheads. She leans close to the mirror and searches her face, starting with her nose. When she sees anything that "doesn't look right" she squeezes and scrapes at it with her fingernails. She concentrates on this one spot until it "feels done." She only does this when she is alone at home. If her husband is home, she waits until he is asleep. Margie always does her checking and picking in the upstairs bathroom, leaning over the sink. She spends five to thirty minutes, often stopping only when her back begins to ache from leaning toward the mirror.

Write a description of your habit. What do you do, step by step? When and where do you do it? Who is around when you engage in your habit? List any other details that help illustrate your habit.

_____

_____

_____

_____

_____

Carl:

I bite my nails. Sometimes I don't realize I am doing it until my fingers are in my mouth and I am biting and chewing. Other times I can see the progression. First I examine my fingers and find one nail that is uneven or jagged. I put my finger in my mouth and feel the jagged edge with my tongue, then I bite until that nail feels even. I might then examine my fingers again. I am usually sitting on the couch, watching TV, driving in my car, or sitting at my desk at work. But it can happen anywhere. Sometimes no one is around, but other times my wife, brother, or close friends are around. What really bothers me is when I bite my nails while my boss or coworkers are around.

Step 5: Practice Relaxation

We've included two relaxation methods in chapter 8. You may have your own special method of relaxing. Entire books are written about relaxation, and we have listed a few of our favorites in the Resources section. Choose a method that feels comfortable to you. Make a commitment to practice your relaxation method daily. Continue daily relaxation practice as you begin work on changing your habit.

Habit Change Strategy

When was the last time your homework included relaxation? Make daily relaxation a habit.

Step 6: Identify Habit-Provoking Situations

Review your Habit Description chart and your answers in steps 3 and 4. Now we are going to look at your habit a little differently. What kind of mood are you usually in when your habit shows up? For example, are you tense, angry, sad, bored, tired, or lonely? Where are you likely to be when you engage in your habit? At what time of day do you seem most vulnerable? Are you usually alone or with someone? Whom are you with? Do you feel more vulnerable during certain activities or in particular situations? Answering these questions below will help you identify when you are most likely to engage in your habit. This awareness will help you be on the lookout for habit-provoking situations.

_____

_____

_____

_____

Carl:

I am usually bored, nervous, or worried when I start biting my nails. Most often, I am in my car, sitting at my desk, or watching TV, but it can be anywhere. I can be alone or with people close to me. Sometimes I am with my boss, colleagues, or strangers. I feel most vulnerable when I am sitting down, doing nothing with my hands.

Habit Change Strategy

When it comes to identifying habit triggers and habit-provoking situations, be your own detective. What were you doing when your habit showed up? Where were you? How did you feel? What were you thinking? Be on guard next time you are confronted with these triggers and situations.

Step 7: Develop a Competing Response

One of the most important steps of habit reversal is to develop a competing response, a behavior you will try to engage in every time you have an urge to start the problem habit. Because you may use it quite frequently, choose a competing response that can be done often and as long as needed. Be sure that the competing response is one you can continue for several minutes. The behavior must be incompatible with your habit. If your habit is hair pulling or twirling, your competing response could be to clench your fist. If you tend to bite your fingernails when you are in class, you could hold a pencil in your hand. You can't chew on your fingernails, twirl your hair, or pull your hair when your hands are doing something else.

Your competing response should also be a behavior that can be done without interfering with other activities. If you pick your skin or twirl your hair while watching TV you can continue watching TV while clenching your fists. If you tend to engage in your habit while driving you can clench the steering wheel. At work or school, you can clench one fist and clench a pencil in the other hand.

Engaging in your competing response should help you be more aware of what you are doing and what you are not doing. In our example, while you are clenching your fist, you can continue to remind yourself of the reason you are doing so—to keep from picking. Paying attention to your habitual, automatic behavior will help keep it from occurring without your being aware of it.

Below, list several possible competing responses you could engage in when you are in a habit-provoking situation. Brainstorm—list the behaviors that come to mind, without over-thinking them. You will select just one, but for now list at least five from which you can choose.

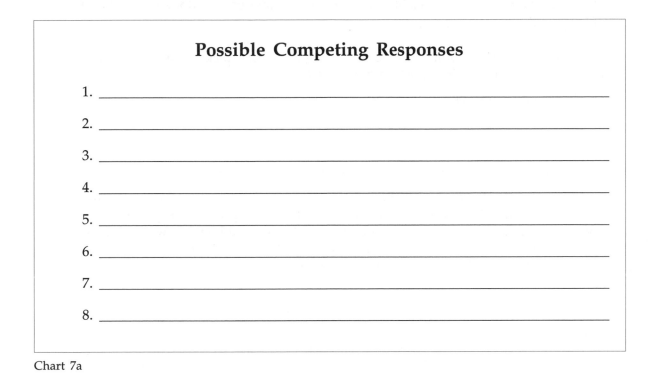

Possible Competing Responses

1. _____
2. _____
3. _____
4. _____
5. _____
6. _____
7. _____
8. _____

Chart 7a

Carl's Possible Competing Responses

1. *Clench both fists.*
2. *Clench one fist, hold onto a table or steering wheel with the other hand.*
3. *Clench a soft ball in each hand.*
4. *Put hands in pockets.*
5. *Fold hands in lap or behind back.*
6. *Hold a pencil in one hand.*
7. *Finger keys in pocket.*
8. *Mentally list all of the states in the Union, then the state capitals.*

Chart 7b

⬨ Habit Change Strategy

Your competing response should be an activity that can be done often and as long as needed, is incompatible with your habit, and can be done without interfering with other activities.

After you have listed your possible competing responses, pick one that seems to fit all of the criteria we discussed. It must be a behavior that:

- is incompatible with your habit
- you can do as often as needed
- you can do as long as the urge continues
- can be done without significantly interfering with other activities

Carl listed eight possible competing responses. Then he compared them with the criteria above. Clenching one fist while holding onto a table, steering wheel, or pencil would work only when such items were available; finding these items could interfere with other activities. This option would work if he only chewed his nails in the car or while sitting behind his desk. Clenching soft balls wouldn't work because he would have to carry the balls around with him all the time. Carl felt that fingering keys or putting his hands in his pockets would draw too much attention. Finally, listing all the states would not keep him from biting his nails because his hands would still be free. Carl chose clenching both fists as his competing response because it met all of the criteria.

From your list, choose the competing response that works for you. You will be replacing your old habit, with all of its disadvantages and negative consequences, with a new, healthy habit—your competing response. In chapter 6 you charted the advantages and disadvantages of keeping and changing your old habit. Let's do the same with your new habit. Make copies of the Competing Response Advantages and Disadvantages chart below. Complete it for the competing response you think will best meet the criteria. If you aren't convinced this is the best option, complete a chart for another competing response. You may even want to line up more than one competing response for different situations. We've provided Carl's Competing Response Advantages and Disadvantages chart as an example.

Competing Response Advantages and Disadvantages

Competing Response: _____

Advantages	Disadvantages

Chart 7c

Carl's Competing Response Advantages and Disadvantages

Competing Response: Clenching fists
_____

Advantages	Disadvantages
I can't bite my nails and clench my fists at the same time.	I might get tired of clenching my fists—but then I could think of a new competing response.
It wouldn't interfere with most activities.	I can't clench my fists when I'm doing something else—but I can't bite my nails when I am doing something else either.
I can do it anytime I have an urge to bite my nails.	
It will give me something to do when I am bored or nervous.	
I will have nice fingernails.	
My fingers won't hurt.	
People won't stare at my fingers and nails.	
My wife will be proud of me.	
My children will see that it is possible to change bad habits.	
I won't look so nervous, even if I feel nervous.	

Chart 7d

Like Carl, you may find that the left-hand column of the chart for your competing response may look much like the advantages of changing your habit on your Habit Advantages and Disadvantages chart in chapter 6. Like Carl, you probably won't be able to come up with many disadvantages of your competing response. Carl wrote down his disadvantages, then immediately argued against them. It was clear to him that his was a good competing response. For many people, their competing response will yield more benefits than just getting rid of an old habit. For Betty, who had a problem with shopping, walking not only helped her resist shopping and spending but also improved her overall health. Reading not only gave George a new form of entertainment besides the Internet, it also added to his knowledge.

When you have found the competing response that works best for you, describe it below. Describe it very specifically this time. Anytime you find yourself engaging in your habit, interrupt it by using your competing response.

My Competing Response

_____

_____

_____

_____

_____

_____

Chart 7e

Carl's Competing Response

I will make fists with my thumbs tucked in and my fingers held tightly over my thumbs. I will hold the fists for three minutes every time I feel the urge to chew on my nails or whenever I find myself starting to feel for rough spots on the edges of my fingernails.

Chart 7f

Step 8: Review the Behaviors that Lead to Your Habit

In step 3 you listed the behaviors that lead to your engaging in your habit. If you didn't list these behaviors, go back and do so now. Whenever you notice these behaviors, begin your competing response. Rehearse the response now. Think about finding yourself doing one of the preliminary behaviors and then stopping yourself. Perform the competing response as you described it in step 7.

Now think about the habit-provoking situations you identified in step 6. If you skipped step 6 because it seemed so obvious and simple, go back and list the situations now. Imagine yourself in one of the habit-provoking situations, performing a few of the preliminary behaviors. Instead of engaging in your habit, start your competing response. Perform your competing response for three to five minutes, then repeat the entire exercise three to five times for a total of fifteen minutes.

As you are rehearsing, talk to yourself, either aloud or in your head. Mentally discuss what you are doing, what steps you are taking, and how you are feeling. Most people have anxiety about the urge or tension that precedes engaging in a habit. It is common to have thoughts such as "I am not going to be able to stand it," "I'm going to go crazy," or "I must do this; I have to do my habit." Talk back to these thoughts, saying, "Sometimes I have resisted my habit, and I haven't gone crazy yet," or "The urges will go away; they always do." Chapters 9 and 10 will give you more pointers on how to talk back to your negative thoughts.

It is important to rehearse your competing response every day. Plan to dedicate at least fifteen minutes to rehearsing each day for seven days. Make a commitment to rehearse as described, at an appointed time every day for a week. Each day, when you have done your rehearsal, check off the days below.

Day 1 ____ Day 2 ____ Day 3 ____ Day 4 ____ Day 5 ____ Day 6 ____ Day 7 ____

By the end of the first week the urges will probably diminish greatly. You may find that the habit almost disappears. Then you can relax a bit and rehearse only when you feel the urges increasing.

Habit Change Strategy

Rehearsing your competing response will prepare you to handle habit-provoking situations when you encounter them.

Step 9: Get Help from Others

In earlier chapters we discussed why habits persist. Now you will utilize that information as you arrange your social environment so that others will be able to help. Start by choosing one or two people who can help you change your habit. Discuss The Habit Change Program with that person. Explain that you need help in the form of positive feedback. Let each person know that nagging and criticizing won't help, and that noticing your progress and praising you for your good work will be more beneficial.

Margie told her mother how hard she was working and proudly showed her the slight improvement of her skin's appearance. Her mother's response was, "You should have been doing that all along." Margie was disappointed by her mother's response. She explained the Habit Change Program to her mother and told her what kind of responses would be helpful. With this added information her mother recognized the effort Margie was making to help herself and she gave Margie the support she needed. At first Margie found it difficult to talk to her mother about her skin picking, but the positive support she received made it worthwhile.

Step 10: Identify Situations You Have Been Avoiding

Carl avoided activities that would make his hands more noticeable. He didn't shake hands and kept his hands in his pockets as often as possible. He enjoyed playing cards, but he avoided this because attention might be focused on his hands. Margie wore long sleeves, even during the summer. She wore her hair close to her face with her bangs covering her forehead, and she never went out of the house without makeup. Her children loved to go swimming at their apartment complex. She took them to the pool but never went swimming herself; she sat by the pool, dressed in long pants and long-sleeved shirts. List the situations you avoid because of your habit.

Carl:

I avoid situations at work that will make me nervous, therefore I try to get out of meetings, especially if my boss or other important people will be there. I keep my hands in my pockets whenever I can. When I do have my hands exposed, I try to keep my fingers curled so they aren't as prominent.

Now, make plans to display your improvement by intentionally putting yourself in situations you have been avoiding. List the things you plan to do and the dates you would like to be able to do them.

_____

_____

_____

_____

Carl:

I will start slowly to put myself in situations I have been avoiding. I'll start with taking my hands out of my pockets the second week, stop curling my fingers the third week, then stop avoiding meetings at work the fourth week.

Habit Change Strategy

Don't let your habit rule your life. Stop avoiding the things that could make your life richer and more enjoyable.

You now have the steps for habit reversal. If you have read this chapter but have not filled in the blanks, go back and do so now. As you have seen, the work you do in one chapter builds on the work you do in the next, so it is important to complete each exercise. The next chapter teaches you some relaxation exercises. Relaxation will help you cope with the anxiety that naturally comes with making major life changes.

8

Relaxation

Sit in reverie and watch the changing color of the waves that break upon the idle seashore of the mind.

—Henry Wadsworth Longfellow

True silence is the rest of the mind; it is to the spirit what sleep is to the body, nourishment and refreshment.

—William Penn

Most habits are ways of relieving stress, nervousness, anxiety, or boredom. You probably feel more relaxed while you are engaging in your habit, or just after engaging in it. Since you are removing these coping methods, you will need to develop other ways of coping with stress. In this chapter you will learn some relaxation exercises; eventually you will be able to use one or more of these when you feel the urge to engage in your habit. First, though, you will need to practice relaxation techniques for several minutes a day. The more you practice, the more you will be prepared to relax when the urge hits.

How Does Relaxation Help?

You may be saying, "I don't have any stress. I'm not nervous. I'm just bored when my habit shows up." However, being bored doesn't mean being relaxed. Think back to a time when you were bored. Carl, our nail biter, described how he feels when he is bored: "My eyes wander around the room. I get squirmy and cross my legs, then I uncross them and change position in my seat. I feel very restless and, before I know it, a finger is in my mouth and I'm chewing on a nail. Nail biting relieves the restlessness and gives me something to do."

Engaging in his habit helps Carl relieve his boredom and restlessness. Engaging in a relaxation exercise can bring about a very similar response. While watching TV, Carl can practice relaxation exercises instead of biting his nails. Whenever he catches himself biting his nails, he tells himself to relax. Even while sitting in a boring meeting he can make himself relax. For Carl, just engaging in a relaxation exercise gives his mind something to concentrate on and relieves his boredom.

Amanda gets the urge to pull her hair when she feels an itch on her scalp. She tilts her head and stiffens her muscles. She searches for the right hair with her fingers. Pinching a hair and pulling gently, she decides it's not the right one. As she searches, her neck, shoulders, and fingers tighten more. When she recorded her actions on her Habit Records, she noticed that she held her breath and felt like she was in a trance. When she slowed her breathing and relaxed her muscles using progressive muscle relaxation (explained below), she found that the trancelike state was broken, the urge to pull was reduced, and she could engage in her competing response. After several days of relaxation practice, Amanda's anxiety was greatly reduced, and she didn't have as many urges to pull her hair.

Matthew found that the abdominal breathing exercise below helped him control his habit of interrupting. When he was in social situations, he often found himself getting overly excited. He felt like he just had to speak. His pastor once told him that he seemed to suffer from undelivered speech. When he feels the urge to interrupt now, he takes a few deep abdominal breaths, and then decides if he should speak. Relaxing helps him slow down, so his brain can catch up with his mouth.

Lucy's urge to play bingo or video poker was strongest when she was worried or anxious. Gambling got her mind off her worries and seemed to calm her. She did get excited when she was winning, but she felt angry with herself and out of control when she was losing, which was most of the time. And losing money she had set aside for something else added to her worries. Using relaxation techniques relieved much of her anxiety and stress. After meditating—her chosen relaxation exercise—she felt more in control of her emotions and her thoughts. She felt she could face her worries.

♟ Habit Change Strategy

Relaxation can bring relief from the emotions that make you more likely to engage in your habit—anxiety, stress, boredom, nervousness, and worry.

Relaxation Methods

You've heard the old doctor's order, "Take an aspirin and call me in the morning." Well, relaxation training is sometimes called "the aspirin of behavioral treatments." Relaxation is considered to be good for nearly everyone.

You may think you already know how to relax. You watch TV, read, sleep, take long walks, eat "comfort foods," or drink alcohol. While these activities seem relaxing in their own way, we are referring to a different kind of relaxation.

Our goal is to relax our bodies and minds. Below we have provided three relaxation methods. Choose the one that most appeals to you or try them all.

If you are taking medications for anxiety, diabetes, or to lower your blood pressure, consult your doctor. He or she might want to adjust your medication dosage as you reduce your stress, anxiety, and tension. If you have a physical problem such as osteoporosis, heart or lung disease, or a mental disorder, one or more of these exercises could have adverse effects on your condition. Ask your doctor which relaxation exercise would be best for you.

Abdominal Breathing

How do you breathe? Take notice of your breathing style next time you are nervous. Does your chest, or your abdomen, rise and fall? Are your shoulders tense and inching upward with every breath? Do your muscles feel tight? Abdominal breathing can help. Cherry has vocal-cord tightness, which sometimes gives her a hoarse voice and makes her stutter, especially when she is nervous. When speaking in public, she had a habit of tensing her shoulders and breathing with her chest, rather than with her abdominal muscles. A friend who was a member of Toastmasters advised her to relax her shoulders and use slow abdominal breathing. As a result of following this advice, Cherry's speaking voice improved because she improved her breathing. In addition, she felt less nervous when she spoke.

When your shoulders and abdominal muscles are tight, you tend to use your chest, not your abdominal muscles, to breathe. Because you are not filling your lungs fully, you probably aren't getting enough oxygen. To compensate, you breathe faster, in shallow breaths. The nervous, anxious feelings worsen. After practicing abdominal breathing, you will learn to recognize your nervous breathing and switch to a more relaxed breathing style. Practice the following exercise for four to five minutes daily:

1. Lie in a comfortable position. Breathe normally for five breaths. Does your chest move up and down with each breath, or is it your abdomen? If you can't tell, rest one hand on your chest and one on your abdomen. Which one rises? If you still can't tell, rest a book on your abdomen. Does it move up and down? Aim to have your abdomen move up and down, while your chest stays fairly still.

2. Close your eyes and breathe in, using your abdominal muscles. Breathe in deeply, pushing your stomach up, keeping your chest relatively still.

3. Take several slow, deep breaths, then open your eyes and look at your abdomen. Is it rising and falling? Breathe gently at your usual speed and depth.

4. If you're still using your chest muscles, press gently on your abdomen as you exhale. Don't worry if it isn't working yet. It takes time to change nervous breathing to relaxed breathing.

5. When you have learned to use relaxed breathing lying down, practice abdominal breathing sitting, then standing.

6. When you find yourself using nervous breathing in a stressful situation, stop and begin your relaxed breathing. In time, it will become more natural.

Progressive Muscle Relaxation

The body often responds to anxiety and stress by tensing the muscles. Tightening your muscles beyond normal tension, then relaxing them, can help bring about relaxation. In this exercise, you will tighten then relax your muscles, one group of muscles at a time. It may help if you record the instructions and play the recording during the exercise. Make sure your recorded voice is relaxed and calm. If you don't like the sound of your voice, record someone else reading the instructions. If you like, you can play soft, relaxing music in the background. This exercise should be done for at least ten to fifteen minutes daily.

1. Lie comfortably, with your arms at your sides and your legs stretched out straight.

2. Take three deep breaths. You may want to precede this exercise with a session of abdominal breathing.

3. Tighten your hands, making a fist, for seven seconds. Then relax your hands and arms for fifteen seconds.

4. Tighten first your forearms, then your upper arms in the same way, tightening for seven seconds, relaxing for fifteen seconds.

5. Continue tightening and relaxing each muscle group, in this order: forehead, muscles around the eyes, jaw, neck and throat, chest and shoulders, upper back, abdominal or stomach muscles, upper legs, lower legs, and feet.

6. Try tightening and relaxing one extremity at a time.

7. Are you relaxed? Review your body, one muscle group at a time. If you feel tension anywhere, repeat the tense-and-relax cycle for that muscle group.

8. After you've practiced progressive relaxation daily for a week or so and you feel comfortable with it, sit up and go through the procedure of tensing and relaxing each muscle group a bit more quickly. Then try it standing. Now you have a relaxation method you can use any time you experience tension and stress.

Meditation

People have been practicing meditation for at least five thousand years. Some practice it for spiritual reasons, but many practice it for health reasons. Meditation not only produces relaxation but can also influence your metabolic rate, decrease your heart rate, increase your alertness, decrease alcohol and drug use, and reduce chronic anxiety. Remember, if you don't like the idea of meditation, you have two other relaxation techniques to pick from. Here is a simple meditation technique.

1. Do what you can to reduce the noise around you. If that's not possible, you may want to play very soft music or nature sounds on your stereo. Sit in a comfortable chair and close your eyes.

2. If you're feeling tense or nervous, spend a few minutes doing progressive muscle relaxation.

3. Focus your attention on a physical or mental image. Concentrate on it, but don't focus too hard.

4. When thoughts come to mind, let them float on by. Don't push them out of your mind, but don't focus on them either. Just accept the thoughts, then let them go. If a thought or worry just won't leave, stop and write it down. The worry is gone now.

5. Focus on a word or phrase. It can be a neutral word, or a word or phrase that has special meaning for you, like "praise God," "relax," or "be still." Dr. Claiborn often recommends focusing on the word "calm." Cherry's preference is a Bible verse.

6. In your mind, say the chosen focus word or phrase with every breath you let out. You may want to stretch the word out for the entire length of the exhaled breath.

7. When thoughts pop into your head, gently remind yourself to stay focused on your word and your physical or mental image. Let the thought float on by.

8. Focus on your word for ten to fifteen minutes daily. At first, you could start by doing this for just five minutes. When you feel nervous or stressed, do a shortened version of this exercise. With time, you'll be able to bring on a relaxed state in just a few minutes.

⬥⬥⬥ Habit Change Strategy

Choose a relaxation technique and practice it daily while you are working on habit change.

Daily relaxation exercises will help relieve your anxiety, stress, tension, and boredom. This will, in turn, help reduce your urges to engage in your habit. Choose a relaxation technique and begin practicing it every day. If one doesn't work well for you, choose another one. Relaxation will also help you as you work through the next two chapters, in which you'll examine the thoughts surrounding your habit and replace them with more realistic thoughts.

9

Changing the Way
You Think

I don't wait for moods. You accomplish nothing if you do that. Your mind must know it has got to get down to business.

—Pearl S. Buck

If you think you can do a thing or think you can't do a thing, you're right.

—Henry Ford

Humans are thinking creatures. We are continuously thinking and processing information. Think about an activity that you do each day. Mentally review each step of the activity. What do you do first? What do you do next? What thoughts are involved in these activities? For example, Cherry usually starts each day with a cup of coffee, a light breakfast, a look at the news on TV, and a few minutes reading her Bible. Then she's ready to start her workday. Cherry's Activity Steps chart illustrates her behaviors, thoughts, and emotional reactions as she starts her day of writing.

Cherry's Activity Steps

Activity: <u>start of workday</u>

Step	Behavior	Automatic Thought	Emotional Reaction
1	Get up from couch and get another cup of coffee.	I'd rather watch more news. I don't feel like working.	Frustration, pleasure at aroma of coffee
2	Go to home office and turn on the computer.	The computer takes a while to warm up. I'll go to the restroom.	Anticipation
3	Go to restroom, take vitamins, comb hair, etc.	Oh, vitamins—can't forget them. This counter is dirty. I'll clean the bathroom this afternoon.	Feelings of tiredness
4	Go back to office, open e-mail program.	I'll check my e-mail first. That's part of my work, even if most of the e-mail is personal.	Varied reactions to e-mail—relaxed feeling, concern, laughter, sadness, interest in learning
5	Exit e-mail, open word-processing program.	Time to start writing. But first I'll take a break and play solitaire. There's Little Kitty. She wants a snack.	Relaxation, enjoyment, guilt for postponing writing
6	Open computer solitaire game, give the cat a snack.	I'll play for just a few minutes. I deserve a break. Here's your snack. Now be good, Little Kitty.	Some guilt, more enjoyment and relaxation
7	Close solitaire, back to word-processing program.	Gotta get to work. I'll open chapter 9 and work on our revision.	Overwhelmed feeling and frustration, then excitement and satisfaction with work

Chart 9a

Most of our behaviors and thoughts are based on what we've learned in the past. Cherry's Previous Learned Behavior and Thoughts form depicts her automatic thoughts and behaviors that involve things she has learned from experience.

Cherry's Previously Learned Behaviors and Thoughts

What automatic thoughts did you have that involved previous learning? *I remembered my usual morning routine; how to turn on the computer; how to open different programs; what each program does; that solitaire is fun; how to get to the coffee pot, office, and restroom; that I like the taste and aroma of coffee; that writing is productive and I need to meet a deadline; and where the cat's snacks are.*

Chart 9b

You can see how much of Cherry's behavior involved things she had learned previously. This is true for all of us whenever we do something that we have done in the past. When you drive your car, you must recall how to drive, the meaning of traffic lights and signs, and how to get where you are going. When you bake a cake, you must remember where the ingredients and utensils are, how to read a recipe, how to turn on the oven, and what the timer's buzzer means. Each of these activities involves the recall of previous learning.

We perform these activities automatically, without much awareness. In addition, we can drive a car or bake a cake while listening to the radio, conversing with others, answering the phone, or thinking about other activities. We all process a massive amount of information through automatic thinking. Just imagine driving a car, baking a cake, or operating a computer without automatically remembering past learning! If we had to pay attention to every detail of our activities, we would get very little done. It is clear that it would be impossible to perform our daily activities without using some type of automatic processing.

Now complete your own Activity Steps chart and Previously Learned Behaviors and Thoughts form. Choose any activity that you do almost daily. Make at least seven copies of these blank forms before you fill them out because you will use them again.

Habit Change Strategy

Get used to listening to your thoughts during everyday activities. Then when your habit shows up, you'll be more in tune with the automatic thoughts that preceded it.

Activity Steps

Activity: _____

Step	Behavior	Automatic Thought	Emotional Reaction

Previously Learned Behaviors and Thoughts

What automatic thoughts did you have that involved previous learning? _____

_____

_____

_____

_____

Chart 9d

Cognitive Therapy for Habits

Cognitive therapy seeks to help people change behavior by changing their thoughts. Many cognitive therapy techniques focus on the type of automatic processing we have described. Dr. Aaron Beck is considered by many to be the father of cognitive therapy. Cognitive therapy based on Beck's work has been used to effectively treat depression and anxiety problems. In fact, in many cases it has worked as well as—or even better than—medication! Cognitive therapy is also effective in preventing relapse, or the return of symptoms, for years after treatment. Cognitive therapy is now being used in combination with behavior therapy to treat addictions and habits. The exercises in this section are based on the work of Aaron Beck and those who have built upon his ideas.

Earlier in this chapter you recorded the steps, thoughts, and behaviors involved in a routine daily activity that probably has little emotion attached. The steps involved in engaging in your habit are likely to be packed with more emotion and stronger thoughts.

Consider Margie's problems with skin picking. Her habitual behavior usually begins when she looks in a mirror and sees a blemish. Her automatic thoughts are, "There's a spot . . . it's rough . . . I need to fix it." These thoughts lead to an emotional response of distress since not being perfect seems bad to her. In fact, she routinely has many automatic thoughts about not being perfect. Before she's aware of these thoughts and emotions, Margie's hand is on her face. "I shouldn't be doing this, I don't need to do this," are her usual thoughts, followed by feelings of tension and stress. Then she gives into the urge and thinks, "I'll just pick a bit . . . it's okay . . . smoothing this spot will make it look better." These are what we call *permission-giving thoughts.* Margie doesn't completely believe them, though, and she feels guilty and angry.

Beware of permission-giving thoughts. They make us much more likely to follow through with the action we are contemplating. They whiz through our minds in a shorthand form. Most people aren't aware of all of their thoughts and may claim that they don't think anything, they just act. However, we know this isn't how our brains work. We think, then we act. But in a habit-provoking situation, the thoughts are there and gone before we have a chance to consciously process what we are doing. Therein lies the problem.

If our thoughts happen so quickly and automatically, how can we change a habit that is perpetuated by these thoughts? Using cognitive therapy techniques, we can slow these thoughts by paying more attention to them. As we look at them, we can make important changes in our automatic thoughts, and then change the way we act in response to the thoughts. Changing our thoughts and actions also brings about changes in our emotions. Filling out the Activity Steps chart is the beginning of this process.

Complete an Activity Steps chart and a Previously Learned Behaviors and Thoughts form for your habit twice a day for the next three days. Mentally review each episode as soon afterward as possible. List the steps you took, along with the related automatic thoughts and emotional reactions. It is easiest to catch the thoughts while they are "hot." If you are trying to figure them out later, imagining yourself back in the actual situation can help. You will probably find that it becomes easier to identify your automatic thoughts and emotional reactions with each chart you complete. The same thoughts and emotions will likely recur. Remember Lucy, our friend with the gambling problem? We've provided her Activity Steps chart and Behaviors and Thoughts from Previous Learning chart as examples.

✗ Habit Change Strategy

When it comes to habits, slow thinking is an advantage. Slow down your thoughts and examine them before acting.

Lucy's Activity Steps

Activity: Going out to play bingo

Step	Behavior	Automatic Thought	Emotional Reaction
1	Phone call from friend inviting me to bingo.	I barely have enough money to pay bills. But maybe I'll win. I could always borrow if I need money later.	Excitement, indecision, guilt comes and goes
2	Accept invitation, get ready to go play bingo.	I shouldn't go. I could still cancel. No, I deserve some fun with all the stress I'm under.	Guilt, overshadowed by more excitement and anticipation
3	Arrive at bingo hall, begin playing bingo.	This is my lucky day. I just know I'll win. And look at this card—it's got my lucky seven on it.	Excitement, happiness, energy; anxiety and stress is gone
4	Playing bingo, win two games in a row.	BINGO! I love to say that. I have more than I came with. I should stop now. No, I could win more. What fun I'll have telling people about this day.	Excitement, feelings of power, exhilaration
5	Losing now. Lost half of money I came with.	Should I keep going? I still have enough money for rent. I could borrow money to pay the rest of my bills. Surely I'll win back what I lost. I have to win it back.	Anxiety, but hope, tension, tiredness; determination to win money back
6	All of my money is gone. Time to go home.	I could kick myself. I should never have come. Why didn't I stop when I was ahead? I'm a terrible person. Who can I borrow from this month? What excuse can I give for borrowing money again?	Depression, guilt, shame, anger with self, stress, tension

Chart 9e

> ## Lucy's Previously Learned Behaviors and Thoughts
>
> **What automatic thoughts did you have that involved previous learning?** *I remembered that gambling relieves my stress and anxiety; that gambling is fun and exhilarating; that I really didn't have extra money to spend; that I could borrow from friends but it is embarrassing and I have already borrowed from a lot of people; that my friend likes to play bingo and is fun to be with; that she accepts my gambling.*

Chart 9f

Questioning Automatic Thoughts

Do some of your automatic thoughts seem silly when you review them? This is quite normal. Many thoughts seem silly in retrospect. In his practice Dr. Claiborn often tells a story about one of his children in order to illustrate where some of these thoughts come from. Years ago, when she was just a little girl, his daughter liked to run under the lawn sprinkler in her bathing suit on hot days. She was doing this one day when she needed to go to the bathroom. She couldn't remove her bathing suit because a knot behind her neck held it fastened, and she had trouble reaching the knot. She came running to her father and started to cry, saying that she would *never, ever* get the bathing suit off. He was able to help her untie the knot, however, in plenty of time for her to get to the bathroom.

This is an illustration of one of the ways children think. Dr. C.'s daughter believed that if she could not solve the problem right away, then there would be no way to solve it—*ever*. This thought was upsetting to her. Unlike adults, young children say aloud the things they are thinking. We may laugh at the things they say, but we understand that this type of thinking, sometimes distorted or irrational, is appropriate for a child. As we grow up our childhood beliefs don't always go away—they can become automatic thoughts in many situations. We don't often say them aloud, but they remain in our minds. This is why we often get upset about little things that, when we look at them later, are really not important or logical things to be upset about.

🦋 Habit Change Strategy

Keep a list of silly, illogical, or irrational thoughts you have. Just writing them down helps us recognize them for what they are—silly thoughts. Remember that everyone has them at times.

When people first start recording their automatic thoughts they are often embarrassed to show them to anyone else, even their therapists. If you feel embarrassed, you need to realize that we all think in irrational, childlike ways much of the time. Usually these thinking patterns are just fine since the simple rules we learned as children work in most situations. If we are doing something more complex, however, we may have to slow down and use more rational, adult ways of thinking. In the rest of this chapter and in the next one, we will look at how to begin changing the patterns of thinking that make up our automatic thoughts. It is not necessary to try to change all, or even most, of our automatic thoughts, but it is important to change the thoughts in those areas of our lives where they are causing problems.

Now let's take a closer look at why some of these automatic thoughts are so upsetting. We will begin with some thoughts from Lucy's example. When she lost her money at the bingo game she wrote down these thoughts: "I could kick myself. I should never have come. Why didn't I stop when I was ahead? I'm a terrible person. Who can I borrow from this month? What excuse can I give for borrowing money again?" Lucy's automatic thoughts are representative of the thoughts many of us have when we are dealing with unwanted habits. Separating Lucy's thoughts into categories will help us deal with our similar automatic thoughts.

- **I could kick myself . . . I'm a terrible person.** Of course Lucy doesn't mean she actually wants to kick herself. She means that she thinks she deserves to be punished because she did something wrong. These statements are *conclusions*.

- **I should never have come. Why didn't I stop when I was ahead?** These thoughts express the reasons Lucy thinks she deserves punishment. If we turn the question "Why didn't I stop?" into a statement, it becomes "I should have stopped." These statements about what she has done wrong are *"should" statements*.

- **Who can I borrow from this month? What excuse can I give for borrowing money again?** These are problem-solving thoughts. In general, problem-solving thoughts are not a source of difficulty and may well be helpful, especially when they're used in the right situations. Lucy could have used a few problem-solving thoughts when she started thinking about going to play bingo in the first place.

Conclusions

Let's think about conclusions as possible problem automatic thoughts. What happens if we just accept conclusions (our own or other people's) without asking some questions? We may find ourselves in trouble. The statement "The world is flat" is a conclusion. We have lots of evidence that this conclusion is not true. In fact, even though you probably haven't tested the idea yourself, you would likely judge the conclusion that the world is flat to be silly. But what about Lucy's conclusions that she is a terrible person and that she deserves to be punished? Where is the evidence to support these conclusions? We might agree with her that she made a poor choice when she went to play bingo. But does that mean that she is a terrible person or simply that she has made a mistake?

☙✠ Habit Change Strategy

Confront and question all conclusions. Ask yourself, Where is the evidence? Does the evidence support your conclusion?

Accepting an *alternative conclusion*, that Lucy has simply made a mistake, might also lead to changing the conclusion that she deserves punishment. After all, we all make mistakes. But even if Lucy did deserve to be punished, let's take a closer look at what punishment does. Psychologists who have studied punishment have found that it has two effects. It *temporarily* suppresses the behavior that occurred immediately before the punishment. This means that if punishment is delayed, it may have little or no effect on the problem behavior. The second effect is that it leads to an emotional reaction, such as fear or anger. What it does not do is teach the person a better way to deal with the situation in which the behavior occurred. In Lucy's case, if she were punished, she might not go play bingo for a little while (temporary suppression) and she would feel bad, but she would not learn a new way to deal with being stressed or bored.

✿ Habit Change Strategy

We need to learn new ways of dealing with anxiety, stress, and boredom. Punishment does not help us deal with these feelings. In fact it produces even more anxiety and stress.

Should Statements

Like conclusions, *"should" statements* are *problem automatic thoughts.* Dr. Claiborn often jokes that he is very grateful for "should" statements since they keep him in business. With conclusions, we looked for evidence that supported them. With "should" statements we will do the same thing. "Should" statements often imply that there is a rule or law that covers the situation. People seem to make up these rules as they go along, often making up new ones after they have broken others.

Lucy thought, "I should have quit while I was ahead," which implies that she broke a rule, "Know when to quit." This is an interesting rule, but who made it up? Is it a moral law or a legal statute? If she means that it is a good idea, that is not the same as it being a rule. She could say, "It's a good idea to quit when you are ahead." If Lucy restates it that way, she hasn't broken a rule and therefore doesn't feel the need to be punished. This simple change in the thought makes it much less upsetting. Consider "should" statements for other habit problems:

- "I shouldn't gamble" becomes "I would be better off if I didn't gamble."

- "I shouldn't pick my skin" becomes "I would look better if I didn't pick my skin."

- "I shouldn't spend money on things I don't need" becomes "I would be better off if I used my money more carefully."

- "I should be able to go to sleep right away" becomes "I would like to be able to go to sleep without a problem."

- "I should exercise daily" becomes "I would feel better if I exercised regularly."

As you can see, these *alternative thoughts* are much less upsetting than their "should"-statement counterparts. The upset is the result of punishing ourselves for breaking the rules of the "shoulds." These rules don't change anything or help us learn anything new, but they do cause anxiety and stress. How do we handle anxiety and stress? By engaging in our problem habits. Engaging in our habits causes more punishing thoughts followed by more anxiety and stress. It's a vicious circle. Changing these automatic thoughts will help eliminate some of the anxiety that keeps us running back to our habits. Alternative thoughts encourage improvement, rather than demand perfection.

Take a look at your Activity Steps charts. Can you find any conclusions and "should" statements? If you are like most people, you will notice several statements appearing over and over. Complete the Alternative Thoughts worksheet, which follows. List the problem automatic thoughts you have identified in your Activity Steps worksheets. Then state evidence to support or negate the thoughts. Finally, replace these thoughts with alternative thoughts that are supported by the evidence.

Alternative Thoughts Record

Problem Thought	Evidence and Arguments to Change the Thought	Alternative Thought

Chart 9g

Lucy's Alternative Thoughts Record

Problem Thought	Evidence and Arguments to Change the Thought	Alternative Thought
I can always borrow if I need money later.	I've borrowed before, but that doesn't mean anyone will lend me money again.	I might be able to borrow money later.
I shouldn't go.	What rule says I shouldn't?	It might be best not to go.
I deserve some fun with all the stress I'm under.	Gambling fun probably won't reduce my stress.	Maybe it won't reduce my stress, but I want to gamble.
This is my lucky day. I just know I'll win. And look at this card—it's got my lucky seven on it.	What makes this day lucky? And what makes this particular number lucky?	I want to gamble today. I sometimes win when seven is on a bingo card.
I should stop now.	Is there a rule for when to stop?	It may be a good idea to stop now.
What fun I'll have telling people about this day.	Will it be fun to tell people about today if I lose?	It will probably be fun to tell people about this day if I keep winning.
I could borrow money to pay the rest of my bills.	There is no guarantee someone will lend me money.	I might be able to borrow money. Or everyone could say no this time.
Surely I'll win back what I lost.	Where is the evidence that I will win what I've lost?	I might win back what I lost, but I often don't.
I have to win it back.	What if I don't?	I want to win it back.
I could kick myself.	Do I deserve to be punished?	I made a mistake. I will try harder next time.
I should never have come.	Is there a law or rule that says I shouldn't have come?	It probably wasn't a good idea to come here.
I'm a terrible person.	Where is the evidence that today's mistake makes me a terrible person?	I've made a mistake, but that doesn't mean I'm a bad person.

Chart 9h

As you can see, conclusions and "should" statements can cause a great deal of anxiety and stress. They can also help us justify and rationalize our behavior. Using more realistic alternative thoughts can eliminate some of the justifications that keep our habits going. In this chapter we have started to look at how our thoughts and emotions are connected and how we can begin to modify them. In the next chapter we will work on some additional ways of looking at and changing our thoughts.

Habit Change Strategy

Test every thought for validity. Are you jumping to conclusions? Are you relying on "should" statements? Tell yourself the truth. Examine the evidence.

10

More about Changing Thoughts

To be conscious that we are perceiving or thinking is to be conscious of our own existence.

—Aristotle

The ancestor of every action is a thought.

—Ralph Waldo Emerson

In the last chapter, we looked at how our ways of thinking are connected to emotional upset and how changing our thinking habits can help us change our behavior and habits. This works because our thinking habits are part of what keeps us practicing overt habits. If we simply change our behavior and do not change the way we think, we will have a much greater risk of relapsing.

Facilitating Thoughts

Consider Lucy's problem with gambling. She had some particular thoughts and beliefs that made her more likely to gamble. For example, she believed that her bad luck just *had* to change. If she made several losing bets in a row, she would think that she was more likely to win the next time. Even when Lucy made an effort to change her behavior and stop gambling, her unchanged beliefs about luck set her up to simply return to gambling. Think of these as *facilitating thoughts*—thoughts that make the habit seem more reasonable.

✺ Habit Change Strategy

A facilitating thought is a setup for failure. It makes the unreasonable seem reasonable. Look for thoughts that facilitate your habit.

Facilitating thoughts are similar to the permission-giving thoughts we discussed in chapter 9. Permission-giving thoughts can include thoughts like "Just this one time won't hurt," "I deserve to do it," or "Everyone else does it so I can too." Facilitating thoughts go deeper. They are born of beliefs we hold before we are faced with the trigger situation. They are blanket permission slips to engage in the habit. Permission-giving thoughts are often related to facilitating thoughts.

You've probably heard a lot of "truths" about dieting. "Food eaten during preparation of a meal doesn't have calories." "Have a piece of cake. I've removed all the fat." "Candy taken out of the kids' Easter baskets has no sugar or fat." "Chocolate is good for you." Oops! That last one might be right, but does it mean that eating a pound of chocolate in one sitting is good for you? We say these things jokingly, but sometimes we seem to really believe them. If we didn't, why would we act on them? Jeff removed all the unhealthy snacks from his desk and brought nutritious lunches to eat at work. But what happened when a box of candy was delivered to his office during the winter holidays? He gave himself permission to eat the candy, since he had not brought it into the office. He also gave himself permission to eat unhealthy snacks when he went to meetings and parties. In fact, he had already given himself permission. His facilitating thought was, "If the food is there, and I didn't do anything to put it there, I can eat it. I'm not responsible for food other people bring in. I'll only have a little and that won't hurt anything."

What kind of facilitating thoughts could be setting you up for relapse? These can be quite difficult to identify, so we've listed as examples the facilitating thoughts of Lucy, Jeff, Betty, George, and Margie. For each facilitating thought you write down, develop a more reasonable thought. We've provided space for three facilitating thoughts, but you'll probably discover many more over time. It might help to print your collection of facilitating and reasonable thoughts on three-by-five-inch cards and tape them up wherever you'll likely run into trigger situations.

Facilitating thought: _____

_____

_____

Reasonable thought: _____

_____

_____

Facilitating thought: _____

_____

_____

Reasonable thought: _____

_____

_____

Facilitating thought: _____

_____

Reasonable thought: _____

_____

_____

Lucy:

Facilitating thought: _It's OK to go out and gamble if I set an amount and don't lose any more than that. I could think of it as the price of entertainment—the price of dinner and a movie._

Reasonable thought: _I have a problem with gambling. It is better for me not to gamble at all. I usually lose more than the price of dinner and a movie. Usually I don't stop until I've gambled everything I have._

Jeff:

Facilitating thought: _Walking is a good competing response and helps with weight loss. But I don't need to walk when it is too hot or too cold, when I am tired, or when my wife can't walk with me._

Reasonable thought: _These are excuses. I'll get a treadmill and when the weather is bad I can walk on it. When I'm tired I'll likely feel better after I've walked. I choose to walk every day. My walking is not dependent on my wife's walking with me._

Betty:

Facilitating thought: _If it's a really good sale, it's OK to buy gifts ahead of time, even if the price is still higher than I had budgeted._

Reasonable thought: _Sales come and go. I can always find a gift for the right price at the right time. A sale is not a good excuse for going over my budget for gifts. Each month I make a list of gifts to buy, and for now that is all I will buy._

George:

Facilitating thought: _It is OK to spend extra time at the computer if I have nothing else to do._

Reasonable thought: _It's a problem for me to spend too much time on one leisure activity, playing on the computer. It is healthy for me to engage in other leisure activities. There is always something else to do. So there is really no time when I have nothing else to do._

Margie:

Facilitating thought: *It's OK to pick at a blemish to smooth it if I am in a hurry to leave the house, going to work for instance.*

Reasonable thought: *It is better for me not to pick at blemishes, especially when I am in a hurry and don't have time to fight against the urges. It is best to wait until I have time to think it over.*

Thought Distortions

Facilitating thoughts are based on beliefs—beliefs we may or may not consciously acknowledge. Often, we just haven't paid attention to them, so we haven't examined them to see if they are valid or reasonable. In chapter 9, we discussed "should" statements and conclusions. These are types of automatic thoughts that result from some of our underlying beliefs. These thoughts and beliefs are frequently distorted. Now, we'll look at some other ways thoughts get distorted, how to identify them, and how to change them.

Remember the story about Dr. C.'s daughter and the bathing suit? That was an example of distorted thinking. We don't completely stop thinking this way when we grow up. Every person, regardless of education, intelligence, age, or social status, has some distorted automatic thoughts. Most of us aren't even aware that we are having these thoughts. We are not telling you that you are bad or wrong for having them. We are, however, suggesting that some of them may get in your way or cause you problems. They may be contributing to emotional upset, which may lead you to engage in the habits you are trying to change, or they may be making it much harder for you to change the habits.

Dr. David Burns has written several good self-help books using a cognitive approach to help people understand their thinking and the distortions in it. We've listed a few in the Resources section. In his book *The Feeling Good Handbook* Dr. Burns (1999) lists ten distortions that show up in most people's thinking. He helps readers identify the distortions in their thinking, then learn to think in a less distorted fashion. Other authors, such as Dr. Albert Ellis and Dr. Aaron Beck, have developed similar lists. When we look at these lists of thought distortions, it seems to us that many of them overlap. For our purposes, it is more helpful to use a shorter list. We've narrowed it down to three kinds of thought distortions—*drawing conclusions without evidence, thinking in absolute terms,* and *making predictions.* These types of thought distortions apply to the majority of cognitive distortions that serve to maintain problem habits and interfere with efforts to change them.

Drawing Conclusions without Evidence

We discussed this type of thought distortions in chapter 9. Those who are familiar with Dr. Burns's list of distortions may understand these kinds of thoughts to encompass *jumping to conclusions, discounting the positive, magnification, minimization, blame, mental filtering,* and *emotional reasoning.* These all have one thing in common—we arrive at a conclusion about ourselves or the rest of the world without evaluating the data. One of these, *mental filtering,* is a process in which we selectively pay attention to data that supports our ideas without evaluating the rest of the information. This process is involved in other types of thoughts, such as discounting the positive, magnification, minimization, and blame. Emotional reasoning is involved when we think "I feel that way so it must be true." The act of using feelings as evidence involves first arriving at a conclusion, then using the conclusion as evidence to support itself. This process can really be problematic for people who are trying to give up troublesome habits. The solution is to evaluate evidence more carefully and remember that feelings aren't facts.

What feelings do you most often mistake for facts?

Feeling: _____

Fact: _____

Feeling: _____

Fact: _____

Feeling: _____

Fact: _____

Jeff:

What feelings do you most often mistake for facts?

Feeling: *I am a failure, especially when it comes to controlling what I eat.*

Fact: *Sometimes I fail to resist certain foods and other times I succeed.*

Feeling: *I have no self-control.*

Fact: *Sometimes I have trouble with self-control, but I am improving.*

Feeling: *I am ugly and fat.*

Fact: *I might look more attractive if I lost weight. I do have attractive qualities, though.*

Habit Change Strategy

Be your own detective. Look for supporting evidence that is based on facts, not on feelings.

Thinking in Absolute Terms

In chapter 9, we discussed "should" statements. The basic problem with them is that they are absolute. In his list Dr. Burns includes other distortions that are examples of absolute thinking—*all-or-nothing thinking, labeling,* and *overgeneralization.* All-or-nothing thinking is a frequent problem in relapse. People think of themselves as having a habit or not having it. They might think, "I am a gambler, skin picker, or insomniac. If I have the problem once, I will always have it. If I slip and start up the habit again, I will never be able to control or change it." An example of labeling is "If I cannot stop the problem habit then I am a failure." This is an absolute statement. It is either true or false. Overgeneralization involves seeing negative events as a never-ending or absolute pattern: "It will never get better."

The problem with absolutes is that they don't fit the real world. There are a few absolutes, but they are rare, and most of us don't encounter them very often. One way to counteract absolute thoughts is to ask yourself if you can think of an exception. If you can, then you can try to come up with an alternative thought that is not absolute but does fit the evidence and data you have. If you have a lapse, it doesn't make you a failure, but it does suggest you have some weaknesses and problems you can benefit from working on. Remember that you don't fail at everything. You just read a sentence and understood it. You didn't fail at that. So you don't fit into the absolute category of failures since you don't fail at everything.

Think of an absolute thought you have about yourself and your habit. _____

_____

Can you think of an exception? _____

With what alternative thought could you replace the absolute thought? _____

_____

Jeff:

Think of an absolute thought you have about yourself and your habit. *I can't resist chocolate, and once I start, I can't stop with one serving.*

Can you think of an exception? *Last Thursday I passed up chocolate candy at work.*

With what alternative thought could you replace the absolute thought? *I love chocolate. I have difficulty resisting chocolate and sometimes have too much when I do eat it.*

⚭ Habit Change Strategy

When it comes to thoughts about your habit, ask yourself, "Am I *absolutely sure* of the validity of this thought?"

Making Predictions

Predicting what will happen in the future is the third type of distortion, and it can be a source of trouble for many people when they are trying to change habits. A common form of prediction is the "what if" thought. This often occurs when a person thinks about trying not to engage in a habit. They think, "What if I don't give in and do it?" Then they mentally answer this question by making a prediction: "If I don't give in to this urge, it will just get stronger and stronger. If I don't get some relief from the tension, I will explode." This type of prediction may seem silly to someone else, but when it is our own we often take it quite seriously.

We often make predictions about not being able to handle things, failing to meet our goals, or being defeated by impossible obstacles. Another form of prediction is the "I can't stand" statement. You may think, "I can't stand to leave this one blemish alone," or "I can't stand to pass up this bargain," or "I can't stand not getting enough sleep." Ask yourself what it means to not be able to stand something. The famous psychologist Albert Ellis says, "You can stand anything, including being run over by a steam roller, until it kills you. Then you don't have to stand it anymore." When we say we can't stand something, we are really making a prediction about what will happen if we try it. The fact is that, in most cases, we will be uncomfortable, but we will be able to stand it.

In chapter 9, we also talked about permission-giving thoughts. These thoughts often come with their own predictions. For example, "I may as well spend the money now because I'd probably just spend it later anyway." The best way to deal with these kinds of predictions is to ask yourself some critical questions. Think about a prediction you've recently made concerning your habit.

What exactly were you predicting? _____

What is the probability of your prediction coming true? Has this type of prediction ever *not* come true? _____

Finally, if it did come true what would the consequences be? _____

_____

Jeff:

What exactly were you predicting? *If I go out to eat, I'll probably have dessert. If I don't have dessert I won't enjoy the meal.*

What is the probability of your prediction coming true? Has this type of prediction ever not come true? *A month ago, the probability would have been about 90 percent. Now it's about 50 percent. I didn't have dessert when I went out to eat two weeks ago and I did enjoy my meal.*

Finally, if it did come true what would the consequences be? *If I ate dessert it wouldn't be good for me, physically, but then I could still continue to try my best to eat healthy foods. If I didn't enjoy my meal, I could think of ways to enjoy a healthy meal next time I go out.*

Habit Change Strategy

Put away your crystal ball! Even if your predictions came true, it wouldn't be the end of the world.

The Distorted Thought Record (DTR), below, will help you examine your automatic thoughts for distortions. It is like the Alternative Thoughts chart you completed in chapter 9, but it takes the ideas much farther and will help you gain a better understanding of how your thoughts about habit change may be distorted. Describe a situation or habit occurrence in the first column. In the second column, in a few words, describe how you were feeling. Then record your automatic thoughts. You may have quite a few, but the most important ones are those that are connected to your emotional response and those that are involved in your giving yourself permission to engage in the habit. In the fourth column, identify the distortions in your thoughts. Label them using the categories we described: conclusions without evidence, absolute statements, and predictions. In the last column, record the evidence you have for the automatic thoughts, along with an alternative automatic thought. We've provided a sample DTR for Jeff, our friend with an eating problem. Notice that the alternative thought is likely to lead to different behavior. Make about six copies of the blank DTR so you can repeat this exercise several times.

		Distorted Thought Record		
Situation	**Emotional Reaction**	**Automatic Thought**	**Type of Distortion**	**Review of Evidence and Arguments to Change the Thought**

Chart 10a

Jeff's Distorted Thought Record

Situation	Emotional Reaction	Automatic Thought	Type of Distortion	Review of Evidence and Arguments to Change the Thought
Someone brings candy into work during holiday season.	Desire, deprivation	I can't resist chocolate.	Conclusion	Sometimes I actually do resist chocolate. So I can resist it, but it's hard.
		It's not my fault. They should know some of us are on diets.	Conclusion	I've decided to stick to my diet even if it's hard. They bring in chocolate every year and it has nothing to do with me.
		I'm blaming others! I'm weak and want to blame others for my weakness.	Absolute	It's easier to blame others, but I can choose to take responsibility for my own actions. A single slip doesn't make me weak.
		If I don't eat the chocolate I will just eat something worse when I get home.	Prediction	If I don't eat the chocolate, I might choose to eat something unhealthy when I get home, but I don't have to. I could feel good about showing self-control.
		That chocolate looks good. I'll be sorry if I don't at least try it.	Prediction	It looks good, but if I don't eat it I will probably not even remember later that I skipped it.
Eat a piece of the candy.	Pleasure, disgust, guilt, anger at myself	I won't be able to have just one piece. I'll overdo it and eat too much chocolate.	Prediction	If I eat one piece, I might choose to eat another. I might choose to eat too much. I might not. One mistake doesn't have to lead to two.
		I had a piece. I'm a failure.	Absolute	I ate a piece of chocolate, which is not on my diet plan. It wasn't a good idea but it doesn't make me a failure.
		I may as well eat lots of chocolate. I've proven I can't resist.	Absolute	I didn't resist the first piece but I may be able to resist eating any more. I have resisted in the past.
		I'll end up eating too much chocolate. I know I will.	Prediction	I might eat too much chocolate. But then, I might not. I don't have to eat any more chocolate. I can choose to stop with one piece.

Chart 10b

Harmful Beliefs That Shape Our Automatic Thoughts

We all have basic beliefs. Sometimes our basic beliefs get us into trouble. Often we're not even really aware of these beliefs. Consider them a kind of form or mold that we use to shape our automatic thoughts. For example, if you have a basic belief that you are powerless, then an automatic thought like "I can't stop doing this," or "I'll never be able to change," might pop into your head. These thoughts are specific ways of expressing the broader basic belief.

The flowchart is one of the best ways to identify these beliefs. Start with an upsetting automatic thought and ask yourself, "If this thought were true, what would it mean?" Keep asking until you find a basic belief that forms or shapes the automatic thought. Jeff used an automatic thought from his Distorted Thought Record.

Jeff's automatic thought: *I can't resist chocolate.*

⇩

If that statement were true, it would mean: *I have no control over what I eat.*

⇩

If that statement were true, it would mean: *I have no control over myself.*

⇩

If that statement were true, it would mean: *I am a weak person.*

Jeff's basic belief that he is a weak person is causing a lot of his problems. Believing that he is weak may lead him to not even try to change the habit or give up at the first sign of trouble. Pick one of your automatic thoughts and see if you can discover the basic belief behind it.

Automatic thought: _____

⇩

If that statement were true, it would mean: _____

⇩

If that statement were true, it would mean: _____

⇩

If that statement were true, it would mean: _____

Once you've discovered some of your harmful beliefs, it is important that you challenge them and work on changing them. Look for the evidence. If you can't find evidence to support the belief, form a more reasonable alternative belief. Completing the Harmful Belief Challenge worksheet will help you do this. At the top of the first column, write the basic belief you have found by doing the flowchart above. Write an alternative, or revised, belief at the top of the next column. During the next week, list the evidence you gather each day that supports the basic belief and evidence that supports the alternative belief. We've provided Jeff's Harmful Belief Challenge worksheet as an example. Make at least twenty-five blank copies of the Harmful Belief Challenge worksheet. We recommend that you complete one of these worksheets each week as long as you are actively working on changing your habit, at least six months.

Harmful Belief Challenge

Day	Original Basic Belief: _____ _____ _____ **Evidence That Supports the Belief**	Revised Basic Belief: _____ _____ _____ **Evidence That Supports the Belief**
1		
2		
3		
4		
5		
6		
7		

Chart 10c

Jeff's Harmful Belief Challenge

Day	Original Basic Belief: _I am weak._ **Evidence That Supports the Belief**	Revised Basic Belief: _I have both strengths and weaknesses._ **Evidence That Supports the Belief**
1	I ate two cookies, which are not on my food plan.	I ate two cookies. But I only ate two, and I stuck to my food plan the rest of the day.
2	I had a small bag of potato chips at lunch.	Although I ate a small bag of potato chips at lunch, I did eat the carrots I had brought with me and I did some extra walking on my lunch break. Getting exercise is also part of my fitness plan.
3		I stuck to my food plan today and I exercised, even though I was tired and didn't feel like exercising today.
4	I only ate four fruits and vegetables today. My plan calls for five.	I ate four fruits and vegetables today. And I ate five during each of the last three days.
5	I didn't exercise after work tonight.	I have exercised four times this week and it is OK to skip a day. That doesn't mean I am going to give it up.
6		Someone brought doughnuts to work this morning and I did not eat any. I wanted to, but I didn't. I exercised today and I stuck to my food plan.
7	I went out to dinner and had fried chicken.	I have not been going to fast-food restaurants as much as I used to. Today I ordered fried chicken at a nice restaurant. I think that was not a good choice. Next time I will choose something healthy from the menu.

Chart 10d

You'll be surprised when you discover some of your harmful beliefs. Most people have a few of these basic beliefs that cause them trouble. They tend to be very broad or generalized and cause a lot of upset when they come up, especially when a person dwells on them. Changing these harmful beliefs to more reasonable ones, as we have suggested, will be helpful in many areas of your life, including your efforts to change your habits, since these beliefs are active in many situations that upset you or leave you feeling bad.

Let us close this discussion of thoughts and beliefs with one more idea that can be helpful in changing harmful beliefs. In these chapters on automatic thoughts we have suggested that you can look at evidence to help change these thoughts. We are really talking about becoming more scientific in your approach to your life. Every day, you can do a little experiment to test the theories included in your basic beliefs, called a *behavioral experiment*. For example, suppose you believe you are a "weak" person. Did you do anything today that was not what a weak person would do? If so, that is evidence that shows you are not weak. You can set up experiments by asking in advance what a weak person would do in a particular situation. What would a person with both strengths and weaknesses do in the situation? Then go out and see what you do when you're in that situation. Which model does it support? You'll probably find that your actions are those of a person with both strengths *and* weaknesses.

Changing the way you think is important in changing the way you act or changing your habit. Our thinking patterns also involve habits. All of the ideas in this book can be applied to thinking habits, just as they can be used for any other habit. You can use competing responses, relaxation, consequences, advantages and disadvantages, rewards, and any other techniques you've learned here to help change the way you think. While you are working on your habit you may need to come back to these chapters and repeat the exercises. Changing habits is hard work, but it *can* be done.

11

Developing Good Habits

The great thing in this world is not so much where we are, but in what direction we are moving.

—Oliver Wendell Holmes

God grant me the serenity to accept things I cannot change, courage to change things I can, and wisdom to know the difference.

—Reinhold Niebuhr

As you've seen, developing good habits to replace bad habits is an important part of habit change. Competing responses—good habits—help fill the void left by the bad habit. You may also be interested in developing good habits that are totally unrelated to the bad habit you are eliminating. If you bought this book with the sole intention of developing good habits and turned directly to this chapter, you'll have to go back to the first part of *The Habit Change Workbook*. Read chapters 1 through 7 to get a good understanding of the principles involved in changing habits. You won't need to complete all of the exercises, but you will need to work the exercises that seem appropriate. You might even discover a bad habit you need to work on.

Cherry wanted to develop good health and fitness habits; specifically, she wanted to eat right and exercise regularly. She soon found that breaking bad habits was very much related to developing good ones. She realized that she needed to eat more fruits and vegetables and fewer desserts. She learned that exercising three to four times a week meant stopping excuses. She discovered that focusing on weight by weighing herself daily was a bad habit—it took her focus off health and put it on weight reduction.

Do You Want to Change?

Motivation and commitment are important factors in any change—you need to believe that you need to develop new habits. Chapters 5 and 6 discussed the consequences of bad habits and the advantages and disadvantages of changing them. We can apply the same principles to developing good habits. When the process of change gets challenging, reviewing your Good Habit Advantages and Disadvantages worksheet and Good Habit Consequences worksheet will remind you of why you are trying to change. In the Good Habit Consequences worksheet, below, describe the habit you would like to develop, then describe the emotional and other consequences of developing the habit. Not all the consequences may be positive. For example, it could cost money to go to the gym or take time away from another activity you value. We've provided Jeff's chart as an example. His goal, like Cherry's, was to develop good eating habits.

Good Habit Consequences

What habit would you like to develop? _____

_____

_____

_____

What would be the emotional consequences of developing this habit? _____

_____

_____

_____

What would be some other consequences of this habit? _____

_____

_____

_____

Chart 12a

Jeff's Good Habit Consequences

What habit would you like to develop? _Good health and fitness habits—better diet and more exercise._

What would be the emotional consequences of developing this habit? _Less anxiety about my health and about my looks. I would feel more attractive. My wife would not feel anxious about my health._

What would be some other consequences of this habit? _I would lose weight. I would have more energy and feel healthier. My cholesterol would likely be lower. My doctor would be happier with me. I might even live longer. I wouldn't be able to eat some of the things I like._

Chart 12b

Now that you have determined the consequences of developing your good habit, think about the advantages and disadvantages of doing so. You may find that they are quite similar to the positive and negative consequences of the habit. The following exercise will help you compare the positive and negative consequences of the habit. What, specifically, are the advantages? What will you gain from developing this habit? And what will the habit cost you? What will you lose? Fill in the boxes in the Good Habit Advantages and Disadvantages chart with benefits and costs of developing your habit. Then look at your results. Are the advantages of developing the habit greater in importance to you than the reasons not to change? If so, you are ready to develop your new habit.

⋈ Habit Change Strategy

Make a copy of your Good Habit Advantages and Disadvantages chart and keep it in a conspicuous place. Review it at times when change seems almost impossible.

Good Habit Advantages and Disadvantages

Advantages	Disadvantages
Results of Developing Habit	Results of Not Developing Habit

Chart 12c

Jeff's Good Habit Advantages and Disadvantages

Advantages	Disadvantages
Results of Developing Habit	Results of Not Developing Habit
I would have better health.	I would not have to put up with feeling deprived because I can't have whatever food I want whenever I want it.
My cholesterol would probably be lower.	
I would probably live longer.	My cholesterol would stay high.
I would look trimmer and healthier.	I probably wouldn't live as long.
My clothes would fit better.	I wouldn't be as healthy.
I wouldn't feel such a strong urge to eat unhealthy foods.	My clothes would stay snug.
I would probably have more energy.	I would stay overweight.
I wouldn't get out of breath when I play with my kids or walk up a hill.	I would stay tired all the time.
	I would continue to get out of breath when I play with the kids.
I would be a good example for my kids and they might learn better eating and exercise habits from observing me.	I would continue to disrespect myself.
I would have more respect for myself.	Others would disrespect me and think I am a failure for trying and failing or for not even trying.
Others will be impressed with my ability to change my health habits.	
I would probably enjoy certain foods more if I had them less often.	
I might discover that I like some foods I hadn't been eating before.	

Chart 12d

Record Keeping

Are you still with us? Are you ready to change? Record keeping is important to changing habits. Your Good Habit Record (GHR) will help you clearly see your progress—you'll see when you are most successful and when you ease up on your determination to change. You may have related habits you want to develop, so we've included space to record two habits. The "comments" column can be used however you wish. Record your feelings, your thoughts, your attitudes, the interference of others—whatever seems pertinent to your efforts to change your habits.

How long should you keep a Good Habit Record? As long as it takes! Make about twenty-five copies of the blank GHR, and keep a GHR until you feel comfortable with your new habit, at least six months. After that, keep a GHR for a few days every couple of months to check up on yourself—or whenever you feel your determination to continue your habit slipping.

George wanted to change the way he spent his leisure time. He determined that his habit of spending hours at his computer every day had negative consequences on his life and the lives of his family members. His habit change plan included making better use of his time. He decided to go for a walk with his wife every night, spend more time playing games with his children, get more involved in church functions, and spend more time with friends. We've included George's GHR as an example. He decided to list walking with his wife and playing games with his children as his two main good habits, since they were to be daily activities. He decided he would mention involvement in church and time with his friends in the "comments" column.

Good Habit Record			
Day	**Habit:** _____ _____	**Habit:** _____ _____	**Comments**
Sunday			
Monday			
Tuesday			
Wednesday			
Thursday			
Friday			
Saturday			
How did you do this week? What can you do differently next week?			

Chart 12e

George's Good Habit Record

Day	Habit: _Go for a walk with my wife every evening._	Habit: _Play games with my children every day._	Comments
Sunday	Walked 20 minutes with my wife.	Spent 2 hours playing games with kids. Really enjoyed myself and they enjoyed themselves too.	Went to church with wife and children in morning.
Monday	Walked with wife for 30 minutes.	Played games with kids for 1 hour.	
Tuesday	Walked with wife for 20 minutes.	All the kids had homework. I played solitaire by myself for 1 hour—the old-fashioned way, without a computer!	
Wednesday	Wife was busy. Went for walk by myself for 25 minutes.	Played games with the kids for 1 hour.	Went to church with wife and children. Enjoyed it. Invited my friend to go out to lunch.
Thursday	Walked with wife for 20 minutes.	Kids had homework so read for 2 hours. Very relaxing.	Went out to lunch with my friend. He was glad to get together with me. Told him about the problems I've had with the computer. He understood.
Friday	Tired. Didn't walk today.	Played games with the kids for 2 hours. Gave my wife a chance to relax and she appreciated it.	
Saturday	Walked by myself, since my wife was out with friends.	Played games with the kids for 2 hours. Wife played too.	Went to men's prayer breakfast at church. Saw guys I haven't seen in a while.

How did you do this week? What can you do differently next week?

Pretty good! I enjoyed myself, playing games with the children. They might get tired of it, though, so we might have game nights maybe three times a week and I might read or play solitaire other nights.

Chart 12f

Tips for Developing Habits

You can do some things to help ensure your success as you endeavor to change your habits. You can also learn to avoid pitfalls that can set us up for failure when we are working to develop good habits. Keep these things in mind while changing your habits.

Do Something

Sometimes we get frozen by indecision. The changes seem too hard or too easy. We're not sure if this is the *right* way to do it or the *best* change we can make. Don't worry about making your changes perfectly. Make a decision and do something. Make the change. Later, you can reevaluate and adjust your plan. Think of this as an evolving process of change.

Keep Habit-Reversal Principles in Mind

In chapter 7, you learned about using habit reversal for breaking bad habits. Most of the habit-reversal principles can also be applied to developing good habits. You've already described the habit you want to develop, listed advantages and disadvantages of changing your habits, and begun to keep a record of your progress. Next, seek social support from others, but don't make your success dependent on them; you are choosing to change your habits, not other people's habits. Use relaxation techniques to cope with anxiety; read chapter 8, choose a relaxation technique that works for you, and practice it daily.

Which relaxation technique will you try? _____

Another important part of habit reversal is identifying situations in which you are more likely to engage in your bad habit. Correspondingly, look for situations that interfere with your developing good habits and watch for ways you can make habit change more likely. For example, encountering unhealthy snacks at work or at parties made it much more difficult for Jeff to stick to his diet plan. Keeping healthy snacks in his desk drawer helped him say no to the unhealthy ones.

What situations interfere with your developing your new habits? _____

_____

What can you do to arrange your environment to make it easier for you to engage in your new habits? _____

_____

George:

What situations interfere with your developing your new habits? *Incoming phone calls interrupt my time with the children.*

What can you do to arrange your environment to make it easier for you to engage in your new habits? *I can take the phone off the hook when we start playing games.*

Keep It Simple

Don't complicate your plans to change. Keep change as simple and effortless as possible. Look for possible roadblocks and do your best to eliminate them. For example, Cherry once signed up for a year-long membership at a fitness center about thirty minutes away from her home. She went twice, and then she stopped. The effort was just too great. Then she got her husband involved. They decided to go for walks every evening, but it was often too hot or too cold. Finally, a fitness center opened at a location just five minutes away from her home. This worked out fine—it was not far away, so there was little room for excuses. Cherry and her husband made exercise as easy and simple as possible.

How could you simplify your plans for change? _____

_____

_____

_____

George:

How could you simplify your plans for change? _I was pressing my wife to go for a walk with me every night. And my children sometimes had homework or other things to do. I realized that I can walk alone when my wife isn't available and I can spend more time reading when my children aren't available._

Make It Convenient

Do all you can to make it likely that your new habit will occur. Keep any supplies you need for your habit change within easy reach. For example, one of Cherry's goals was to read her Bible more often, so she decided to keep her Bible, highlighter, and pen (her studying supplies) next to her favorite chair so she doesn't have to go looking for them. To help herself eat more healthful foods, she keeps ready-to-eat fruits and vegetables in the kitchen, and she keeps hard candies in her desk drawer, because they seem to reduce her craving for high-fat, high-sugar snacks.

What can you do to make it more convenient to engage in your new habits? _____

_____

_____

George:

What can you do to make it more convenient to engage in your new habits? _Because the games were in the closet, I kept forgetting about my plans to play games with the children until bedtime. I put the games in a convenient spot in the living room, right next to the TV. Now, when I look at the TV, I think of the games._

As you work on developing your new habits, you'll probably encounter some opposition from a surprising source—yourself! Negative thoughts and emotions can make accomplishing change difficult. Chapters 9 and 10 will help you understand more about the effects of automatic thoughts. You will learn how to evaluate these thoughts and modify them so they don't interfere as much with your habit change plans.

12

Maintaining Your Gains

By perseverance the snail reached the ark.
                              —Charles Haddon Spurgeon

You may have to fight a battle more than once to win it.
                              —Margaret Thatcher

By the time you get to this chapter, you will probably be well into the action stage and entering the maintenance stage of action. Many people think this is the end of the process of change. They feel that they've made it. But they don't realize that they must take steps to hold on to the changes they've made. Don't make this mistake. Maintenance is every bit as important as action. This chapter is geared to helping you make your habit changes permanent.

Relapse Prevention

When researchers have looked at the outcome of the treatment of substance abuse, it has become clear that they needed to come up with some new ideas. A high percentage of people were not able to maintain the gains that they made in treatment—relapse rates were disturbingly high. Think about your past efforts to change your habits. You may have started out well then slipped back, gradually or suddenly, to the old way of doing things—you relapsed.

One researcher working on alcohol treatment came up with an idea he called *relapse prevention*. Dr. Marlat (1985) examined what went wrong in the treatment of people with alcohol problems. How did relapse occur? He developed a set of ideas about what could be done differently and what could be added to treatment that would improve the disturbing relapse rate. These ideas are now used in working with a range of behavioral problems. We will discuss some of them here, along with our own thoughts and recommendations regarding relapse prevention.

Don't Talk about Relapse?

Does it scare you to think about relapse? It is a common fear. Many people, even well-meaning mental health professionals, think it is a bad idea to talk about relapse. They believe it is important to keep a positive attitude. "Believe you've beaten the habit and it will be so." They think that just considering relapse could make it more likely to happen. While a positive attitude is important, dismissing the possibility of relapse can make you even more vulnerable to relapse. It is better to accept the possibility and prepare for it.

In chapters 9 and 10, we discussed the problem of making predictions without evidence. The idea that discussing a problem can make it more likely to occur is that very type of thinking distortion. A more realistic approach is to look at the evidence about how people successfully maintain changes and learn what makes them more likely to relapse. Accepting the possibility and understanding the risks of relapse can help us to plan ways to deal with it.

What Is a Relapse?

Before we discuss it, we need to be clear about what a relapse is. You've probably heard the word used to describe any return to habits. We've heard people describe a one-time event as a relapse. A recovering-alcoholic friend of Cherry's referred to one night she spent drinking as a "relapse." But this is not a relapse. We use the word to mean a return to your old *pattern* of behavior, or going back to where you were before you started working on your habit.

There is a more appropriate word for a brief episode of the problem behavior: a *lapse*. Cherry's friend had a lapse, and then she resumed her abstinence. If the friend had continued to drink, the episode would be termed a relapse. Let's consider some of the people you have read about in this book. Margie worked hard to get her skin picking under control. Her arms looked better and her face was clearing up. She went weeks without picking. Then she had a bad day at work and found herself picking at her arms on the way home. In the bathroom that evening she examined her face and picked at a blemish. She stopped after a few minutes, realizing she stood at a crossroads. Margie faced a choice—to lapse or relapse? Continue picking tonight and tomorrow, or stop now and increase her habit-change maintenance efforts? Margie stopped picking that night and continued to maintain her habit change. She has had many *lapses*, but she has not *relapsed*.

After making significant improvement in his gambling habit, Fred had a death in the family. Saddened and grieved, he reflected on the brevity of life. "Life is too short and chances of bad things happening are too great not to live every moment to the fullest," he thought. Fred remembered how much he had enjoyed gambling, especially when he was worried or bored. He called one of his gambling friends and went to a casino. The next day he went out alone to place some sports bets and play poker. All the old feelings of excitement returned. He won a little money at first but then started losing. He wound up with the same financial problems he had overcome, and he became depressed. Then he remembered how much better he had felt having less chaos in his life and went back to work on his habit, using the skills he had learned, and he got himself back on track.

Because Fred's lapse lasted several weeks, it could be considered a relapse. Lapse or relapse? He took longer to stop than Margie did, but he still faced the same question she had faced—return to the habit or get back to habit change? Although his behavior was falling back into the same pattern he had before he started working, Fred's return to habit change makes his slip look like a lapse. So was it a lapse or a relapse? We could argue this point endlessly. However, it is our opinion that, no matter how long you have strayed from your habit-change program, you can still get back on track. Any relapse can be turned into a lapse. It will always be your choice—lapse or relapse.

Absolute Ave. or Habit Change Way?

Why do we make a point of distinguishing between lapses and relapses? Because the difference is critical in spotting the distortions in thinking that are part of the problem. We discussed thinking in absolutes in chapter 10. Also known as an *abstinence violation effect* (AVE), absolute thinking can turn a lapse into a relapse. When people try to change a habit they often think about it in absolute terms: "I used to have that habit but I broke it. I don't do that any more." If they have a lapse, they may switch to the opposite position and start telling themselves they do have that habit: "I changed for a while, but then I went back to the habit." They think of the habit as uncontrollable, or they think of themselves as powerless over the habit.

"I have done this for years; I can't change my habit." This type of absolute thinking is part of the abstinence violation effect. An easy way to remember the principle of AVE is to imagine yourself choosing (or not choosing) to walk down "Absolute Ave." When Margie had a stressful day, she lapsed for a few hours, but she chose not to walk down Absolute Ave., she chose not to start thinking that she couldn't control the problem. Margie made a decision: "I don't want to get back into this habit. I need to use the tools I learned in order to get it back under control." Thinking of yourself as powerless or as defined by the habit are both forms of absolute thinking and are sources of trouble. How can we avoid the AVE? How do we bypass Absolute Ave.? Following are a few detours that will send you away from Absolute Ave. and help you continue down Habit Change Way. But first, a warning: Expect lapses in your behavior and be prepared for them.

Challenge Your Thoughts and Beliefs about Your Lapse

Our first detour sends you back to chapters 9 and 10. So what do you do when a lapse happens? When it happens, examine your thinking about your lapse. Investigate the thoughts and beliefs that are making you so distressed. This will cut off your walk down Absolute Ave. and send you back down Habit Change Way.

Complete a Distorted Thought Record whenever a lapse occurs. Describe the habit occurrence in the first column. Then record your emotional reactions and automatic thoughts. Identify the distortions in your thoughts, labeling them using the categories we described in chapter 10: conclusions without evidence, absolute statements, and predictions. In the last column, record the automatic thought and the evidence and arguments to change the thought. Then choose one of your automatic thoughts and use a flowchart to discover a harmful belief that is behind it. You can create flowcharts for several automatic thoughts until you find the harmful belief that seems to be causing the most trouble, then complete a Harmful Belief Challenge worksheet. In the first column, write the basic belief; in the next column, write an alternative belief. Each day during the next week, list the evidence you gather that supports the basic belief and evidence that supports the alternative belief. We've provided Margie's worksheets as examples.

Distorted Thought Record

Situation	Emotional Reaction	Automatic Thought	Type of Distortion	Review of Evidence and Arguments to Change the Thought

Chart 12a

Margie's Distorted Thought Record

Situation	Emotional Reaction	Automatic Thought	Type of Distortion	Review of Evidence and Arguments to Change the Thought
Stressful day at work. Driving home.	Feeling fatigued, overwhelmed, frazzled.	I'm so tired. This has been a horrible day. Why did my boss talk to me like that? I should have stood up for myself. I'm a failure. I'm so weak.	Conclusion	I'm tired and stressed out. I feel like a failure. I feel weak. Feeling like a failure doesn't make it a fact.
		I can never stand up to people.	Absolute	Sometimes I don't stand up to people but, I have stood up to people in the past.
		I'll never be able to stand up for myself.	Prediction	I have difficulty standing up for myself and may have this problem the rest of my life. Or I might learn to stand up for myself.
I have an itchy spot on my arm, a sore that has been healing. I realize I am scratching it.	Feeling fatigued, overwhelmed, frazzled, stressed out. Worried about job.	Oh, my arm itches and I'm scratching. I've disturbed that spot and it was healing so well. I may as well pick at it to smooth it over now.	Conclusion	I itched, I scratched, and now the spot that was healing is open again. I've picked at it, but I don't have to continue. I can choose to clench the steering wheel instead. I can stop picking now or whenever I choose.
		I should be clenching the steering wheel. But I have to pick at this spot.	Absolute	I can choose to clench the steering wheel, not picking, but I am choosing to pick. I can stop when I choose to.
		I'm just not able to stop now, not when I am so stressed out. I'll work on my habit when I am less stressed.	Conclusion	I am stressed and anxious and that is when I am most likely to pick—and when it would be the most helpful to work even harder on habit change.
Continue to pick at spot on arm.		I may as well keep picking now.	Conclusion	I can still choose to stop picking at any moment.
		I'll never be able to stop. I knew I couldn't do it.	Prediction	I have stopped in the past and can this time too.
		I'm so weak.	Absolute	I can stop picking, but I am having setbacks. I'll keep trying.

Chart 12b

Automatic thought: _____

⇩

If that statement were true, it would mean: _____

⇩

If that statement were true, it would mean: _____

⇩

If that statement were true, it would mean: _____

Margie:

Automatic thought: _I can't stop picking when I am under stress._ _____

⇩

If that statement were true, it would mean: _I have no control over my habit when I am under stress._ ____

⇩

If that statement were true, it would mean: _I can't control myself when I am under stress._ ____

⇩

If that statement were true, it would mean: _I am weak when I am under stress._ ____

Harmful Belief Challenge

Day	Original Basic Belief: _____ _____ **Evidence That Supports the Belief**	Revised Basic Belief: _____ _____ **Evidence That Supports the Belief**
1		
2		
3		
4		
5		
6		
7		

Chart 12c

	Margie's Harmful Belief Challenge	
Day	**Original Basic Belief:** *I am weak when I am under stress.* **Evidence That Supports the Belief**	**Revised Basic Belief:** *I can be weak or strong when under stress.* **Evidence That Supports the Belief**
1	I picked at my arm in the car. I picked at my face in the bathroom in the evening.	I picked at my arm in the car and didn't stop when I got home. I picked at a blemish on my face, but I did stop after a few minutes. Before, I might have continued for an hour.
2		I had an argument with my friend. I was very upset, but I didn't pick. I practiced my competing response.
3	I was nervous in a meeting at work and just found myself picking at the spot on my arm.	I did pick at the spot on my arm, but I stopped after less than a minute, as soon as I realized what I was doing, and clenched a pencil instead.
4		Driving home, I touched the spot on my arm and started to scratch, which usually precedes picking. I stopped and clenched the steering wheel.
5	I was nervous and went into the bathroom, looked at my face in the mirror, and picked for about 10 minutes.	I picked for 10 minutes, not 15 minutes, 20 minutes, or an hour. I went back to the living room and worked on my crocheting project.
6		I was bored. Boredom is stressful for me. I called a friend and talked on the phone. She knows about my problem and offered encouragement.
7		I felt worried about my mother, who is sick. I started to pick at the skin on my arm, but I stopped with only scratching, no picking. I am proud of myself for stopping. I can do this.

Chart 12d

Deal with High-Risk Situations

Our next detour will help you handle *high-risk situations* (HRS). These are unique to each individual and probably to each particular habit. An HRS for Margie seemed to be a stressful day. Stressful times are usually high-risk situations for most people, and it is a good idea to keep this in mind. Barbara had a problem with insomnia. As she followed her habit change plan, she was sleeping much better and waking up rested most mornings. Then she went on vacation and started staying up late and sleeping late in the morning. The insomnia didn't show up again until she went back to work and had trouble going to sleep at night. Barbara realized that she had lapsed into some problem habits connected with her sleep. She needed to reassess the situation and apply the techniques she had learned. It was important for Barbara to recognize that going on vacation was an HRS for her.

High-risk situations can be ordinary, predictable events, such as walking past a mirror for a person with skin-picking or hair-pulling problems, joining in the office Super Bowl betting pool for the gambler, or going on a vacation for the insomniac. Or they can be unique, unexpected events. You've probably already run across some high-risk situations for you. Think of other problem situations you might encounter. List them below.

High-risk situations:

1. _____

2. _____

3. _____

4. _____

5. _____

Margie:

1. *When I'm bored and don't have an activity planned* _____

2. *When I've had a busy day at work and am having trouble calming down and relaxing* _____

3. *When I'm nervous and thinking about or doing something I don't feel prepared for* _____

4. *When I've had a dispute with someone, a friend, relative, coworker, or boss* _____

5. *When I'm in the bathroom and I see a blemish on my face* _____

Fred:

1. *Stress—problems at work, death of my brother* _____

2. *Friend calls and suggests placing a bet, going to a casino, or going to a card game* _____

3. *Big sports games* _____

4. *Worry over money problems—I still think I could make money gambling* _____

5. *Boredom and feeling a need for excitement* _____

High-risk situations can get us heading down Absolute Ave. Handling them appropriately is a detour that will get us back on Habit Change Way. High-risk situations are dangerous because of a couple of types of automatic thoughts that happen in these situations. In chapters 9 and 10, we discussed the effects of facilitating thoughts on problem habits. Unfortunately, they may still be around long after you have changed the habit. When Fred hears about the Super Bowl pool at work, he thinks, "It's not really gambling. Maybe I'll win. It won't do any harm." These are facilitating thoughts. When Margie sees a blemish on her face she thinks, "I will just fix this one. If I don't fix it, everyone will stare at it. I can make things perfect by fixing this one spot." These are facilitating thoughts.

Write down some of the facilitating thoughts you might have when you get into the high-risk situations you listed above. For each facilitating thought, develop a more reasonable thought. You can use some of the facilitating thoughts you listed in chapter 10. We've provided examples of Margie's and Fred's facilitating thoughts.

1. High-risk situation: _____

Facilitating thought: _____

_____

_____

Reasonable thought: _____

_____

_____

2. High-risk situation: _____

Facilitating thought: _____

_____

_____

Reasonable thought: _____

_____

_____

3. High-risk situation: _____

Facilitating thought: _____

_____

_____

Reasonable thought: _____

_____

_____

4. High-risk situation: _____

Facilitating thought: _____

_____

_____

Reasonable thought: _____

_____

_____

5. High-risk situation: _____

Facilitating thought: _____

_____

_____

Reasonable thought: _____

_____

_____

Margie:

High-risk situation: *Busy day at work; having trouble calming down and relaxing.*

Facilitating thought: *I have enough to worry about with my stressful job. I need to relax. Picking at my skin helps me relax. I can work on my habit when I am under less stress. Maybe I should just try to stop later.*

Reasonable thought: *Life is stressful and I might never be under less stress. I could learn better ways to handle stress and better ways to relax. I could try a different relaxation technique and find other activities that would be relaxing.*

Fred:

High-risk situation: *Brother's death. Grieving, depressed.*

Facilitating thought: *I can't handle this. I need to have some way of handling this. Besides, life is too short. I should be able to enjoy life.*

Reasonable thought: *I can handle this. It hurts, but other people have experienced the death of a loved one without gambling. Life is short. I can choose to enjoy it however I want or I can be productive and take care of my family.*

The important thing to remember in relapse prevention is that lapses are quite common and likely to occur. You are better able to handle such problems if you plan ahead. Identify high-risk situations and plan for how to deal with them. Understand what sort of thoughts and beliefs make them a problem. Be especially attentive to absolute statements about your character and strength. For example, telling yourself that a lapse means you are a failure will make that lapse more likely to turn into a relapse. If, on the other hand, you tell yourself that this is actually a common problem, and that it is simply teaching you something new so you will be better able to handle an HRS in the future, the lapse will be a valuable experience.

Regroup

Our last detour is simple. When a lapse has occurred, just go back to the tools that have helped before. Examine each part of your Habit Change Program for weak links. In this chapter we've already discussed thinking habits and habit-provoking situations. What about the rest of the program? Review chapters 5 through 8, and read the chapter on your particular habit. Below, check off the areas you need to give more attention.

❑ Record keeping
Are you still keeping habit records? When you begin a lapse, it is especially important for you to keep records of your habit so you can clearly see when and how much you are engaging in your habit.

❑ Advantages, disadvantages, and consequences
The further you get from your habit, the easier it is to forget the disadvantages and consequences of the habit. Review the advantages, disadvantages, and consequences you recorded at the beginning of your program. Remind yourself of what life with your habit was really like.

❑ Relaxation
Are you practicing your relaxation exercise daily? If it's not working for you, try one of the other relaxation exercises. Or consult the Resources section for books that can help you find a relaxation method that works better for you.

❑ Competing response
Is your competing response working? Does it make it impossible to engage in your habit? Sometimes we develop ways of doing the competing response and participating in our habit at the same time. If your competing response isn't working, you may need to choose another competing response, one that really does interfere with your habit. Review chapter 11. Is there a good habit you could develop that would make your bad habit more difficult to engage in?

❑ Social support
Do you have a support person? Does your support person know what type of support you need? Discuss your needs openly and honestly. Read chapter 20 for ideas about how your support person can help. Consider joining a support group or forming your own group.

❑ Reward
We can run into two major complications here: too much reward and not enough reward. Can you afford your reward? If you decided on having dinner out every week but can't afford the dinner, then it isn't a reward. Promise yourself a reward that fits your budget. And is your reward worth the effort of habit change? If not, you need to come up with something that will motivate you enough to change. Don't limit yourself to tangible rewards. Refer to your Habit Advantages and Disadvantages worksheet and your Good Habit Advantages and Disadvantages worksheet. The advantages of changing are also rewards. Put more focus on these intangible rewards.

Habit change is a challenge. For some people it is a minor task that requires some effort for a short while. For the rest of us, habit change is a lifelong endeavor—a very worthwhile endeavor, rich with rewards. Ths concludes our journey together, but we hope it isn't the end of your habit change effort. Continue on your course down Habit Change Way. When Absolute Ave. beckons, put a detour sign up and turn back to Habit Change Way.

Supposing you have tried and failed again and again. You may have a fresh start any moment you choose, for this thing that we call "failure" is not the falling down, but the staying down.

—Mary Pickford

Part III

Detailed Guidance on Specific Habits

13

Nervous Habits, Trichotillomania, Skin Picking, and Nail Biting

Avoiding danger is no safer in the long run than outright exposure. The fearful are caught as often as the bold.

—Helen Keller

The great thing in this world is not so much where we are, but in what direction we are moving.

—Oliver Wendell Holmes

Nervous habits are the annoying things people habitually do when they are nervous or bored. We all have a nervous habit or two. No big deal. But quite often those habits get out of control: we engage in them too often, and they interfere with our lives—or the lives of those around us.

Nervous Habits

You've seen nervous habits in other people. They may have annoyed you, or perhaps you made some assumptions about the people because of their habits. Often we assume someone is nervous or bored when they are jangling keys or coins in a pocket, twirling their hair, bouncing a leg up and down, chewing on a pencil, or swaying back and forth while speaking. And, probably, the person *is* nervous or bored.

You may have a nervous habit you would like to be rid of. Perhaps you want to come across as calm and relaxed—even when you're nervous. This chapter will help you change your nervous habit. You will learn how to stop engaging in your bad habit and replace it with a more acceptable habit. The core of your Habit Change Program will be habit reversal, but you will also use some cognitive techniques to help you change your "thinking habits." You will learn what situations make you more susceptible to engaging your habit. Besides stressful situations, in which you tend to be nervous or anxious, situations in which you are bored are likely times to encounter your habit. Identifying these situations will help you anticipate the times when you will be vulnerable to engaging in your habit.

⚭ Habit Change Strategy

Ridding yourself of nervous habits will help you appear calm and collected even when you are nervous or bored.

We have included nervous habits, trichotillomania, skin picking, and nail biting in the same chapter because the Habit Change Program is basically the same for these problems. What is the difference between nervous habits, trichotillomania, skin picking, and nail biting? Some are labeled disorders while others fall into the category of nervous habits. These labels are arbitrary, the result of some decisions made long ago, without any real basis for making a distinction. One factor that may distinguish one habit from another is how much interference or distress the habit causes. Trichotillomania, for example, often leads to great distress and interferes with the person's ability to live a normal life; nail biting, which is probably one of the most common problem habits, is usually mild enough that it doesn't really interfere with a person's life and is thought of as simply a bad habit.

Trichotillomania

The word *trichotillomania* comes from three Greek words: *trich* (hair), *tillo* (to pull), and *mania* (an abnormal love for, or morbid impulse toward, a specific object, place, or action). A French physician, Francois Henri Hallopeau, first recognized the disorder as an identifiable medical syndrome and gave it a name in 1889. Trichotillomania (TTM) is characterized by the following:

- Recurrent pulling of one's hair with significant hair loss as a result.

- An increasing sense of tension immediately before pulling out hair or when trying to resist hair pulling.

- A sense of tension relief, pleasure, or gratification when pulling out a hair.

- A lack of relationship to another medical condition or mental disorder.

- Significant impairment or distress in occupational, social, or other areas of functioning.

The most common areas for hair pulling are the crown, occipital, and parietal sections of the scalp. A tonsure pattern, which resembles the shaven crown or patch worn by monks, is also a common manifestation. Eyelashes; eyebrows; hair on the extremities; and nasal, abdominal, perianal, and pubic hair may also be pulled. Some people with TTM pull the hair of others—spouses, parents, other family members, pets, and dolls. If you have trichotillomania you may also have one or more nervous habits, such as nail biting, skin picking, thumb or finger sucking, tongue or mouth chewing, nose picking, scratching, and body rocking.

Scalp hair is likely to be pulled when the mind is otherwise occupied, such as while watching TV, reading, or driving. Eyebrows and eyelashes are often pulled when a person is focusing on grooming. Some people experience itching, sensitivity, irritation, burning, or pressure before hair pulling. The irritation and itching may actually be due to the hair pulling, so it can lead to a cycle of itching, pulling, itching, and pulling again. Most people with TTM say that they do not experience pain from hair pulling; many experience a pleasurable feeling, or simply relief from the itching, irritation, or tension.

Touching or stroking of hair often precedes pulling. More than half of the people with TTM search for and pull hairs of a certain textural quality. Hair is generally pulled with the fingers and hands. Some grasp the hair between the tips of the thumb and index finger, and others wrap the hair around the index finger and pull. A few use tweezers to pull hairs. Hair may be manipulated or played with, the roots of hairs are sometimes broken or bitten off, or hair may be used like dental floss. The hair is sometimes pulled across the lips or played with. Some people squeeze or smear the root. Most dangerous, hair is sometimes swallowed.

Trichotillomania can lead to some serious complications, including *alopecia* (hair loss), skin trauma and scarring, skin infections, and trauma to the hair follicles. If a person swallows hair, it can lead to gastritis, iron deficiency, anemia, and bowel obstructions from *trichobezoars* (hairballs). Repetitive hair pulling can contribute to muscle strain and carpal tunnel syndrome from the pinching and pulling motions.

As you may know, trichotillomania can have a devastating effect on a person's social life. You may be avoiding certain activities, which can lead to isolation and loneliness. If hair loss is severe enough, many people wear wigs, scarves, or hats whenever they go out in public. They may give up or avoid swimming, bicycling, skiing, or other activities because they fear people seeing their bald spots or losing their wig or hat. Many people with TTM avoid going to the hairdresser, and when they do, they may visit a different one each time to avoid the embarrassment of sharing their secret.

Trichotillomania is actually a common problem occurring in approximately 1 to 2 percent of the population. Women seem to make up 75 to 93 percent of TTM sufferers. There may be an even higher prevalence, however, since people with TTM are often reluctant to seek help or they may not realize their hair-pulling symptoms are part of a known psychiatric disorder that can be treated. Many people are too embarrassed and ashamed to seek treatment once they know they have an illness. It is our hope that, as the public becomes more aware of TTM, the shame will be reduced, and more people will be willing to seek help.

Habit Change Strategy

If you have trichotillomania, know that you are not alone. At least one out of every one hundred people has trichotillomania.

Possible Causes of Trichotillomania

Because of the shame and humiliation related to TTM, people may not want to admit, even to themselves, that they pull their hair. They may think of TTM as a "crazy habit," a weakness, or some other type of problem. Just finding out that they are not alone and that they suffer from a neurobiological disorder often helps to alleviate the shame and humiliation, making them more accepting of treatment.

Research about the cause of TTM is in its infancy. One explanation is that there is a chemical imbalance in the brain, possibly involving the serotonergic, dopaminergic, and opoid systems. Studies have revealed some small differences in the brain structure of people with TTM. Some of the structural differences are similar to those found in people with Tourette's syndrome (TS) and obsessive-compulsive disorder (OCD). Researchers have found that there are elevated rates of TTM in people with both OCD and TS, in comparison to the general population. This fact, and the fact that these disorders tend to run in families, support the idea that they may be different expressions of a similar genetic abnormality (Stein, Sullivan, van Heerden, Seedat, and Niehaus 1998).

One theory is that the genetic difference involves the setting of a threshold for some behaviors. TTM in particular looks very much like a grooming behavior that is out of control. It may be that a control mechanism for this type of behavior is different in people who develop TTM, leading to excessive or out-of-control grooming behavior. This breakdown of the control mechanism could be activated by stress, bacterial or viral infection, or autoimmune diseases (Warmbrodt, Hardy, and Chrisman 1996). Environmental influence may also be involved. Precipitating events may be stressful or traumatic experiences including early physical or sexual abuse, loss or perceived loss (e.g., of a job, relationship, or loved one), injury to the scalp or hair, parental shaving or haircuts as punishment, and witnessing another person pull hair (Christenson and Mansueto 1999).

Treatment of Trichotillomania

There are two basic styles of hair pulling. You may experience increasing tension, which is relieved when hair is pulled. This is sometimes called *focused* hair pulling. This type of hair pulling may be ritualized, and the person may feel a need to create symmetry. Focused pulling is the main type of pulling for about one-fourth of trichotillomania patients.

It is more common to have *automatic*, or *habitual* hair pulling, which is the main form of pulling seen in about three-fourths of trichotillomania patients. Automatic pullers don't describe tension before hair pulling. They are more likely to pull when they are bored, watching TV, or focusing on a particular task. Many people with TTM practice both focused and automatic pulling. For example, Amanda had both types of pulling. She would have a feeling of tension or tightness that was difficult to ignore. She'd search for just the right hair and pull it, but the tension would continue. Sometimes she spent hours searching for the right hair, positioning her fingers tight around it and pulling, then searching and pulling again, over and over. At other times, Amanda found herself pulling random hairs absentmindedly while watching TV or reading. Like many people with TTM, Amanda found that treatment using ideas from cognitive behavioral therapy and habit reversal can help change both types of pulling.

Depression, obsessive-compulsive disorder, and other anxiety disorders are more common in people with TTM than in the general public. People who have TTM often have problems with self-esteem, assertiveness, social confidence, interpersonal relationships, and emotional well-being. Addressing these issues and seeking treatment for anxiety and depression will increase the chances of improvement of TTM symptoms. Conversely, treating TTM helps the improvement of depression and anxiety. For women, hair pulling may be more of a problem during the premenstrual period. It is important for you to be especially consistent about applying your habit change skills during this or other high-risk times. You will want to be prepared to fight back when you know you will be facing increasing urges.

A number of different medications have been tried as treatments for TTM. Some, such as clomipramine, fluoxetine, and naltrexone, have been helpful in some patients with TTM. However, relapse after initial improvement is very common. Combined treatment using medication and cognitive behavior therapy may offer the most hope for improvement. Before starting treatment for a problem like this, get a checkup from your primary-care doctor. Consultation with mental-health professionals can be a big help but only if they know how to treat this type of problem. Since cognitive behavioral therapy, including habit reversal, stimulus control, and stress management training, have proven effective in the treatment of TTM, you will need to seek help from a professional trained in these methods. Standard forms of talk therapy are not likely to be helpful in treating TTM. Whether you use the self-help methods in this book, go to a cognitive behavioral therapist, or take medication, the risk of relapse is still fairly high.

Being prepared for relapse and keeping in mind that TTM is usually a lifelong problem will help you maintain your improvement and make relapse less likely. Don't let the prospect of relapse scare you. We will help you learn to recognize the signs of relapse, keep the gains you make, and catch a minor lapse before it becomes a relapse. It is important to recognize the improvement you make. Instead of expecting a complete cure, you need to praise yourself for your achievements: fewer hairs pulled, less time spent hair pulling, and longer time periods between episodes. When it happens, relapse can be a time of refocusing and looking for ways to improve your habit change skills.

Habit Change Strategy

Focus on improvement rather than complete eradication of a habit.

Trichotillomania in Children

Trichotillomania usually begins in childhood or adolescence, and is most often a chronic disorder. Some children who begin before the age of five may "outgrow" the problem. About 1 percent of children are affected by hair pulling. While among adults and adolescents more women and girls than men and boys are diagnosed, among children boys and girls seem to be equally represented. Like adults, children may pull hair from the scalp, eyebrows, eyelashes, arms, and legs. They may also pull hair from pets, dolls, and other family members. Recently found evidence shows that TTM, OCD, and TS, as well as other disorders in childhood, may be associated with streptococcal infection in a small percentage of children. Dr. Susan Swedo hypothesizes that the body forms antibodies to fight the bacteria and that these antibodies also attack brain tissue (Reeve 1999).

For some children, other self-soothing habits, such as thumb sucking or nail biting, may be associated with hair pulling. Treatment of thumb sucking may reduce or eliminate the hair pulling. In young children with other self-soothing habits, hair pulling occurs mainly at bedtime and when the child is bored or tired, or under stress, such as when they are separated from their parents.

Young children frequently stop hair pulling by the time they enter school. Parental support is usually sufficient to help the child cope until he or she outgrows the disorder, but treatment should be considered if hair pulling persists beyond preschool age or if it causes distress for the child. Parents can benefit from receiving education about the disorder to help calm their own anxieties and fears. Cognitive behavioral therapy can be helpful in older children and adolescents.

Skin Picking

Everyone bites their nails occasionally, and everyone scratches, picks, or squeezes blemishes or irregularities in their skin at times. When it causes physical damage or interferes with daily activities it becomes a problem in need of change. Repetitive skin picking is a self-injurious behavior that is sometimes called *neurotic excoriation, dermatillomania,* and *self-inflicted dermatoses.* It often begins as ordinary grooming behavior, in which the person may try to remove or smooth out small irregularities on the skin. The behavior can range from minor skin picking to digging deep into the skin. Fingernails are often used, but tweezers, needles, pins, and other instruments may also be used.

Estimated prevalence of chronic self-injurious skin picking ranges from 2 to 4 percent of the general population. Since data on this habit is limited, however, this figure is just a guess. Women presenting with this problem outnumber men by seven to one. The average age of onset is fifteen years. There appear to be two groups of people who pick at their skin. One group picks at blemishes on their face out of fear that the blemishes will disfigure them. They mentally overestimate the severity and size of a small pimple and decide that it has to be made right. This preoccupation is much like that of people with body dysmorphic disorder (BDD), in which people have such a preoccupation with an imagined defect in their appearance that it causes them significant distress. Not surprisingly, many people with BDD also have a skin-picking problem. The second group picks automatically to satisfy an urge, similar to the hair-pulling urge experienced by people with TTM. For these people, picking relieves tension and stress. As with TTM, a *thought* usually triggers picking in the first group, while those in the second group have a *feeling* before they start to pick. Many people with this problem describe being in a trancelike state as they pick.

Little research has been done on self-injurious skin picking, although Dr, Sabine Wilhelm and her associates published a retrospective study revealing quite a bit of information about skin picking (Wilhelm, Keuthen, and Deckersbach 1999). The research found that the intensity of skin picking waxed and waned over time, although complete remission was rare. Thirty-nine percent of the patients interviewed had a dermatological illness, usually acne, at the time of their first episode of skin picking. People in the study picked at more than one body area. The most frequent sites were pimples and scabs, but they also picked at red, swollen, or infected areas, mosquito bites and scars. Fifty-two percent of study participants reported picking at healthy skin. For many women, skin picking changed with their menstrual cycle, occurring at a higher frequency during or shortly before menstruation.

Habit Change Strategy

Skin picking can be more of a problem before and during the menstrual period. Be especially careful to use your Habit Change Program during this time.

People in the study reported picking their skin for an average of eighty-three minutes per day; nearly half indicated that they picked for less than five minutes per episode. During skin-picking episodes, they felt mesmerized, but they also felt increasing satisfaction. Picking led to a feeling of reduced tension. These emotional effects may explain why the behavior is so difficult to resist. Feelings of shame, guilt, and physical pain also followed picking episodes. The emotions are similar to those described by people after bulimia nervosa, kleptomania, and trichotillomania episodes. People with skin-picking problems often have other self-injurious and impulse-control problem behaviors. For some people, skin picking helps them to regulate intense emotions and may serve as a self-soothing mechanism.

Skin picking appears to be related to OCD and BDD. Approximately half of the people in the Wilhelm study met the criteria for OCD and nearly one-third met the criteria for BDD. Many people with skin-picking problems have been described as being perfectionistic or having obsessive-compulsive traits. Wilhelm also reports high rates of other anxiety disorders, depression, substance abuse, borderline personality disorder, obsessive-compulsive personality disorder, hypochondriasis, gynecologic symptoms, and migraine or tension headaches among skin pickers. Nearly half of study participants had first-degree relatives who picked their skin. As with TTM, people often don't seek help for skin picking because of feelings of embarrassment and shame. When they do seek treatment, they are often first seen by a dermatologist, and they usually deny having a psychiatric problem.

Many of the skin pickers in the Wilhelm study had current or past *stereotypies* (stereotyped, or repetitive, behaviors), such as body rocking, nail biting, thumb sucking, knuckle cracking, cheek chewing, head banging, teeth flicking, and lip biting. Major episodes of skin picking were triggered by stress or significant changes in family, marriage, work, or health status.

Nail Biting

As with skin picking, most people bite their nails or cuticles at least occasionally. But for some people, it can be a serious problem. They may feel embarrassed to be seen biting their nails and cuticles, or they may feel shame at having the results of severe nail biting noticed. Besides embarrassment, injuries to the nails and nail bed, and bleeding and disfigurement of the fingers and nails, can occur. Despite the commonness of this habit little research on nail biting and its treatment has been done. Most people who have this problem seem to have started in childhood. Often they have been punished or had bad-tasting substances put on their fingers to try to stop their nail biting. These treatments rarely seem to work. Like skin picking and TTM, these behaviors look like grooming behaviors that have gotten out of control. If skin picking or nail biting is a problem habit for you, the Habit Change Program can help.

Your Habit Change Plan for Nervous Habits, Trichotillomania, Skin Picking, and Nail Biting

You can change your habits. You may have given up hope, but there are proven techniques for changing these types of habits. If you haven't worked through chapters 5 and 6, do so now. It is important for you to convince yourself that you do indeed have habits in need of change. You need to recognize the negative consequences. When the going gets rough—and it will—your Habit Advantages and Disadvantages worksheet and Consequences chart will remind you of why you are trying to change.

After reading chapter 5, you kept a record of your habit. You discovered the emotions, automatic thoughts, triggers, and consequences associated with your habit. Look at the worksheets you completed, think back to the last few times you have engaged in your habit, and answer the following questions. We've provided Margie's and Amanda's answers as examples.

What *feelings* do you typically experience before, during, and after engaging in your habit?

Before: _____

During: _____

After: _____

What *automatic thoughts* do you have before, during, and after engaging in your habit?

Before: _____

During: _____

After: _____

What are the most frequent *emotional triggers* for your habit? _____

_____

What are the most frequent *situational triggers* for your habit? _____

_____

Margie:

What *feelings* do you typically experience before, during, and after engaging in your habit?

Before: *Disgust, anxiety, fear, or worry about things.* _____

During: *Nervous and hurried feelings, then relief when I give in, anger with myself, disgust, guilt.*

After: *Guilt, disgust with myself, anxious, tired, depressed feelings.* _____

What *automatic thoughts* do you have before, during, and after engaging in your habit?

Before: *I'll just do this to get rid of those spots, then I'll quit. I just have to look OK today.* ____

During: *Oh, I'm picking again. Well, I have to finish now. I'm disgusting.* _____

After: *I am disgusting and have no self-control. Why couldn't I have stopped?* _____

What are the most frequent *emotional triggers* for your habit? *Most often, I feel worried or nervous. Sometimes I am lonely or bored. Other times I feel disgust at the looks of a blemish on my skin.*

What are the most frequent *situational triggers* for your habit? *Seeing a pimple or a piece of loose skin. Being in the bathroom, in front of the mirror. Sometimes if I am nervous I find myself scratching my arm or hand.*

Amanda:

What *feelings* do you typically experience before, during, and after engaging in your habit?

Before: *Sometimes boredom, like when I'm watching TV. Other times, I feel anxiety, tension, or like I just have to pull a particular hair. Itching or burning sensation where the hair grows.*

During: *When I'm bored I pull absentmindedly and don't feel anything. When I deliberately pull, I feel relief, but disgust; at other times I am kind of zoned out and feel nothing.*

After: *I feel calm and less anxious on one hand, but I feel guilt and disgust with myself on the other hand. The anxiety is relieved, but it has been replaced by depression.*

What *automatic thoughts* do you have before, during, and after engaging in your habit?

Before: *I might just find myself pulling and think, "I'm doing it again! Stop it!" Or, when I'm deliberately pulling, "I have to pull this hair; it will relieve the itch."*

During: *"I'm disgusting. I must be the only one who does this. How will I hide this bald spot? I need to get rid of the itch. though." But sometimes I don't seem to have any thoughts.*

After: *"I did it again! I'll never be able to stop. I'm disgusting. I'm sure no one else does this. I've got to hide this bald spot. No one must know. Someday I'll get help."*

What are the most frequent *emotional triggers* for your habit? *Boredom when I'm watching TV or reading. Before I deliberately pull, I feel anxious or stressed out or worried. Or I might be bored and go into the bathroom.*

What are the most frequent *situational triggers* for your habit? *Having an argument with someone. Being at home alone and going into the bathroom to the mirror. Touching and feeling my hair with my hands. Watching TV or reading.*

In chapter 5, you learned about your habit by filling out Habit Records and Triggers and Consequences Records. In chapter 6, you discovered the advantages and disadvantages of keeping and changing your habit. At the end of chapter 6, you made a commitment to change. You are taking the first step toward change by continuing to record your participation in your habit, using the Habit Records and Triggers and Consequences Records. How long should you continue to fill out these records? As long as it takes! Keep them until you have significantly changed your habit, but for at least six months. After you stop keeping these records, check up on yourself regularly every six months: keep Habit Records and Triggers and Consequences Records for several weeks so that you can assess yourself for relapse. You may even want to continue keeping records indefinitely.

⚘ Habit Change Strategy

Keep records of your habit as long as you have the habit. Record keeping is your best defense against doing the things you don't want to do.

We cannot overemphasize the importance of the record keeping. Cherry had a problem with spending a few years ago. In typical fashion she bought not one but three books on the subject of overspending. She flipped through them and noted that record keeping was an important factor in spending reduction. So she kept a record of every penny she spent for several months. Seeing the patterns of her habit on paper made her want to change. The overspending improved greatly. Just seeing the extent of your habit will make *you* want to change, too. And motivation to change will bring about change.

While you continue to keep track of your habit on your Habit Records and Triggers and Consequences Records, bookmark this page and read chapters 7 through 10. In chpater 7 you will be asked to develop a competing response. Carefully review and understand the steps in habit reversal described in chapter 7. Decide what you will do when you have the urge to engage in your habit. In chapter 8, you will learn relaxation techniques. Choose your favorite technique and incorporate it into your habit change plans. Chapters 9 and 10 will help you recognize the automatic thoughts that contribute to your problem habit. When you have finished reading chapters 7 through 10, meet us back here to continue your individual journey toward changing your specific habit.

Below we have listed tips for applying habit change principles to most nervous habits. Then we've provided more specific tips for skin picking and trichotillomania. Check off the ideas that might help you change your habit. Then we'll help you develop a personalized plan for changing your habit.

Tips for Changing Nervous Habits

❑ Resume old activities and start new ones you have been avoiding because of your habit.

❑ When the urge is *overwhelming*, do all you can to avoid trigger situations (but don't allow this to become long-term avoidance).

❑ Get treatment for any physical or mental problems that might be contributing to your habit.

❑ Print encouraging statements on three-by-five-inch cards and place them in areas that tend to be associated with triggers for your habit—on the bathroom mirror, on the TV, in the car, or by your favorite chair, for example.

❑ Learn better ways to handle stress—don't forget your daily relaxation exercise. Do the thought-changing exercises in chapters 9 and 10.

❑ If nail biting is a problem, keep your nails neatly manicured. File rough edges immediately—but don't overdo it.

❑ Keep fingernail files available in triggering environments, if nail biting is a problem.

❑ Continue keeping Habit Records and Triggers and Consequences Records for at least six months or as long as you have a problem with nervous habits, skin picking, or TTM.

Habit Change Strategy

Don't avoid life! Use avoidance of habit-provoking situations only when the urge to engage in your habit is overwhelming.

Tips for Skin Picking and Trichotillomania

❑ Consider seeing a dermatologist, especially if you have acne, extra-dry skin, rashes, redness, itching, allergies, or persistent dandruff.

❑ Pay special attention to skin care. Moisturized, well-cared-for skin is healthier and less tempting to pick.

❑ Keep lotion handy at all times. Whenever you are tempted to pick, moisturize instead.

❑ Use mild skin-care and laundry products. There is no reason to irritate the skin any more than necessary.

❑ Limit your use of makeup. Using too much concealer will decrease the negative consequences of skin picking and may interfere with healing.

❑ Get rid of all implements you have used for skin picking or hair pulling—tweezers, cuticle nippers, needles, pins, scissors, toothpicks, and so on.

❑ If you use tweezers for plucking your eyebrows (or cuticle nippers for trimming tempting loose hangnails) in order to stop yourself from picking, keep them available in several convenient spots—but *not* if you often use them to the point of worsening the situation.

❑ If you need tweezers and cuticle nippers for skin and eyebrow care but often tweeze too far, use them only in the presence of your support person.

❑ Give artificial nails a try. They can make picking and pulling more difficult and often change the way it feels, thus decreasing the urge.

❑ Keep handy a supply of rubber fingertips, the kind found in office-supply stores. When the urge hits, put one on. Don't let this be your *only* prevention, though, because they won't always be handy.

❑ Keep your hands busy when you are in trigger situations: play with a puzzle, squeeze a ball, or do needlework.

❑ Consider temporarily removing or covering mirrors in your home until you have made some progress in hair pulling or face picking, especially if looking in the mirror is a high-risk situation for you. Bringing back or uncovering the mirrors can be a reward, a symbol of your accomplishment. Painting mirrors or decorating them with cling-on scenes can be a fun project.

❑ Stop hiding your habit. Gradually begin to expose your hair, face, or hands to others. Start with family, close friends, and your hairstylist, then move on to the rest of the world. You'll be surprised at the support you receive. And exposure will increase the negative consequences of engaging in your habit.

❑ Get to know your hairstylist or manicurist. Enlist him or her as a support person and ask for hair-, skin-, and nail-care advice for your particular hair and skin type.

❑ Be creative with your self-monitoring. Collecting or counting pulled hairs can help you first see the severity of your habit, then later appreciate your progress.

❑ Don't touch your hair unless you are combing or styling it.

❑ When the temptation to pick or pull is *overwhelming*, cover your hair, wear a scarf or hat, or put on gloves. Don't let this be a permanent solution, though. Covering up should be used as a response to overwhelming urges, not as camouflage for the results of engaging in your habit.

❑ Make your hair unappealing to pull by applying gel or hair spray. These products change the "feel" of your hair, which changes the experience.

❑ Try keeping your hair out of your face by using barrettes, combs, or headbands.

❑ Keep your hands away from your face and other problem areas.

❑ The Trichotillomania Learning Center is a nonprofit educational foundation with a mission of providing education, creating an active support network, and raising support to identify effective treatments for this disorder. Keep in touch with them to stay updated on the latest information. See the Resources section for contact information.

Developing Your Habit Change Plan

Did you notice that the title of this section is *Your* Habit Change Plan? That's because it will be *your* plan. Now you are ready to put what you have learned into action and create your own Habit Change Plan. You've discovered the habits that are interfering with your life. You've learned some ways to make changes in your life and ways to deal with the negative thoughts and beliefs that have kept you from changing.

You probably have some general goals in mind. Of course, your main goal is to stop picking, or pulling, or nail biting, or jangling your keys. But after giving it a little thought, you will probably be able to create a couple of related goals. For example, Amanda decided to learn to play tennis. She'd always wanted to learn to play and she realized this would increase her overall confidence in herself. Besides wanting to stop the skin picking, Margie wanted to take better care of her skin, which would provide a competing response and help repair the damage she had already done to her skin. Putting some concentration on positive goals helps with motivation. Now, you'll break your goal of stopping your habit into smaller goals and develop a step-by-step plan for achieving those goals. For a few pointers on making your plan, look over chapter 15. Some of the principles discussed there will apply here.

Step 1: Develop Long-Term Goals

Choose a general achievement you would like to accomplish—a long-term goal. Then list a couple of related goals. What are your long-term goals? How will you know when you have met your goals? Complete the Long-Term Goals worksheet. We've provided Margie's and Amanda's long-term goals as examples.

❀ Habit Change Strategy

Make specific goals that are challenging, yet attainable. They don't have to be perfect though—you can always change them later.

Long-Term Goals

My long-term goals are:

1. _____

2. _____

3. _____

How will I know when I have met these goals? _____

_____

_____

_____

Chart 13a

Margie's Long-Term Goals

My long-term goals are:

1. *Stop picking my skin.* _____

2. *Take better care of my skin and bring about the healing of my damaged skin.* ___

3. *Spend more time crocheting. Complete three projects this year.* ___

How will I know when I have met these goals? *I will know I have accomplished these things when my skin is clear, with no scabs or sores, and when I am no longer picking at blemishes that occur. Damaged areas will be healed. I will have crocheted three projects.*

Chart 13b

Amanda's Long-Term Goals

My long-term goals are:

1. _Stop pulling my hair._

2. _Take better care of my hair and go to the beauty parlor every month._

3. _Learn to play tennis._

How will I know when I have met these goals? _I will no longer be pulling my hair. My hair will look nicer, and there won't be any bald spots. I'll be going to the beauty parlor every month. I will be playing tennis and learning the rules of the game._

Chart 13c

Step 2: Make a Plan

Looking at these goals and imagining achieving them all at once can feel overwhelming. But you can break them into smaller parts, so that they don't seem so overwhelming. Now you will make plans for achieving your goals. An important part of your plan will be making short-term goals. Your major focus will be on meeting these short-term goals instead of the long-term ones. For example, when we first decided to write this book, the project seemed overwhelming. How would we ever get it written by the deadline? When we divided it into chapters and gave ourselves mini-deadlines to meet, it seemed much less daunting because we had a plan and goals for carrying out our plan.

We've provided a Habit Change Plan worksheet for you to complete. Make copies of the blank worksheet so you can make revisions if it needs adjustment later. As you create your plan for change, include some of the things we mentioned earlier. Use the ideas you've gathered in this book: record keeping, competing responses, relaxation, triggers, changing the way you think and deal with feelings, social support, and rewards. We've provided Margie's and Amanda's worksheets as examples.

Habit Change Strategy

In your plan include something from every category—record keeping, competing response, relaxation, triggers, thoughts and feelings, social support, rewards—they are all important to your success.

Habit Change Plan

Record
Keeping

Competing
Response

Relaxation

Trigger
Management

Challenging
Avoidance

Thoughts
& Feelings

Social
Support

Rewards

Margie's Habit Change Plan

Record Keeping

I will continue to keep Habit Records and Triggers and Consequences Records for at least six months, and after that as long as I have a problem with skin picking.

Competing Response

When I am driving, I will clench the steering wheel. When I am at work I will clench a pencil. When no pencil is available, I will clench my fists. I need something to do with my hands, so I will take up crocheting for when I am watching TV.

Relaxation

I'm going to practice progressive relaxation daily and whenever I am feeling worried, tense, anxious, or bored.

Trigger Management

When I go in the bathroom, I will do what I need to do, then leave. I won't spend as much time on grooming—in fact, I will allow myself only a certain amount of time to put my makeup on. As soon as I feel an itch or an urge to pick, I will institute a competing response.

Challenging Avoidance

I will use makeup that is good for sensitive skin and not too heavy. When I'm around the house or just running to the store or picking up the kids at school, I won't wear makeup and I'll let my skin "breathe." I'll get rid of the implements I've used to pick at my skin.

Thoughts & Feelings

I'm going to question the idea that picking will help my skin look better. I'll refute the belief that I am disgusting and weak when I do give in to the urge to pick at my skin and the idea that if I start picking at a blemish I need to finish. I can stop if I choose to.

Social Support

I'm going to ask for my husband's and children's support and encouragement and keep them updated on my progress. The kids just might gain confidence by seeing that their mom can change.

Rewards

I'll reward myself by taking care of my skin and moisturizing it. I guess that is also a competing response. When I go an entire week without picking I'll buy myself a new outfit. I'll reward myself for sticking to my plan by buying yarn to crochet a really special project.

Chart 13e

Amanda's Habit Change Plan

Record Keeping

I will continue to keep Habit Records and Triggers and Consequences Records for at least six months, and then as long as I still have a problem with hair pulling.

Competing Response

Pinching my forefinger and thumb together will be my main competing response. I will do that as soon as I get the urge to pull a hair. When I am reading or watching TV I will keep a squishy ball in my right hand to remind me not to pull. I'm going to learn to play tennis, something more active I can do for entertainment.

Relaxation

I'm going to meditate and do abdominal breathing daily and whenever I am bored, worried, tense, or anxious.

Trigger Management

As soon as I feel an urge to pull, or when I touch my hair, I will pinch my finger and thumb together. Hair gel will remind me not to pull. I'll find something to do when I feel bored. I will be extra vigilant when I go into the bathroom and won't linger there.

Challenging Avoidance

I'm going to the beauty parlor to get my hair cut and will go every month. I'll tell my hairdresser about my TTM problem. I might wear hats for a while longer, but I'll stop wearing wigs. Around the house, no hat.

Thoughts & Feelings

I will remind myself that I have a disorder, a problem with my brain, but that I do have choices and can stop pulling my hair. When I do give in, I'll refute the belief that I am disgusting or weak, or that there is no hope for me.

Social Support

There are other people with TTM! I'm going to join the support group here in town. I'll enlist the help of a couple of good friends who will be understanding once I explain it to them. And, of course, my hairdresser will be a major support person.

Rewards

I'll reward myself by taking care of my hair and going to the beauty parlor every month. Every week that I improve I will go out to eat with one of support people—kind of a celebration dinner.

Chart 13f

Step 3: Develop Short-Term Goals

What will you accomplish tomorrow and in the next few days? Assess your Habit Change Plan and your Habit Records, and set one to three short-term goals for the coming week. Make copies of the Short-Term Goals worksheet and at the beginning of each week set goals for the following week. Evaluate your work in the previous week and decide how you could improve. Your short-term goals should be based on behaviors you need to change, so that you can better meet your long-term goals. We've provided Margie's and Amanda's Short-Term Goals worksheets, both for their second week, as examples.

⬙⬙ Habit Change Strategy

Remember, goals should be specific, challenging, and attainable. Be a bit easy on yourself the first few weeks to help yourself build confidence, then get more challenging.

Short-Term Goals   Week No. _____

My short-term goals are:

1. _____

2. _____

3. _____

How will I know when I have met these goals? _____

_____

_____

_____

Did I meet my goals last week? If I didn't, what could I do differently in the next week?

_____

_____

_____

Chart 13g

Margie's Short-Term Goals

Week No. __2__

My short-term goals are:

1. _Do competing response when have urge to pick at skin—clenching fist, clenching pencil, etc._

2. _Find out what kind of skin-care products are best for my skin._

3. _Buy yarn and begin crocheting project._

How will I know when I have met these goals? _I will be doing competing response often when I have an urge to pick. I will have found out what skin-care products are best for my skin. I will have begun my crocheting project._

Did I meet my goals last week? If I didn't, what could I do differently in the next week? _I remembered to do my competing response about half of the time, but it was still hard to keep from picking. I want to take better care of my skin, so it won't be as tempting to pick._

Chart 13h

Amanda's Short-Term Goals

Week No. __2__

My short-term goals are:

1. _Use competing response when have urge to pull hair—pinch finger and thumb together._

2. _Purchase squishy ball for competing response during TV watching._

3. _Find out where I can take tennis lessons._

How will I know when I have met these goals? _I will be using my competing responses often when I have an urge to pull my hair. I will have a squishy ball and begin using it when I watch TV. I will have information about tennis lessons._

Did I meet my goals last week? If I didn't, what could I do differently in the next week? _I found it hard to resist hair pulling. I think it will help to have a ball to squeeze._

Chart 13i

Now you have a plan for changing your habit. Try to look at this as a long-term project. It took a while for your habit to get out of control. It will take a while for you to get it under control. Read chapters 11 and 12 now. You'll learn more about quitting your bad habits and developing healthy habits, including your competing response. You'll probably think of a few more habits that you would like to incorporate into your life. Focusing on the good habits will take your mind off the bad habits you are trying to eliminate. Habit changing just might become a habit!

You might be wondering how you are going to keep the changes you make. Will they end up being only short-term changes, or will you be free of your bad habits and keep the healthy ones for good? Chapter 12 will help you fight back against temporary lapses in your Habit Change efforts.

Do you know others who might like to change their habits? Chapter 20 can help you make habit changing a family affair or a group effort. You don't all have to be interested in changing the same type of habit, only in changing whatever habits each of you finds troublesome in his or her life.

14

Sleeping Habits

God bless whoever invented sleep, the cloak that covers all human thoughts.
—Miguel de Cervantes

I will not go to bed just because my husband is sleepy and has to get up early in the morning.

—Erma Bombeck

Sleep is a basic human need, an appetitive behavior. However, while people can starve themselves to death, most can't stay awake for more than two to three days. Sleeping problems are very common. Approximately 30 to 35 percent of adults have insomnia at least once a year. Many people describe insomnia as a chronic problem. Most don't realize there are non-drug methods to improve their sleep. Indeed, the non-drug methods have been shown to work better, over a long period of time, than sleeping pills (Morin, Hauri, Espie, Spielman, Buysse, and Bootzin 1999; Morin, Colecci, Stone, Sood, and Brink 1999). Other sleeping problems, such as nightmares, can also be effectively treated using non-drug methods.

Causes of Sleep Disturbances

Situational stress, psychiatric or medical disorders, and chronic sleep disorders may cause sleep disturbances. If you have a sleep problem that has lasted more than a few weeks or you are excessively sleepy during the day, the first thing to do is visit your primary-care doctor. Your doctor can evaluate you and determine if the sleep problem is due to a medical problem in need of treatment. In this chapter, we will discuss some of the more common sleep problems.

Clinical depression is a common cause of sleep problems. Depression is often associated with a type of insomnia that causes a person to wake up very early in the morning and not be able to get back to sleep. Other symptoms of depression, such as sadness, lack of enjoyment, appetite changes, and hopelessness are also likely to be present. If you have these symptoms, we recommend that you seek treatment for depression.

Do you have trouble going to sleep due to a creepy feeling in your legs? Do you feel like you have to move your legs or get up and walk around when you are trying to go to sleep?

This could be a sign of a problem known as *restless legs syndrome*, which is usually treated with medication. Do you snore? Is your snoring loud enough that others in your home complain, or do they say that you sometimes seem to stop breathing? Do you ever wake up gasping for breath? Are you excessively sleepy during the day? These symptoms may be a sign of a problem called *sleep apnea*, a common sleep disorder that involves breathing problems in your sleep. Most people with sleep apnea do not know they have it. Describe your symptoms to your doctor. You may be referred to a sleep evaluation center. Problems like sleep apnea can have a major effect on your health and need to be evaluated and treated.

Many prescription and over-the-counter drugs can affect sleep, as can caffeine, alcohol, and illicit drugs. If prescription drugs are causing a sleep problem, your doctor may be able to substitute another medication. Some of the medications used to treat problems such as depression can cause sleep problems. Sometimes the medications prescribed to help with sleep become part of the problem, especially when you try to stop taking them. In many cases the cognitive behavioral therapy techniques described in this chapter will help.

Sleep problems often increase with age. Up to 40 percent of older adults report chronic sleeping problems. Daytime sleepiness, light sleep or nonrefreshing sleep, frequent awakenings, and waking up too early are common complaints. Many older people believe that as they get older they don't need as much sleep. While this is not true—their sleep needs don't actually change—some sleep changes are part of what naturally seems to occur with age. In addition, changes in lifestyle, such as reduced activity levels and the increased need for prescription medications, are likely to have an impact on sleep.

Personal and Social Consequences

Sleeping difficulties can adversely affect a person's quality of life. When we don't get enough sleep we may experience increased fatigue, a desire to nap, decreased alertness, or excessive sleepiness that lead to falling asleep at awkward or dangerous times. Often, attempts to correct the sleeping problem, such as staying in bed longer, taking more daytime naps, taking sleeping aids, or consuming alcohol before bedtime, end up making the problem worse. Worrying about getting enough sleep, especially for people with insomnia, is very common; paradoxically, worry interferes with sleep, which leads to more worry.

One of the most serious consequences of sleeping problems occurs on our roadways. The National Highway Traffic Safety Administration has reported that an estimated one-hundred thousand car accidents every year in the United States are caused by sleepy drivers (Idzikowski 1999). Each year fifteen hundred of these crashes are fatal.

Treatment Options

Sleep-inducing medications, also known as sedatives or sleeping pills, are not recommended for people with chronic sleeping problems or with a history of chemical dependency. However, sedatives can be useful in the treatment of temporary sleeping problems induced by acute stress. Side effects can include daytime drowsiness, performance deficiencies, memory impairment, and rebound insomnia, or insomnia that occurs when you stop the medication. Rebound insomnia often leads people to think they cannot sleep without taking the medication. Falls and accidents are an additional risk, especially for elderly people, as a result of the effects of the drug lasting into the next day or impairing their ability to get up at night to use the toilet. These medications can be habit forming when used for prolonged periods and they can lose their effectiveness with time. If you are using a medication to help you sleep and want to stop, see your doctor before altering the dosage. He may want to instruct you to gradually taper to smaller dosages for several nights before discontinuation. Even so, you should expect some rebound insomnia.

Cognitive behavioral techniques are very effective in the improvement of sleeping problems. Our goal is to help you develop behaviors, thought patterns, and environmental conditions that promote adequate sleep.

The Habit Change Plan for Insomnia

As we have done when confronting other habit problems, we need to begin by getting a good look at what is going on now. Included in this chapter is a sleep diary. To understand your insomnia, you will need to fill out the sleep diary. It is probably best to do this for two full weeks before trying to change your sleep habits. Make six copies of the blank Sleep Diary and keep records as you learn to understand and change your sleep problem. We've included Barbara's Sleep Diary as an example.

Habit Change Strategy

Behavioral and thinking habits can affect your sleep. Changing them can help you sleep better.

Sleep Diary

Instructions: Fill in the starting time and length of any naps. Fill in any alcohol or medications you used. Fill in the time that you get into bed for the night and the time you turn out the lights to go to sleep. Estimate the amount of time in minutes it takes you to fall asleep. Fill in the number of times you wake up in the night and estimate the amount of time you are awake each time. Fill in the time you wake up for the day. Fill in the time you get up for the day. Calculate efficiency by dividing the length of time asleep by the length of time in bed. Multiply this answer by 100 to get a percentage of time asleep. It is best to convert hours to minutes for these calculations. Rate how restoring the night's sleep was from 0 to 5 with 0 being not restorative and 5 being completely restorative. All notations should be made when you get up in the morning except for naps, which can be noted before bed. This means filling out the form for day 1 on the morning of day 2, and so forth.

	Day 1	Day 2	Day 3	Day 4	Day 5	Day 6	Day 7
Nap start time and length							
Sleep aids or alcohol used							
Time you got into bed							
Lights-out time							
Time it took to fall asleep after lights out							
Interruptions and length							
Time you woke up for the day							
Time out of bed for the day							
Sleep efficiency (time asleep/time in bed)							
Restored feeling 0–5							
Minutes asleep							
Minutes in bed							

Chart 14a

Barbara's Sleep Diary

Instructions: Fill in the starting time and length of any naps. Fill in any alcohol or medications you used. Fill in the time that you get into bed for the night and the time you turn out the lights to go to sleep. Estimate the amount of time in minutes it takes you to fall asleep. Fill in the number of times you wake up in the night and estimate the amount of time you are awake each time. Fill in the time you wake up for the day. Fill in the time you get up for the day. Calculate efficiency by dividing the length of time asleep by the length of time in bed. Multiply this answer by 100 to get a percentage of time asleep. It is best to convert hours to minutes for these calculations. Rate how restoring the night's sleep was from 0 to 5 with 0 being not restorative and 5 being completely restorative. All notations should be made when you get up in the morning except for naps, which can be noted before bed. This means filling out the form for day 1 on the morning of day 2, and so forth.

	Day 1	Day 2	Day 3	Day 4	Day 5	Day 6	Day 7
Nap start time and length	None	4 P.M.; 30 min.	4:30 P.M.; 30 min.	4 P.M., 30 min.	None	4:30 P.M., 45 min.	5 P.M., 45 min.
Sleep aids or alcohol used	Ambien	Ambien	Ambien	Ambien	Ambien	Ambien	Ambien
Time you got into bed	10:30 P.M.	10:30 P.M.	10:30 P.M.	10:45 P.M.	12:35 A.M.	12:35 A.M.	11:00 P.M.
Lights-out time	11:30 P.M.	11:00 P.M.	11:20 P.M.	11:30 P.M.	1:00 A.M.	1:00 A.M.	11:50 P.M.
Time it took to fall asleep after lights out	30 min.	45 min.	45 min.	40 min.	40 min.	45 min.	40 min.
Interruptions and length	2:10 min., 15 min.	1:10 min.	2:10 min., 10 min.	2:15 min., 10 min.	1:10 min.	1:15 min.	1:15 min.
Time you woke up for the day	6:30 A.M.	6:10 A.M.	6:20 A.M.	6:20 A.M.	8:15 A.M.	8:15 A.M.	6:30 A.M.
Time out of bed for the day	7:00 A.M.	7:00 A.M.	7:30 A.M.	7:30 A.M.	10:30 A.M.	11:30 A.M.	7:30 A.M.
Sleep efficiency (time asleep/time in bed)	72 percent	74 percent	65 percent	66 percent	60 percent	57 percent	67 percent
Restored feeling 0–5	3	3	2	2	1	1	2
Minutes asleep	365	375	355	345	385	375	345
Minutes in bed	510	510	540	525	595	655	510

Chart 14b

Understanding your sleep habits is the first step toward learning new sleep habits and making your sleep more satisfying. As you can see, Barbara's Sleep Diary shows that she has difficulty getting enough sleep. She has trouble falling asleep and has difficulty getting up on time for work. She tries to catch up on sleep by taking afternoon naps and staying in bed later on weekends. There are a number of problems in the way Barbara deals with her sleep, and these methods contribute to her persistent sleep problem. She is getting about six and one-half hours of sleep a day, which is not enough for her, so it is not surprising that she is unhappy about it. Most people need more than this amount of sleep. In addition, Barbara's sleep pattern is not very efficient. Her average sleep efficiency is about 65 percent. Sleep experts agree that a sleep efficiency below 85 percent is a problem.

Set Your Biological Clock

It is important to understand that sleep is a natural process that is coordinated with rhythms in the body. When your body's set of rhythms gets uncoordinated, your body doesn't work as well and you don't feel quite right. Humans have a *biological clock* built into the brain that helps coordinate biological rhythms including sleep and wakefulness. However, it's not a very good clock. It doesn't run accurately. It tends to run on something other than a twenty-four-hour schedule. For many people the clock may even run on a twenty-five-hour schedule.

As a result, we are likely to go to sleep a little later each day and wake up a little later each day. If we give in to this tendency, our sleep may become a problem in a short time. For example, suppose you go to sleep a little later than usual Friday night, knowing that you don't have to get up early Saturday. You may sleep in a little Saturday morning. Then you do it again Saturday night and Sunday morning. By Sunday night you may have shifted your clock an hour or more and not be able to get to sleep on time. Then you have a problem getting enough sleep by Monday morning. Because of the inaccurate pattern of the clock we advise people to reset it each day. One of the best ways to do this is to get up each morning at the same time. Yes, even on weekends, vacations, and holidays. It will help you sleep better.

⚘ Habit Change Strategy

Get up at the same time each day, even on the weekends!

Make Helpful Associations with Being in Bed

Most people want to associate being asleep with being in bed, but people with sleep problems usually associate tossing and turning, worrying about not getting enough sleep, and other activities with being in bed. Some people do all sorts of things in bed, including eating, talking on the phone, reading or studying, watching TV, paying bills, and arguing with their spouses. If you want to become a good sleeper, you need to do only two things in bed: sleep and have sex.

All other activities, including lying around when you are not sleeping, should be done elsewhere. Many people with sleep problems think they need to stay in bed even when they are not asleep, because they believe (or hope) they are getting at least some of the rest they need anyway. In fact, however, the rest they get is not really all that good for them, and lying in bed when they are not sleeping creates a harmful association. Bed becomes associated with tossing and turning. Try the following strategy: If you are not asleep within fifteen to twenty minutes of going to bed, get out of bed, go to a quiet part of your home, and engage in a quiet activity. Do not return to bed until you are sleepy. Remember that being sleepy is different from being tired. *Sleepy* means feeling like you could easily fall asleep.

Many people who give advice about sleeping problems will tell you to go to bed at the same time every night. However, this conventional wisdom is not helpful if you are going to bed before you feel sleepy. You need to stay up until you are sleepy, then go to bed. Remember, if you are not asleep in fifteen to twenty minutes, get out of bed until you are sleepy. This rule also applies when you wake up in the middle of the night and can't get back to sleep or when you wake up early in the morning and know you probably won't get back to sleep. If you're not asleep in fifteen to twenty minutes, get up. In other words, never allow yourself to lie in bed for long periods when you aren't sleeping.

Some people with sleeping problems don't sleep in their beds much—or at all. They may sleep in a chair or on the couch instead. This is not a good idea, for the reasons we explained above. You need to associate the place you sleep with sleeping and not with other things. The couch is likely to be a place where you do many other things, so if the couch becomes your bed this will weaken the link between your "bed" and sleeping, which will in turn contribute to sleep problems.

⚭ Habit Change Strategy

Go to bed when you are sleepy. If you aren't asleep in twenty minutes, get up. Sleep only in bed.

Arrange a Comfortable Environment

The environment in your bedroom is important to your getting a good night's sleep. You want to make your bedroom a good place to sleep, which involves arranging conditions for your greatest comfort. Make sure your bedroom is cool, dark, and relatively quiet. Light is a problem for many people. Bright light, such as sunlight, wakes up your brain. Making a small investment in good shades or drapes is often helpful. Drapes may also help with sound. Also, keep your bedroom temperature cool—most people seem to sleep better in a cool room.

Paying attention to environmental sound in the bedroom is also important. Most people sleep better in a quiet environment. Even while you are asleep, your brain processes what you hear. If it detects something important you will wake up. This is why a parent may wake upon hearing the soft cry of a baby but can sleep through louder noises that don't mean as much. Make an effort to keep your bedroom quiet. This may mean asking other family members who are on a different schedule to turn down the TV or requesting that they try to be quiet when you are sleeping. Some people sleep better with a masking noise, sometimes called *white noise*. You may be able to purchase a machine that makes a simple swooshing noise or more complex sounds like ocean waves. Other people use a fan or similar device. Soft music can also help, depending on your individual preferences and habits. If you find yourself waiting for the sleep timer on the radio to go off and the music to stop or if you sing along with the radio it may not be a good idea to have music in your sleep environment.

If a particular background noise is present most of the time, you will have trouble sleeping when it is not there. Dr. C. learned this years ago, when he spent a weekend at a friend's home in New York City. His friend slept peacefully but Dr. C. couldn't get to sleep because of the traffic noise. When things were reversed and his friend stayed at Dr. C.'s home in the woods of Connecticut, the friend couldn't sleep because it was too quiet.

✖ Habit Change Strategy

Make your environment comfortable and conducive to sleep. Avoid changes of light, noise, and temperature.

Exercise to Improve Sleep

It is important to treat your body in ways that help with sleep. Making positive changes in your fitness and exercise habits can help with sleep problems. See chapter 15 for help with making these changes.

In addition, pay careful attention to the timing of exercise. We have a daily rhythm of body temperature changes. If you were to take your temperature several times a day, you would see that it goes up and down in a regular pattern. We sleep better when our body temperature is going down. This usually starts in the late afternoon or early evening. Exercise causes a change in body temperature and can alter the pattern of temperature changes. Because of this, it is most helpful to exercise late in the afternoon. For most people, getting regular daily exercise will improve sleep. However, exercise near bedtime is likely to get your temperature going the wrong way and cause problems falling asleep. On the other hand, taking a hot bath just before bed may be helpful. The bath tends to bump your body temperature up a bit, but when you get out of the tub your temperature starts to drop again almost immediately.

✖ Habit Change Strategy

Exercise is conducive to sleep, but not if it is done too close to bedtime.

Eat Properly to Promote Good Sleep

When it comes to sleep, making a few simple changes in your eating habits can help a great deal. Eating a big meal may leave you feeling sleepy, but for most people the best plan is to have a small snack before bed; eating a few crackers or something similar may be helpful, since eating a snack made up of carbohydrates may be beneficial. Remember that it is best not to do anything in bed but engage in sleep and sex, so if you have a snack, don't eat it in bed. Also, pay attention to other things you eat or drink that might affect sleep. Caffeine is a common ingredient in some drinks, like coffee, tea, and colas. If you have any sleep problems, avoid caffeine after early afternoon. Some people are very sensitive to the effects of caffeine and do better if they eliminate it entirely. See chapter 15 for help with making changes in your dietary habits.

Drinking alcohol also interferes with sleep. Many people believe that having a drink, or a "nightcap," at bedtime will help them sleep. While it is true that alcohol makes people sleepy, the fact is that alcohol has a complex and disruptive effect on sleep. The sleep you get when you first go to sleep with alcohol in your system is actually changed. Alcohol alters the stages of sleep and you do not get the deep sleep you need. Then, in a few hours, when all the alcohol is metabolized, both alertness and REM sleep bounce back when the suppressing effects of the alcohol are no longer present. In addition, alcohol makes sleep apnea problems much worse.

🦋 Habit Change Strategy

A small bedtime snack is helpful, but caffeine or alcohol is not.

Make Changes to Improve Your Sleep

We've given you information that can help you improve your sleeping habits. Now it is up to you. It's time to make some decisions. What will you do now, tonight, that will help you sleep?

- Pick a time to get up every morning. What time will you get up? _____

- Don't go to bed until you are sleepy. If you are not asleep in fifteen to twenty minutes, get up and go to another part of your home. List some things you will do during these times.

  _____

  _____

- Remember, do only the two *S* activities in bed—*sex* and *sleep*. Are there any other things you do in bed that you are going to have to give up, like reading or watching TV? List them here.

  _____

  _____

- How can you arrange your environment to make it more conducive to sleep? List changes you will make here.

  _____

  _____

  _____

- Do you need to make exercise, diet, activity, or medication changes that would help you sleep? List changes you will make here.

  _____

  _____

  _____

- Chapter 8 includes descriptions of some simple relaxation methods. Choose one and practice it during the day until you feel comfortable with it. Then start practicing it at bedtime each night. Which relaxation method will you try first?

  _____

- Keep using the Sleep Diary while you are working on your sleep problem. Seeing improvement in your sleep efficiency will help you stop worrying about sleep. If you don't see any improvement, consult your doctor.

Barbara:

- Pick a time to get up every morning. What time will you get up? _7:00 A.M._

- Don't go to bed until you are sleepy. If you are not asleep in fifteen to twenty minutes, get up and go to another part of your home. List some things you will do during these times.

  I'll go to the living room and read, watch a quiet TV program, or play solitaire when I can't sleep. I'll keep the lights low so I can better relax and become sleepy. I definitely won't do things that take a lot of concentration, such as paying bills.

- Remember, do only the two S activities in bed—_sex_ and _sleep_. Are there any other things you do in bed that you are going to have to give up, like reading or watching TV? List them here.

  I often read, watch TV, or talk on the phone in the bedroom. I'll move the TV out of the bedroom. I have also done paperwork, such as sorting mail or paying bills, which I'll now do in the kitchen instead.

- How can you arrange your environment to make it more conducive to sleep? List changes you will make here.

  I'll purchase some better drapes that block out most of the light. Our older children go to bed later than my husband and I do. I'll have them stay away from the bedroom door and the hall as much as possible, turn the TV down, and be quieter.

- Do you need to make exercise, diet, activity, or medication changes that would help you sleep? List changes you will make here.

  I'll ask my doctor to help me reduce and then stop the Ambien that I take to help me sleep. I'll eliminate coffee altogether and have a small carbohydrate snack before I go to bed. And I need exercise anyway—I'll start exercising every afternoon after work.

- Chapter 8 includes descriptions of some simple relaxation methods. Choose one and practice it during the day until you feel comfortable with it. Then start practicing it at bedtime each night. Which relaxation method will you try first?

  I'm going to start with the progressive muscle relaxation exercises.

Nightmares

Nightmares—what are they and what can you do about them? The technical name for nightmares is _anxiety dreams_. But there are several types of nighttime experiences that can be mistaken for nightmares. A nightmare, or anxiety dream, is an actual dream that is upsetting. It is most likely to occur late in the night's sleep or close to morning, during REM sleep. If you wake up feeling panicky, or if you sit up in bed and even scream but can't describe a dream, it is probably not a nightmare. People who have panic disorder or related anxiety disorders will sometimes experience _nocturnal panic attacks_. They may find themselves awakening in a panic attack and think they must have had a nightmare, but often they can't describe any such dream. Nocturnal panic attacks are not usually associated with REM sleep, which is the stage of sleep in which we dream. The self-help method described below will not help nocturnal panic. But people who have panic attacks can get cognitive behavioral therapy and usually end up panic free. And when they get control of their daytime panic attacks the nocturnal ones also go away.

Another problem sometimes confused with nightmares is *sleep paralysis*, also called "riding the witch." This happens when a person wakes partially out of REM sleep, or dreaming sleep, but can't move. During REM sleep we are actually unable to move. This is fortunate because otherwise we would try to act out the things we dream about. Our brain protects us by shutting down our ability to move. This process works well unless this ability to move is not turned back on promptly when we wake up. This happens occasionally to many people and can be frightening. If it happens to you very often you need to see a sleep specialist to find out what is causing the problem.

Many children and a few adults experience episodes of *night terrors* when they are asleep. People with this problem may sit up in bed screaming, walk in their sleep, thrash around, or even strike a bed partner. They may be difficult to awaken and are likely to be very confused if anyone does manage to wake them. They will usually go back to sleep quickly if allowed to do so. Night terrors are common among children but rare in adults. They occur during non-REM sleep and are not associated with clearly defined dreams. They almost always occur in the first third of the night's sleep, during slow-wave sleep. When an episode occurs, the best thing to do is simply allow it to run its course and then get the individual settled back in bed. Despite the myth to the contrary, it is not dangerous to wake people in this state, although if they are awakened they will be confused and may strike out.

An opposite myth has it that it *is* important to wake people during night terrors or nightmares. This is not true either. It is very difficult to wake someone out of a night terror, and it is not likely to change the duration of the event. If you wake someone from a nightmare they are likely to have trouble getting back to sleep, so you will not have done them a favor. If these episodes become frequent, have a consultation with your doctor or a sleep specialist.

Many people wonder what their dreams mean. This can be a major question or concern if the person is having nightmares. Researchers studying sleep have tried to understand dreams but have not yet reached agreement. The theory most supported by recent research is that dreams are part of a mechanism in the brain for storing events in memory. This theory holds that the actual images in dreams are probably not important and don't tell us a lot about the individual. Others have argued that dreams can tell us what is going on in the unconscious or even predict the future. But this book is focused on how to change problem habits, and regardless of their meaning we think of nightmares as a problem habit.

If you are having a problem with nightmares—that is, you are having frequent, frightening dreams and you sometimes fear going to sleep because of them—we have a simple suggestion that will probably help. In some cases it is enough on its own to solve the problem. The idea is to learn a relaxation skill and practice it at bedtime. Progressive muscle relaxation and a meditation relaxation method are described in chapter 8. First learn these relaxation techniques and practice them at another time of day until you feel comfortable with them, then start practicing them at bedtime every night. This simple solution is often enough to help you get to sleep and to eliminate nightmares. Even if it doesn't entirely fix this problem it is the first step in a more complete treatment.

If the nightmares continue after you learn and practice the relaxation, then you will need to try one or both of the methods we describe below. The first one is best to use if the nightmares have a consistent theme or repetitive nature. The second one should work for most nightmares.

✂✂ Habit Change Strategy

Practicing relaxation exercises is the first step toward getting rid of nightmares. Often, it is the only step needed.

Systematic Desensitization

This method, developed many years ago, is used to effectively treat phobias. It involves the idea that exposure to small amounts of something, then gradually increasing the exposure, leads to desensitization and a different response. The concept is similar to that of allergy shots. Allergy shots involve exposing the body to a small amount of the substance that the body is sensitive to. Gradually, with repeated exposure, the body becomes desensitized and stops reacting to the substance. The same concept is used here to expose people to the anxiety-producing content of nightmares. You will be asked to write out the content or images of the dream that make you upset and then develop a plan to gradually expose yourself to these images, while learning to not be as sensitive to them. After a while you will be able to work with images that appear in the scariest parts of the dream and become desensitized to them as well. The dream will lose its ability to make you distressed. Systemic desensitization works especially well with dreams that are repeated. Larry often had nightmares about a traumatic assault that had happened to him many years before. He kept dreaming of the event over and over. We've provided his systemic desensitization plan as an example.

Write out a description of the events in your dream.

_____

_____

_____

_____

_____

_____

_____

_____

Larry:

Write out a description of the events in your dream.

I am walking along a sidewalk. The wind starts to blow and it looks like it might rain. The sidewalk starts to get narrower and narrower. When I look down, there is a deep, dark chasm on each side of the sidewalk. Then there is nothing left but the sidewalk and the chasm, no trees, buildings, or cars. Nothing. I am all alone. It begins to rain, first sprinkling, then raining harder. The wind gets stronger and the rain comes down in a downpour. I look down and around me and see that the sidewalk is narrower now. It's slippery, too. One false step and I might fall into the dark chasm. I don't know what is down there, but I don't want to fall. I am scared I'll fall down there. The sidewalk begins to wind all around with sharp turns. It's like a maze and I can't find my way home or even find my way out. I am feeling desperate because I can't find my way out. Then I hear footsteps. They get closer and closer, louder and louder. I notice there are no other sounds. Only the footsteps and my heartbeat. I walk faster and faster, and then I start to run, but the footsteps get closer, and someone grabs me from behind. I scream out, but no one comes. This is when I wake up.

Next put the scary parts of the dream in order according to how upsetting they are. Give them a score from 0 to 100 with 0 being not bothersome at all and 100 being the scariest thing you can imagine. Use the space here to place the different images in order from scariest to not scary at all.

_____   _____

_____   _____

_____   _____

_____   _____

_____   _____

_____   _____

_____   _____

_____   _____

_____   _____

_____   _____

_____   _____

Larry:

0	*Walking along a sidewalk*
10	*Raining as I walk along sidewalk*
20	*Wind blowing as I walk along sidewalk*
30	*Walking along a narrow sidewalk*
40	*Dark chasm surrounding the sidewalk*
50	*Dark chasm surrounding the sidewalk, no trees, buildings, cars, all alone*
60	*I am in a maze, lost, and can't find my way home.*
70	*I hear footsteps behind me as I walk along the sidewalk, no other sounds.*
80	*I'm running, footsteps are louder. Someone seems to be following me.*
90	*Someone grabs me.*
100	*I scream, but no one comes.*

Now you are ready to start systematic desensitization. Bookmark this page and turn to chapter 8 now. Read it and choose one of the simple relaxation methods described there in, and practice it during the day until you feel comfortable with it. Then return to this page. Pick a time to work on your nightmare when you won't be interrupted for about thirty minutes. Get yourself into a very relaxed state using the method you have been practicing. Then imagine as vividly as you can a scene you described that caused a moderate amount of distress. Start with a scene that you rated about 50 on your 0 to 100 scale. For example, Larry started by imagining walking alone along a sidewalk with a dark chasm surrounding it and with no trees, buildings, or cars in sight.

While you are imagining the scene, notice if you start becoming anxious. Keep the image in mind for a few minutes, then stop and repeat some of the relaxation exercise so that you are more relaxed again. Go back and forth between the upsetting image and the relaxation until the image really doesn't bother you much—until the score has dropped a significant amount. Then move up the scale to the next scary item. Keep working at this until the thirty minutes are up for the day. If you wish, you can do this a little longer but we would recommend not making it any shorter than thirty minutes. Try to do this exercise daily.

Each day, start with the image that you last worked on the previous day. This way, you will be moving up the scale in small overlapping steps with each day's practice. Eventually you will get to the top of your scale and all the images from the dream will have lost their power to scare you. If you have more than one scary recurring dream, use this method for each one. If you can't identify an image to start with or if all the images seem just as scary, start with scenes from the beginning of the dream. Each day, rate the images of your dream. Don't be surprised to see that the score decreases dramatically. Also, keep track of the occurrence of the dream you are working on. Even if it goes away, it is best to finish the desensitization.

Lucid Dreams and Scripts

Systematic desensitization works well for nightmares that are repeated, but what about scary dreams that don't seem to be repeated? The following method for dealing with dreams can help. The ideas may sound funny, but try them out. We think you will find them helpful and maybe even fun.

Do you usually know you are having a dream? Some people say they do and some say they don't. For this method it is helpful to be certain you are having a dream, so the first step is to learn how to know for sure. Your brain can tell the difference—you just need to learn to ask. For example, as you read this now, you know you are awake. If you asked yourself, "Am I awake?" your answer would be "Yes." If you asked yourself during a dream the answer would be "No." During a disturbing dream most people don't ask themselves this question. However, if we make asking the question a habit while we are awake, the question will show up in our dreams and we can make use of it. Start now and ask, "Am I awake?" Ask this question a number of times during the day. Tell yourself to ask it when you are sleeping as well. You may not be sure you are going to remember to ask the question during sleep, but try to remind yourself before going to sleep that you need to ask from time to time.

Next, we need to think about the dream world. Many dreams include things that could not really happen. People talk about flying in dreams or talking to people who are long dead. Monsters appear and lots of impossible events happen in dreams. This tells us that the dream world is not restricted to logic or to things that could happen in real life. We need to make use of this fact to deal with scary dreams. If you can tell yourself that you are asleep and that what is going on must be a dream, you can also decide to change the dream.

Anything can happen in a dream. If something scary is happening you can use the superpowers of your favorite superhero to change things. You can fly faster than a speeding bullet, leap tall buildings in a single bound, or bend steel with your bare hands. You can use the ray gun from *Honey, I Shrunk the Kids* to shrink your enemy. If you have a recurring scary dream or dreams with a similar theme, while you are awake you can plan which of these tools you want to use in your dream. Making the event a humorous one is also a helpful idea.

Habit Change Strategy

In the world of dreams, anything can happen. You determine what happens.

Dr. C. suggested that Larry try the suggestions described here. He worked out a script that included sticking a pin in the attacker. The attacker would then fly around the room like a balloon with a hole in it. After a few weeks, Larry reported that the dreams were no longer waking him up for the first time in years. Sometimes this method succeeds and people sleep through the dreams and never remember what they dreamt.

If you have a repeating dream, write out a script describing how you would like to change it. Since magical things can happen in a dream world, write in whatever you would like to happen. If you don't have a repeating dream, work with one that you do remember. Write out the script below.

_____

_____

_____

_____

_____

_____

_____

_____

_____

_____

_____

_____

_____

_____

_____

_____

Larry

I am walking along a sidewalk, and then I start to skip. The wind starts to blow and it looks like it might rain. I notice that the clouds look like giant puffs of cotton candy. Butterflies flutter through the air, floating on the wind. The sidewalk starts to get narrower and narrower, but I snap my fingers and it widens and turns a brilliant gold. I think I might be on the yellow brick road. When I look down, there is a deep, dark chasm on either side of the sidewalk. I look again and discover there is a giant net below. If I fall, it will catch me. Then the trees, buildings, and cars disappear. But instead there are superheroes on both sides of the sidewalk. Some are playing ball and others are standing around talking to each other. Superman and Silver Surfer are playing chess together. I think that is funny because one is a DC character and the other is a Marvel character. It begins to rain, first sprinkling, then raining harder. I snap my fingers again, and a giant umbrella appears. The wind gets stronger and the rain comes down in sheets, but I'm not worried because I have my umbrella. I look down and around me, and see that the sidewalk is getting narrower again. I sigh, then snap my fingers again and it widens. It's slippery because of the rain. One false step and I might fall into the chasm. I slip and fall into the chasm, but I land on the net below and bounce back to the sidewalk. The chasm no longer scares me. The sidewalk begins to wind all around with sharp turns. Silver Surfer and I jump on his surfboard and have great fun sliding around the curves. He whooshes me right to the street where I live. Then we shake hands and he goes back to his chess game with Superman. Then I hear footsteps. They get closer and closer, louder and louder. I notice there are no other sounds. Only the footsteps and my heartbeat. I'm not scared, though, because I have my secret weapons, given to me by Silver Surfer and Superman. Then someone grabs me from behind. I turn around and laugh, and then I poke the attacker in the side, all the air escapes from him, and he floats off into the air. I find out the "attacker" was only a balloon filled with air. This is when I wake up, smiling and feeling quite rested.

Next, begin visualizing the revised script after you have practiced the relaxation. At first, you may have to read it, but you'll soon have the scenario memorized. Do this every day for at least two weeks. This method can be combined with the systematic desensitization method described above. Remember to keep asking yourself if you are awake. When you do dream try to ask that question and, when the answer is "No," remember that you can change what happens in the dream so that it is no longer scary. Some people trying this method say they dreamed they were awake. If that happens to you, try to do something that you could only do when dreaming, such as flying.

Like any of the other habits you try to change, you will need to practice these techniques regularly. If the problem gets better, you can stop practicing, but if the frightening dreams return, start again. Continue to practice the relaxation exercise regularly for at least six months. It's a good habit for anyone to get into.

Read chapters 9 through 12 next. In chapters 9 and 10 you will learn to recognize the automatic thoughts that contribute to your sleep problems. In chapter 11, you'll learn how to incorporate good habits into your life, such as the habits you've learned about in this chapter. Chapter 12 will help you fight back against temporary lapses in your habit change efforts.

Do you know others who might like to change their habits? Chapter 20 can help you make habit changing a family affair or a group effort. You don't all have to be interested in changing the same type of habit, only in changing whatever habits each of you finds troublesome in his or her life.

15

Health and Fitness Habits

Now learn what and how great benefits a temperate diet will bring along with it. In the first place you will enjoy good health.

—Horace

Those who think they have not time for bodily exercise will sooner or later have to find time for illness.

—Edward Stanley, Earl of Derby

What would you like to achieve? If you haven't worked through chapters 5 and 6, do so before doing the exercises in this chapter. It is important to acknowledge that you do indeed have a particular health and fitness habit that has negative consequences. You need to be ready to make a real change. When the going gets rough—and it will—referring to your Habit Consequences and Habit Advantages and Disadvantages worksheets will remind you of why you are trying to change your habit.

If you know you have some negative health habits but you don't know what they are or which ones need changing most, reading the first part of this chapter will help you decide. You may want to do further reading on health and fitness. Your doctor can also help you decide which of your health habits need to be changed. It is important to talk to your doctor about your plans to change before starting. He may want to do some tests or a physical exam before you start, or he may give you instructions, restrictions, or advice on how to proceed.

Our Favorite Bad Health and Fitness Habits

Americans are becoming more and more overweight and sedentary. The prevalence of obesity was 25 percent in the 1960s. Today, 33 percent of the population is overweight. Seventy-five percent of adults in the United States get more than 30 percent of their total calories from fat in their diets. Experts recommend thirty percent or less. Sodium intake is on the increase. Smoking had declined but is now increasing again. Physical activity is on the decline. Around

70 percent of adults over age forty-five don't exercise at all. Physical activity begins to decrease at age six and continues to decrease throughout life. These statistics don't paint a pretty picture of Americans' health and fitness habits.

Cardiopulmonary risk reduction involves five areas of dietary change: reduced intake of fat, increased intake of fiber, increased intake of fruits and vegetables, reduced intake of salt, and reduced prevalence of obesity. These dietary recommendations, along with adequate exercise, constitute a good recipe for healthy living and long life. Experts tell us our diet should include no more than 30 percent of its calories from fat, with no more than 10 percent from saturated fat. In general, fat from plant sources is less of a problem than animal fat. Diets high in animal fat can put us at greater risk for obesity, coronary heart disease, stroke, colon cancer, osteoporosis, diabetes, hypertension, gallbladder disease, breast cancer, and prostate cancer.

Increased fiber intake has been found to influence glucose and lipid metabolism, reduce hypertension, help prevent colon cancer, and improve weight control. A daily intake of twenty to thirty grams of fiber per day is recommended. Increasing consumption of high-fiber foods can also help with weight loss because fruits, vegetables, and many other high-fiber foods are filling and yet low in calories and fat. Eating plenty of fruits and vegetables helps reduce the risk of cardiovascular disease and cancer. Three to five servings of vegetables and two to four servings of fruit or fruit juices each day are recommended. Sodium reduction helps prevent and control hypertension and may reduce the risk of developing osteoporosis and gastric cancer.

Adequate physical activity is an important part of any health plan, but 60 percent of us get insufficient exercise. Physical activity helps reduce the risk of premature death, coronary heart disease, hypertension, adult onset diabetes mellitus, osteoporosis, colon cancer, depression, and anxiety. Research now shows that exercise can work as well as antidepressant medications in alleviating depression symptoms. The recommended activity level is at least thirty minutes of moderate physical activity five days each week or twenty to sixty minutes of vigorous activity three days a week. Only 40 percent of American adults get this much activity.

Most likely, you have multiple health-related behaviors to change. Should you change one at a time, or all of them at once? That is your decision to make. But many behavioral changes complement each other. For example, reducing fat intake, increasing fiber intake, eating more fruits and vegetables, increasing exercise, and losing weight naturally go together. On the other hand, quitting smoking and losing weight clash since some weight gain is common with smoking cessation. A more realistic goal would be to stop smoking with a little weight gain, then to attack the weight problem.

✿ Habit Change Strategy

Could any of your health and fitness habits be adversely affecting your health?

Your Health and Fitness Plan

Did you notice that the title of this section is *Your* Health and Fitness Plan? That's because it will be *your* plan. We aren't going to tell you what to change, or how to change. You will set your own goals and make your own plans for change, but we will provide the tools for you to develop the plan and make it work. You can adapt a diet or exercise plan recommended by your doctor or another health professional. You can do your plan alone, with a formal support group, with a friend, or with your family. If the first plan doesn't seem to be working, you can make another plan. We do recommend that you avoid diet fads or unsubstantiated advice, however.

✕✕ Habit Change Strategy

Check with your doctor before making any changes in your diet and exercise. Make him a part of your habit change team.

Things to Keep in Mind

Before you begin work on your Health and Fitness Plan, read and work through chapters 7 through 10. You may need to adjust some of the exercises in those chapters, depending on the habits you are working on. When you've finished reading chapter 10, meet us back here. The following guidelines will help you develop your plan.

- **Consider the stage of change you are in.** If you are in the precontemplation or contemplation stage, you need to do a bit more research on the habit you are thinking about changing, and its consequences. Speak to your doctor, and read articles and books. Some insurance companies and many community agencies provide free classes on such subjects as smoking cessation and weight loss; find out if you can attend one of those classes. Reading this book should help you move from the preparation to the action stage.

- **Be fully committed to the health and fitness plan you adopt.** If your plan is too challenging, reassess it and make the necessary changes. For example, if you've decided to give up desserts but you find them to be too tempting, you may want to allow yourself a dessert once a week or allow desserts that are relatively low in fat and sugar. Make your goals attainable, but challenging. If you set goals that are too high, you might feel defeated if you can't adhere to your restrictions, and you might have difficulty becoming motivated to attempt lifestyle changes in the future. If you set goals that are too low, your efforts might not show adequate results and you could become discouraged.

- **Challenge yourself.** Should you make gradual changes or major changes from the first day? We recommend challenging yourself with major changes from the beginning. Often it is easier to make major changes than gradual changes. With gradual change you may find it tempting to let go of your changes when you are under stress, bored, or anxious, or you may feel that the changes are unimportant. Remember, go for goals that are attainable, but challenging.

- **Make sure your plan is sustainable.** Think of this not as a temporary change, but as a permanent lifestyle change. So while you are making your plan challenging but attainable, make sure it is also one you will be willing to live with long term, not just short term. A major key to success is choosing behavior that fits you. For example, if you are striving to increase physical activity, do you want a structured exercise or more varied exercise? Do you want to take up a sport, or start regular walks? Do you want to exercise at home or at a gym? Five days a week or three? Make it fit your lifestyle. If you find that your original choice doesn't fit after all, evaluate and adjust your plan as needed.

- **Be optimistic.** Attempts to change health habits generally arise as a response to a health threat or a desire to improve your life in some way. The advantages of change outweigh the advantages of staying the same. Optimism about your ability to change makes your success more likely. Having failed to change numerous times before can make you feel less optimistic about changing this time, but past failure doesn't predict the future. This time, you have new skills to help you change. Also, you've learned from the past—now you know about what pitfalls to avoid, what situations are the most tempting, what worked, and what didn't work. It's hard to stay optimistic when our minds are telling us things that sabotage our efforts and damage our optimism. The ideas in chapters 9 and 10 will help you refute this negative self-talk.

- **Remember, life happens!** Make your plan and make the changes a part of your lifestyle. Try your best, but keep in mind that you *will* miss your scheduled exercise or eat something that is not in your diet. When this happens, remember that a slip is no reason to quit. If you mess up too often, reexamine your plan. When and why are you not meeting your goals? How can you adjust your plan to better fit your lifestyle?

- **Focus on behavior change, not just the measurable results.** Weight loss is a good example—try to view your plan as a lifestyle change that is never finished. Otherwise, you will meet your goal and think you are done, and soon, the weight would be back. If you focused only on measurable results you could also feel discouraged when you hit the inevitable plateau. But if you concentrate on the good things you are doing for your body and your overall health, you won't feel so discouraged.

- **Self-monitoring is an important part of changing health and fitness habits.** You will need to make your own habit record, personalized to meet your goals and follow your plan. Your habit record can be as simple or as complicated as you like. Just make sure you faithfully keep the record. We've provided a Diet and Exercise Record at the end of this chapter. You may want to use it, or you can make your own.

  The results of an interesting study illustrate the importance of self-monitoring with such a record. Participants were asked to keep a record of their exercise and the foods they ate during December, when it's often difficult to maintain a diet. Only the people who were the most consistent in keeping their records lost weight during the holidays. Only the least consistent record keepers gained weight (Baker and Kirschenbaum 1998). Why is self-monitoring so effective in maintaining weight control or other habit changes? The reason is that it may be a useful coping response in high-risk situations. Self-monitoring can help people cope with the negative feelings associated with occasional overeating or other slips. They can more easily see the episode as a temporary problem instead of a more permanent relapse, they can view the situation as more controllable, and they can recognize the effects of triggers and environmental influences. Many of us, when we try to change a habit, have difficulty because the behavior is largely automatic. Self-monitoring helps us recognize what we are doing so we can better work on it.

- **Include a competing response in your plan.** There may be blocks of time in your day during which you previously would have engaged in unhealthy habits. Find something else to do instead of snacking on junk food. Have healthy foods available to munch on, or read a book during the time you would normally be eating. You could plan on doing your exercise during the time you would previoulsy have been stopping for a latte.

- **Reward yourself for good work.** Changing health and fitness habits is hard work. Reward yourself with something special when you meet your goals. Perhaps you could buy yourself a new dress or a book you've been meaning to read. Don't let your reward interfere with your plan, though. For instance, an extra dessert shouldn't be your reward for sticking to a diet. Cherry tried this, but she found that thoughts of the dessert reward took her focus off healthy eating.

- **Make relaxation a part of your plan.** Review chapter 8, and choose one of the relaxation methods described therein. Relaxation will help you deal with the stress and anxiety that you once relieved with your habits. It will also help you deal with the inevitable stress that results from changing.

- **Change the way you think.** Do you use excuses for not eating healthy foods, for not exercising, or for not getting yearly physical exams and dental visits? Reading chapters 9 and 10 will help you challenge thoughts and beliefs that are interfering with your plans to change.

- **Make plans for high-risk situations.** You will find that it is more difficult to stick to your plan in certain situations. You have learned to identify triggers for your habit. Make plans now for how you will handle these situations. If you are trying to eat in healthy ways and you go to a party, how will you handle the situation, what will you eat? You could eat before you leave home and snack on the healthiest items at the party, but what if you just can't or won't resist the treats? Pick just one, and eat it after you've eaten the healthiest foods. Keep in mind that old habits never die; they're always ready to be renewed. They aren't unlearned completely. You are learning new habits, new ways of coping with stress, nervousness, and boredom, but you aren't unlearning the old ways.

- **Get social support.** For many, it's easier to change with a group. It could be a formal group, such as Weight Watchers, or it could be a small group of friends who have decided to support each other in their habit changes. Family support should be an important part of your health and fitness plan. Read chapter 20 for information about making habit change a group effort.

One change leads to another. Once you have made one health and fitness habit change, you will have the confidence to attempt another change.

✕✕ Habit Change Strategy

Still not sure which health and fitness habits you need to change? Ask for input from those who know you best—your spouse, relatives, close friends, and doctor.

Developing Your Health and Fitness Plan

Now you are ready to put what you have learned into action. You've discovered the health and fitness habits that are interfering with your life. You've learned some ways to make changes in your life and ways to deal with the negative thoughts and beliefs that have kept you from changing. You probably have a general goal in mind. Now, you'll break that goal down into smaller goals and help you make a step-by-step plan for achieving those goals.

Step 1: Develop Long-Term Goals

Choose a general achievement you would like to accomplish—a long-term goal. You might have more than one long-term goal. Cherry and Jeff each had two related goals. She wanted to improve her overall health and lose weight. Jeff wanted to lose weight and lower his cholesterol. His biggest problem was snacking and eating too many fast foods. We've provided a sample of his long-term goals. What are your long-term goals? How will you know when you've met those goals? Complete the Long-Term Goals worksheet.

Long-Term Goals

My long-term goals are:

1. _____

2. _____

3. _____

How will I know when I have met these goals?_____

_____

_____

_____

Chart 15a

Jeff's Long-Term Goals

My long-term goals are:

1. _Lose weight—about forty pounds_ _____

2. _Lower my cholesterol by reducing fat_ _____

3. _Learn to prepare balanced meals and healthy snacks_ _____

How will I know when I have met these goals? _I will know I've lost weight when my scale says so. My doctor wants my cholesterol to be below 200, so the lab work will tell us that. I would like to learn to prepare twenty healthy meals and have twenty snack ideas._

Chart 15b

☽{}☾ Habit Change Strategy

Make specific goals that are challenging, yet attainable. They don't have to be perfect though—you can always change them later.

Step 2: Make a Plan

Looking at these goals and imagining achieving them all at once can feel overwhelming. But you can break them into smaller parts, so that they don't seem so overwhelming. Now you will make plans for achieving your goals. An important part of your plan will be making short-term goals. Your major focus will be on meeting these short-term goals instead of the long-term ones. For example, when we first decided to write this book, the project seemed overwhelming. How would we ever get it written by the deadline? When we divided it into chapters and gave ourselves mini-deadlines to meet, it seemed much less daunting because we had a plan and goals for carrying out our plan.

We've provided a Health and Fitness Plan worksheet for you to complete. Make copies of the blank worksheet so you can make revisions if it needs adjustment later. Again, we've provided Jeff's plan as an example. If diet is your problem, you may already have a formal plan, perhaps given to you by your doctor. If not, you will need to do a little research. There must be hundreds of diet and fitness plans available. Choose one that seems to fit your needs. If you get started and decide it's not working for you, choose another one. Keep your goals in mind as you make your choices. In our opinion, a healthy, balanced diet is best. Look for a diet plan you can keep for life—you will simply modify it after you meet your goals.

As you create your plan for change, include some of the things we mentioned earlier. Use the ideas you've gathered in this book: record keeping, competing responses, relaxation, triggers, changing the way you think and deal with feelings, social support, and rewards. When you have developed your personal health plan, consult your doctor. Ask him or her to review it and suggest changes.

Health and Fitness Plan

Record
Keeping

_____

_____

_____

Competing
Response

_____

_____

_____

Relaxation

_____

_____

_____

Trigger
Management

_____

_____

_____

Thoughts
& Feelings

_____

_____

_____

Social
Support

_____

_____

_____

Rewards

_____

_____

_____

Chart 15c

Jeff's Health and Fitness Plan

Record Keeping

I will keep a record of everything I eat and evaluate it daily, then weekly. I'll see what areas I am weakest in and try to correct them.

Competing Response

I will use several competing responses when I am nervous or bored—walking, reading, working on special projects around the house or in my workshop.

Relaxation

At work I will practice a relaxation exercise—I'll try progressive muscle relaxation first.

Trigger Management

I will get rid of unhealthy snacks and replace them with healthy ones, bring fruits and vegetables and a few crackers to work each day, and not keep extra food items in my office. If I don't think I will have time for lunch, I'll bring a healthy lunch to work. I'll let myself stop for dinner once or twice a week on the way home—but at regular restaurants, not fast-food ones—and I'll choose healthy foods.

Thoughts & Feelings

I will concentrate on changing the way I think, using the ideas in chapters 9 and 10. I will challenge the belief that I can't lose weight and that I am a failure. I will choose better ways to cope with negative feelings.

Social Support

I have a few friends who are also trying to lose weight. I'll share my goals with them and we can support each other as we stick to our diets.

Rewards

For a reward, I will buy myself a new shirt whenever I lose five pounds. When I lose twenty pounds and forty pounds I'll buy new clothes that fit my new body.

Chart 15d

Habit Change Strategy

In your plan include something from every category—record keeping, competing response, relaxation, triggers, thoughts and feelings, social support, rewards—they are all important to your success.

Health and Fitness Habits 167

Step 3: Develop Short-Term Goals

What will you accomplish tomorrow and in the next few days? Assess your Health and Fitness Plan and your Habit Records, and set one to three short-term goals for the coming week. Make copies of the Short-Term Goals worksheet and at the beginning of each week set goals for the following week. Evaluate your work in the previous week and decide how you could improve. Your short-term goals should be based on behaviors you need to change, so that you can better meet your long-term goals. We've provided Jeff's Short-Term Goals worksheet for his second week as an example.

⚭ Habit Change Strategy

Record keeping is an important part of the Habit Change Program. You can use the Diet and Exercise Record we have provided, or develop a record-keeping system that works better for you.

Short-Term Goals　　　　Week No. ____

My short-term goals are:

1. _____

2. _____

3. _____

How will I know when I have met these goals? _____

_____

_____

_____

Did I meet my goals last week? If I didn't, what could I do differently in the next week?

_____

_____

_____

Chart 15e

Jeff's Short-Term Goals   Week No. __2__

My short-term goals are:

1. *Clear my kitchen of all unhealthy foods, and clear my office of all food.*

2. *Avoid fast food, eat out twice a week, choosing healthy meals.*

3. *Keep a record of everything I eat; follow the diet recommended by my doctor as closely as possible.*

How will I know when I have met these goals? *There will be no food in my office and no unhealthy foods in my kitchen. I will have a completed record of everything I've eaten for every day of this week. I will have come close to following my doctor's diet plan.*

Did I meet my goals last week? If I didn't, what could I do differently in the next week?

I put off removing unhealthy foods from my kitchen and snacks from my office. I will do this next week for sure. I kept a record of everything I ate, but I only partially followed my diet plan and noticed how many snacks I ate. I ate healthy meals when I went out to eat, and I stayed away from fast-food restaurants.

Chart 15f

✎ Habit Change Strategy

Remember, goals should be specific, challenging, and attainable. Be a bit easy on yourself the first few weeks to help yourself build confidence, then get more challenging.

Now you have a plan for changing your health and fitness habits. We have concentrated on diet and exercise, but this plan can easily be adjusted to help you change any type of health and fitness habit. For example, many people neglect to have yearly dental and physical exams, screening tests, and other tests their doctor has ordered. This neglect can become a habit in need of change. Handling stress is another area many of us have difficulty with, especially as we try to deal with lifestyle changes. Be creative—when you feel empowered in one area, attack another health-related habit.

✎ Habit Change Strategy

Receiving family support is especially important when we are trying to change health and fitness habits. Chapter 20 offers ideas for getting your family involved in lifestyle changes. You could make health-related habit changes a family affair!

Read chapters 11 and 12 now. You'll learn more about quitting your bad habits and developing healthy habits, including your competing response. You'll probably think of a few more habits that you would like to incorporate into your life. Focusing on the good habits will take your mind off the bad habits you are trying to eliminate. Habit changing just might become a habit!

You might be wondering how you are going to keep the changes you make. Will they end up being only short-term changes, or will you be free of your bad habits and keep the healthy ones for good? Chapter 12 will help you fight back against temporary lapses in your Habit Change efforts.

Do you know others who might like to change their habits? Chapter 20 can help you make habit changing a family affair or a group effort. You don't all have to be interested in changing the same type of habit, only in changing whatever habits each of you finds troublesome in his or her life.

Diet and Exercise Record

Day	Diet	Exercise	Comments
Sunday			
Monday			
Tuesday			
Wednesday			
Thursday			
Friday			
Saturday			

How did you do this week? What can you do differently next week?

Chart 15g

Jeff's Diet and Exercise Record

Day	Diet	Exercise	Comments

Sunday	Breakfast: muffin, eggs, juice
	Lunch: sandwich, salad,
	    chips, banana
	Dinner: chicken, potato,
	    green beans, roll, margarine
	Snack: apple, crackers, cheese
		Walked 30 minutes	I could have done without the chips.

Monday	Breakfast: cereal, milk, juice
	Lunch: sandwich, apple, carrots
	Dinner: hamburger patty,
	    rolls, peas, broccoli, margarine
	Snacks: crackers, cheese, celery,
	    carrots
		Didn't walk today	I didn't get around to walking today. It might take me a while to get into the habit.

Tuesday	Breakfast: diet drink, banana
	Lunch: chef's salad, carrots
	Dinner: beef stroganoff, green
	    beans, bread, margarine
	Snacks: apple, toast, margarine,
	    celery
		Walked 30 minutes	I was in a hurry this morning and drank a diet drink for breakfast. Pretty good—better than stopping for fast food. Then I took a banana to work with me.

Wednesday	Breakfast: diet drink, apple
	Lunch: sandwich, banana, carrots
	Dinner: spaghetti, garlic bread,
	    margarine, salad
	Snacks: peaches and milk,
	    carrots
		Went to gym, looked around. I can try it for a week.	

Thursday	Breakfast: cereal, milk, canned plums Lunch: sandwich, salad, frozen yogurt Dinner: barbecued chicken, potatoes, margarine, cauliflower, okra Snacks: diet drink, carrots, celery	Went to the gym, walked on the treadmill.	I might join the gym or I might keep trying to walk every day.
Friday	Breakfast: cereal, milk, banana Lunch: taco, refried beans, salad Dinner: hamburger, French fries, milkshake Snacks: toast, margarine, jelly	Walked for 30 minutes	I went out after work and had a hamburger. I felt stuffed. I think I am getting used to eating better and feel bloated when I overeat.

Saturday	Breakfast: pancakes, margarine,
	    eggs, bacon, juice
	Lunch: chef's salad, crackers
	Dinner: steak, potato, green beans,
	    pie
	Snacks: milkshake, apple
		Went to the gym, tried out the weights, walked for 20 minutes in the evening.	I ate a lot of fat in my breakfast and had a full feeling. I didn't really need the pie for dinner, but it sure was good.

How did you do this week? What can you do differently next week?

I think I did pretty well. Toward the end of the week, I ate more fattening foods. I am going to come up with some more menus to provide variety. I'll think about joining the gym, but it might be too far to drive and I'd give up. It might be better to continue with daily walks.

Chart 15h

16

Relationship Habits

I like tidy habits.

—Felix Unger, *The Odd Couple*

Talking is like playing on the harp; there is as much in laying the hands on the string to stop their vibration as in twanging them to bring out the music.

—Oliver Wendell Holmes

We all have habits. Good habits enhance our lives and our relationships. However, many habits, even "good" habits, can have negative effects on our relationships. For an example we need look no further than Felix and Oscar, the ultimate odd couple. All of Felix's habits seem "good," but they bother the people around him, especially his roommate, Oscar. If you've read chapters 1 through 6, you are probably committed to changing a habit that is negatively affecting your life and your relationships. Perhaps you are a perfectionist like Felix, or maybe you're a clutter bug like Oscar. Or maybe you have problems with procrastination, tardiness, dishonesty, using inappropriate language, interrupting, or talking too much.

Whatever your habit, you've likely tried and failed to change before. You know what the problem is and what you'd like to change. So how do you change these habits and change for good? You'll be glad to know you're at least halfway there already. If you haven't worked through chapters 1 through 6, do so before completing the exercises in this chapter. It is important that you believe that you do indeed have habits that are harmful to your relationships and in need of change. In order to change them, you need to recognize the negative consequences of these habits. When the going gets rough—and it will—your Habit Advantages and Disadvantages worksheet and Habit Consequences worksheet will remind you of why you are trying to change. Recognizing the negative consequences is especially important when you are changing relationship habits; it helps us imagine how life would be better without the habit. Review chapters 5 and 6 and answer the following questions. We've provided Matthew's and Barbara's answers as examples.

What relationship habit are you thinking about changing? _____

_____

_____

What are the consequences of your relationship habit on your life?_____

_____

_____

_____

What are the advantages of changing? _____

_____

_____

_____

What would your life be like without your habit? _____

_____

_____

_____

Matthew:

What relationship habit are you thinking about changing? *Interrupting people. It was fine when I was growing up because my entire family did it, but it's not fine now, especially at work.*

What are the consequences of your relationship habit on your life? *When I interrupt people they look startled and often turn away. Sometimes they turn their chairs away. Sometimes they completely ignore me. I don't appear professional or well mannered. I think my coworkers don't invite me to lunch often because of this habit.*

What are the advantages of changing? *I think people would have more respect for me and pay attention to what I say. I would appear more polished and well mannered. I would get invited to lunch and be able to develop closer relationships, both at work and in social situations. I would have more confidence in my abilities to communicate.*

What would your life be like without your habit? *I think I would have more friends. I would have more confidence at work and in social situations. I think I would have more opportunities for promotions at work. If I went looking for another job, I would be more effective in the interviewing process.*

Barbara:

What relationship habit are you thinking about changing? _Procrastination and tardiness. I'm late for everything. Putting things off until the last minute makes me even more late._

What are the consequences of your relationship habit on your life? _I've lost jobs because of being late and putting things off, then not getting them done on time. It makes me nervous rushing around and worrying about getting things done yet not actually doing them. My friends and family are bothered by my lateness and procrastination._

What are the advantages of changing? _My boss would trust me to get things done and might even give me a promotion. I think I would have less anxiety and even sleep better if I knew I was prepared and wouldn't be late. My friends and family would probably want to do more things with me, even go to events where we must be on time._

What would your life be like without your habit? _My job would be more secure and I would have more potential for promotion. I would feel less anxious about my job and about getting things done. I might have more friends and closer relationships with the friends I have. My family would have more respect for me and trust me to be on time._

Habit Change Strategy

Each day, review the consequences and disadvantages of keeping your habit and the advantages of changing. See if you can add to them. Are there consequences, disadvantages, and advantages you didn't think of when you first answered the questions?

Your Relationship Habit Change Plan

After reading chapter 5, you kept a record of your habit. You discovered the emotions, automatic thoughts, triggers, and consequences associated with your negative relationship habit. Look at the charts you completed and think back to the last time your habit interfered with your relationship, and then answer the following questions. We've provided Matthew's and Barbara's answers as examples.

What _feelings_ do you typically experience before, during, and after engaging in your habit?

Before: _____

During: _____

After: _____

What *automatic thoughts* do you often have before, during, and after engaging in your habit?

Before: _____

During: _____

After: _____

What are the most frequent *emotional triggers* for your habit? _____

_____

What are the most frequent *situational triggers* preceding your habit? _____

_____

Matthew:

What *feelings* do you typically experience before, during, and after engaging in your habit?

Before: *Urgency, like I just have to say something.*

During: *Excitement, pride.*

After: *Anxiety, embarrassment.*

What *automatic thoughts* do you often have before, during, and after engaging in your habit?

Before: *I just gotta tell them this story—or make this suggestion. I can't wait.*

During: *This is a great story—or suggestion. I know they're impressed.*

After: *I should have waited. Why can't I wait my turn? Why do I always interrupt?*

What are the most frequent *emotional triggers* for your habit? *Excitement while in a conversation or in a meeting. Or feeling insignificant, in need of acknowledgement.*

What are the most frequent *situational triggers* for your habit? *Being in a conversation or a meeting with coworkers. Having lunch with friends or coworkers.*

Barbara:

What *feelings* do you typically experience before, during, and after engaging in your habit?

Before: *Tired, bothered that I need to do something. Anxious that it isn't done.*

During: *Hurried, anxious, irritable, out of control.*

After: *Depressed, ashamed, out of control.*

What *automatic thoughts* do you often have before, during, and after engaging in your habit?

Before: *I can sleep a few more minutes. Just a few more minutes, then I'll go.*

During: *Why didn't I start earlier? Why did I put it off? I'm so lazy.*

After: *I'll never get things done on time. I'm a failure. Nobody trusts me, and no wonder.*

What are the most frequent *emotional triggers* for your habit? *Being tired, overwhelmed by stuff to do and life in general. Enjoyment of doing something else and not wanting to stop.*

What are the most frequent *situational triggers* for your habit? *Being busy with a lot of things. Having had trouble sleeping or planned activities too close together.*

Recognizing emotional and situational triggers is essential to changing. You will use this information to bring about changes in your relationship habits. Read chapter 7 now to get a basic understanding of the principles of habit reversal, but don't do the exercises in chapter 7 yet. Then meet back here. We'll apply the principles to changing your habit, below.

Competing Response Practice

You know how you would like to behave when you are faced with situations that trigger your habit, but you don't act that way. You fall into your old habits because—well, because that's your habit. You forget all about the consequences, advantages, and disadvantages, and you do what you know best. So how can you change? By practicing. Your competing response will be your desired response to trigger situations and emotions. This response can become your new habit by repetition. You developed your bad habit by repetition, and you can also develop your new, healthy habit by repetition.

Imagine a typical situation in which you find yourself engaging in your habit. Write out the situation just as it usually happens. We've provided Matthew's habit script as an example.

_____

_____

_____

_____

_____

_____

_____

_____

Matthew:

I'm in a meeting at work. We are talking about a new project and everyone is talking. I'm talking too, making suggestions. I get excited about an idea. I have to tell everyone all about it now. I speak up and can't finish my sentence because others are talking. I try again, but still people are still talking. I speak louder. Finally, heads turn in my direction, and I tell them my idea. Everyone pauses and looks at me. Then they start talking again without responding to me. It was a good idea. Why didn't they pay attention? Then I notice that the others have turned their chairs away from me. It's like they've put up a wall to keep me from talking. I come up with another idea and want to tell about it. I can't wait. I get excited and blurt it out. No one hears me. They don't stop talking. Finally, the meeting ends and everyone starts talking about where they're going for lunch. I hang around, but no one asks me to go to lunch. I go back to my desk.

Now, again imagine a typical situation in which you would ordinarily engage in your habit. This time, let's change the script. Instead of engaging in your habit, respond differently. Since you are using your imagination, you can respond exactly as you want. You can write out your script, examine it, think about it, change it, and add to it. Anything can happen in your imagination, and you can do anything. If you tend to interrupt others, imagine yourself in a room full of people where you get the urge to interrupt. Interrupting is often the result of concentrating on what you want to say instead of listening to what is said. In your imaginary scenario, see yourself listening to the others, turning your head from one person to another. Listen intently to each one. When there is a break in the conversation, say what you have to say. Notice that everyone turns toward you and listens with interest. Notice the difference. You have their attention. When you've interrupted in the past, people may not have even stopped talking, or they might have listened only halfheartedly. But what if you forget what you were going to say before there is a lull in the conversation? Or what if the subject changes? See the positive in this, too. You'll have a story you can tell another time. Also, imagine the difference in people's attitudes toward you. They see you as a caring person; you listen to them because you care about what they are saying. Changing the interrupting habit can transform people's opinions of you.

If your problem is tardiness, imagine yourself doing all you can to be ready on time. You set your clothes out the night before. You gather everything you need to take with you and place it by the door. You even plan what you'll do if you arrive early by bringing a book to read, paperwork to review, or a pad to doodle on while you are waiting. As you write out your script, you'll think of many other things you can do to make certain you are on time. After you read the script a few times, add to it. Make a checklist of things you can do to ensure you will be on time.

Below, write out your alternative script. This is your competing response. Use a pencil or erasable pen so you can change it. We've provided Matthew's competing response script as an example.

_____

_____

_____

_____

_____

_____

Matthew:

I'm in a meeting at work. We are discussing a new project and everyone is talking. I'm talking too, making suggestions. But I think about what I'm going to say first. I listen to others, nod my head, and respond when appropriate. I get excited about an idea. I wait until others have contributed, then I speak. I have less to say than I would have with my old habit of interrupting because I have listened and don't repeat what others have already said. Heads turn in my direction, and I tell them my idea. Everyone pauses and looks at me. They listen, and then they respond to what I've said. A couple of guys are excited and we discuss the idea for a while. Then the conversation moves on. I notice that people have their chairs turned toward me. I am asked what I think about a couple of things. I come up with another idea and want to tell about it. I wait and speak when there is a lull in the conversation. When the meeting ends, I go out to lunch with some of my coworkers.

When you have written out your competing response script and have it just right, act it out daily for three weeks. It may seem silly, but do it anyway. When you are confronted with situational and emotional triggers, you will begin more and more often to respond in your new way, just as you do in your script. It might help to have a friend or family member act out your script with you. If you absolutely cannot or will not act out the script, read it several times daily, imagining the situation unfolding just as it does in your script.

⋈ Habit Change Strategy

Don't worry about acting silly. What could be sillier than holding on to habits that have negative consequences?

Rewards

What are the rewards for changing relationship habits? Rewards for changing relationship habits are closely tied to the consequences of changing. Rewards can include improving your relationships—possibly even keeping your job, strengthening your marriage, or saving friendships. But these rewards are so nebulous, you may think. The immediate rewards of our habits often overshadow the future rewards of changing. A few extra minutes of sleep are felt now, while being on time for work is a future reward. Lying can make life easier, at least temporarily, while a reputation of honesty and integrity is a future reward.

Look back at your answer to the question "What would your life be like without your habit?" Using your answer as a guide, below list the rewards for changing your habit. We've listed Matthew's and Barbara's rewards as examples.

1. _____
2. _____
3. _____
4. _____
5. _____
6. _____
7. _____
8. _____
9. _____
10. _____

Matthew:

1. *People would pay more attention to me when I speak.*
2. *I wouldn't feel so discouraged after conversations.*
3. *People would respect me more.*
4. *I would respect myself.*
5. *I would appear more professional and well mannered.*
6. *My coworkers would be more likely to invite me to lunch and associate with me.*
7. *My relationships with other people would improve.*
8. *I would feel more confident in conversations.*
9. *I might have more opportunities for promotions at work.*
10. *If I looked for another job, I would do better in the interviewing process.*

Barbara:

1. *I would have more job security.*
2. *My boss would be happier with my work and might even give me a promotion.*
3. *I would feel less anxiety and worry about getting things done.*
4. *I would get more respect from my boss, friends, and family because I'd be on time and things would get done on time.*
5. *I would feel respect for myself and pride about being on time and getting things done on time.*

6. _We would have fewer family arguments when we are trying to get ready for school and work._

7. _My children would learn from my example to be on time and not procrastinate._

8. _My relationships with friends would improve._

9. _I would be more organized and get more things done in the long run._

10. _I wouldn't be rushing around so much, so there would be less chance of accidents._

⚭ Habit Change Strategy

Make the rewards of changing your habit a major focus. Make copies and post them where you'll see them frequently.

Next, read and do the exercises in chapters 8 through 11. You can change your habits and be happier as a result, but, as you are probably realizing, changes cause some stress and anxiety. Relaxation can help relieve stress. As you read chapter 8, choose a relaxation exercise, and practice it daily. Reading chapters 9 and 10 will help you confront the automatic thoughts that keep you chained to your habit. Continue working on your Habit Change Program as you read chapter 11. You'll learn more about quitting your bad habit and developing healthy habits, including your competing response. You'll probably think of a few more habits that you would like to incorporate into your life. Focusing on the good habits will take your mind off the bad habits you're trying to eliminate. Habit changing just might become a habit!

You might be wondering how you're going to keep the changes you make. Will they end up being only short-term changes, or will you be free of your bad habits and keep the healthy ones for good? Read chapter 12 to help yourself fight back against temporary lapses in your Habit Change efforts.

Do you know others who might like to change their habits? Chapter 20 can help you make habit changing a family affair or a group effort. You don't all have to be interested in changing the same type of habit, only in changing whatever habits each of you finds troublesome in his or her life.

17

Excessive Spending and Shopping

Resolve not to be poor: whatever you have, spend less.
—Samuel Johnson

The answer to all your problems is in this little bottle.
—Lucy Ricardo, selling Vitameatavegamin tonic
I Love Lucy

For some people shopping is a necessary chore, and for others it's entertainment, but for still others it's a devastating problem behavior. When we shop and overspend to relieve anxiety, stress, depression, loneliness, or boredom it can become a habit that greatly interferes with life. When we shop to fulfill our needs for status, power, and self-worth, we are using money to look for something that is unattainable. Contrary to the promise of Lucy's Vitameatavegamin girl, the answer to all our problems cannot be found in a bottle of tonic—or in a new dress, a new pair of shoes, a new car, or a new golf club.

Like we can with any habit, we can change our spending and shopping habits. We can learn to make better choices with our money. Do you have an overspending problem? If you haven't worked through chapters 5 and 6, do so before completing the exercises in this chapter. It is important for you to be convinced that you do indeed have spending habits that are destructive and in need of change. You need to recognize the negative consequences. When the going gets rough—and it will—reviewing your Advantages and Disadvantages worksheet and Consequences worksheet will remind you of why you are trying to change.

Your Spending Reduction Plan

After reading chapter 5, you kept a record of your habit. You discovered the emotions, automatic thoughts, triggers, and consequences associated with your spending habits. Look at the records you completed and think back to your latest shopping and spending episodes to answer the following questions. We've provided Betty's answers as an example.

What *feelings* do you typically experience before, during, and after excessive spending?

Before: _____

During: _____

After: _____

What *automatic thoughts* do you often have before, during, and after excessive spending?

Before: _____

During: _____

After: _____

What are the most frequent *emotional triggers* for your excessive spending episodes?

_____

_____

What are the most frequent *situational triggers* for your excessive spending episodes?

_____

_____

Betty:

What *feelings* do you typically experience before, during, and after excessive spending?

Before: *Bored or worried. Excited when I decide to go, then get ready to go shopping.*

During: *Excited and happy. All worry is gone. Sometimes I feel blank, with no feelings.*

After: *Angry with myself, defensive, worried, tired, anxious.*

What *automatic thoughts* do you often have before, during, and after excessive spending?

Before: *I need to shop for this gift. I won't spend much, I promise. I can control myself.*

During: *I can't pass up this great buy. Won't she love this gift? Who cares about debt?*

After: *Why did I spend so much? It was a good buy. I really saved. But how will I pay rent?*

What are the most frequent *emotional triggers* for your excessive spending episodes?

Boredom, nervousness, anxiety, excitement, and anticipation. Overwhelmed by stress and desire to escape.

What are the most frequent *situational triggers* for your excessive spending episodes?

When birthdays of friends and relatives are coming up, Christmas, any event that gives me an excuse

to shop or buy, a day without planned activities, going to the mall, reading advertisements.

In chapter 5, you learned about your habit by filling out Habit Records and Triggers and Consequences Records. In chapter 6, you discovered the advantages and disadvantages of keeping your spending habits and changing them. Since you've read this far, you are probably quite ready to change. The first step is to record your discretionary spending. This is all the spending of which you have control. While you may want to find ways to decrease living expenses, such as rent, utilities, and insurance, the expenditures we're aiming to change here are those things that you can choose to buy or not buy and things you can choose to spend more or less for. We all have to buy groceries, but we can choose between steak and hamburger, brand names or generic products.

We've divided expenditures into four categories: household items, personal items, groceries, and miscellaneous items. Make about thirty copies of the blank Daily Spending Record (DSR). Record every expenditure—every cup of latte and every stick of gum. How long should you keep a DSR? As long as it takes! Keep a DSR until you feel comfortable with your spending habits, but for at least six months. After you stop, check up on yourself at least every six months; keep a DSR for several weeks so you can assess yourself for relapse. You may want to continue keeping a DSR indefinitely.

As you keep your DSR, you'll probably find that some things just have to be purchased, while other items are more discretionary. You may want to eliminate all discretionary spending until you get your finances under control. Or perhaps you will want to allow some discretionary spending but eliminate things that you know to be frivolous or over your budget. Underline those purchases that you see as problem expenditures. Review your DSR once a week. You may want to underline additional items during your review of your DSR. For many, credit card purchases are especially problematic. It's easy to lose track of how much you're spending, which leads to a sometimes unpleasant surprise at the end of the month when you get your account statement. Use cash as often as possible, but when you do use a credit card, write a *C* next to those expenditures that you charge.

🦋 Habit Change Strategy

For many, it is best to stop all use of credit cards. It's more difficult to see how much you are spending when you use plastic. Instead use cash, money you can see and hold.

We cannot overemphasize the importance of using the DSR. Cherry had a problem with spending a few years ago. In typical fashion she bought not one but three books on the subject of overspending. She flipped through them and noted that record keeping was an important factor in spending reduction. So she kept a record of every penny she spent for several months. Seeing the patterns of her habit on paper made her want to change. The overspending was significantly reduced. Just seeing where your money goes each month will make *you* want to reduce your spending, too. And motivation to change will bring about change.

When Betty began keeping her DSR, she was greatly surprised to find that her discretionary expenditures totaled over $2,000 the first month! Betty's problem purchases (the underlined items on her DSR) totaled $1,229—purchases where she felt she could have reduced the amount spent or completely eliminated the expenditure. She found that she had put $1,008 on her credit cards. Betty realized that without the use of credit cards she wouldn't have spent that money, because she didn't have the cash to spend!

While you are continuing to keep track of your spending on your DSR, read chapters 7 through 10, then meet us back here on this page. In chapter 7, you will be asked to develop a competing response—an activity that you will do whenever you're tempted to overspend. What will you do with the time you once spent shopping or thinking about shopping? What will you do instead of watching the shopping channels or "surfing the Net" for bargains? Line up several activities to take the place of excessive spending. Be ready with an alternative activity, a competing response, when the urge to spend or shop hits. In chapter 8, you will learn relaxation techniques; choose your favorite technique and incorporate it into your spending reduction plan. And in chapters 9 and 10 you will learn to recognize the automatic thoughts that contribute to your spending problems.

Daily Spending Record

Date	Groceries	Household Items	Personal Items	Miscellaneous

Chart 17a

Betty's Daily Spending Record

Date	Groceries	Household Items	Personal Items	Miscellaneous
1/1	$105			
1/2		$107—kitchen grill	$27—makeup - C	$4—latte
1/4		$47—Christmas gift wrap		$11—lunch out - C
1/8	$125		$108—dress - C	$62—dinner out - C
1/10		$7—vacuum bags	$23—socks - C	$4—latte
1/13			$11—hair supplies	$89—gifts - C
1/15	$102		$19—makeup	
1/16		$35—office supplies		$73—dinner out - C
1/19		$27—school supplies	$43—blouses on sale	$208—kids' clothes
1/20			$32—blouses on sale	$14—lunch out - C
1/22	$147			
1/23		$207—new curtains		$4—latte
1/25			$97—pants on sale - C	$53—gifts - C
1/27		$39—tools - C		
1/29	$96			$89—dinner out - C
Total	**$575**	**$469**	**$360**	**$611**

Chart 17b

Developing Your Spending Reduction Plan

Did you notice that the title of this section is *Your* Spending Reduction Plan? That's because it will be your plan. We aren't going to tell you what to change, or how to change. Although we are providing tools to help you with the planning, you will set your own goals and make your own plans for change. Review your Habit Records and Daily Spending Records. What are your problem areas? What items do you spend too much on? When and where do you spend the most? Where can you cut down? You probably have some general goals in mind. Now, you'll break that goal down into smaller goals and develop a step-by-step plan for achieving those goals. For a few pointers on making your plan, look over chapter 15. Most of the principles discussed there will apply here.

Step 1: Develop Long-Term Goals

Choose a general achievement you would like to accomplish—a long-term goal. You may have more than one long-term goal. After keeping a DSR for a month, Betty saw three problem areas: credit card use; impulse buying, especially of sale items; and over-indulgent gifts. We've provided her long-term goals as an example. What are your long-term goals? How will you know when you have met your goals? Complete the Long-Term Goals worksheet.

Habit Change Strategy

Make specific goals that are challenging, yet attainable. They don't have to be perfect though—you can always change them later.

Long-Term Goals

My long-term goals are:

1. _____

2. _____

3. _____

How will I know when I have met these goals?_____

_____

_____

Chart 17c

Betty's Long-Term Goals

My long-term goals are:

1. *Stop all use of credit cards*

2. *Set a price limit on gifts and give more of my time instead*

3. *Think before I buy—no underlined problem purchases on my DSR*

How will I know when I have met these goals? *I will know I am succeeding when there are no new purchases on my credit card, and when my DSR shows a dramatic decrease in spending.*

Chart 17d

Step 2: Make a Plan

Looking at these goals and imagining achieving them all at once can be overwhelming. But you can break them into smaller parts, so that they don't seem so overwhelming. Now you will make plans for achieving your goals. An important part of your plan will be making short-term goals. Your major focus will be on meeting these short-term goals instead of the long-term ones. For example, when we first decided to write this book, the project seemed overwhelming. How would we ever get it written by the deadline? When we divided it into chapters and gave ourselves mini-deadlines to meet, it seemed much less daunting because we had a plan and goals for carrying out our plan.

We've provided a Spending Reduction Plan worksheet for you to complete. Make copies of the blank worksheet so you can make revisions if it needs adjustment later. Once you get started, you may find you need to adjust your plan, adding more ways to decrease spending or eliminating ideas that don't work. Refer to Betty's plan as an example. As you create your plan for change, include some of the things we mentioned earlier. Use the ideas you've gathered in this book: record keeping, competing responses, relaxation, triggers, changing the way you think and deal with feelings, social support, rewards, and spending limits.

Spending Reduction Plan

Record Keeping

_____
_____
_____

Competing Response

_____
_____
_____

Relaxation

_____
_____
_____

Trigger Management

_____
_____
_____

Thoughts & Feelings

_____
_____
_____

Social Support

_____
_____
_____

Rewards

_____
_____
_____

Spending Limits

_____
_____
_____

Chart 17e

Betty's Spending Reduction Plan

Record
Keeping

Keep a DSR and evaluate it each week. I'll look at each purchase and decide if it was needed or if it was an impulse buy. I'll underline excessive spending with the intent of reducing it.

Competing
Response

Make gifts and give of my time when possible. Get several novels from the library. When I feel like using shopping to escape, I'll escape by reading. I'll also start walking and take a class at the community college. I'll tell my husband when I feel like spending money and I'll ask for his help to find something else we can do together.

Relaxation

I'll practice deep breathing exercises every day after lunch when I usually feel the urge to go shopping.

Trigger
Management

I will look at sale advertisements with a more critical eye, then discuss items I'm considering buying with my husband. Going to the mall is a big trigger. Instead, I'll shop at individual stores, getting a particular item and then leaving. After six months, I'll try going shopping at the mall, but only with a friend or with my husband, and I'll discuss purchases with them.

Thoughts
& Feelings

Admit that I do indeed have feelings. When I have the urge to go shopping, I will ask myself what those feelings are and how I can better cope with them. I'll refute the thought that there is no other way to cope and the thought that gifts will help relationships.

Social
Support

My husband will be my support person. I'll explain my goals and plans and then I'll ask him to discuss purchases with me and help me review my DSR.

Rewards

My reward will be dinner out with my husband each month that I decrease my spending by 10 percent.

Spending
Limits

Make a list of all gifts I need to purchase each month and set price limits. Keep one credit card for emergencies (real emergencies!) only.

Chart 17f

❀ Habit Change Strategy

Include something from every category in your plan—record keeping, competing response, relaxation, triggers, thoughts and feelings, social support, rewards—they are all important for your success.

Step 3: Develop Short-Term Goals

What will you accomplish tomorrow and in the next few days? Assess your Spending Reduction Plan and your DSR, and set one to three short-term goals for the coming week. Make copies of the Short-Term Goals worksheet and at the beginning of each week set goals for the following week. Evaluate your work in the previous week and decide how you could improve. Your short-term goals should be based on behaviors you need to change, so that you can better meet your long-term goals. We've provided Betty's Short-Term Goals worksheet for her second week as an example.

❀ Habit Change Strategy

Remember, goals should be specific, challenging, and attainable. Be a bit easy on yourself the first few weeks to help yourself build confidence, then get more challenging.

Short-Term Goals   Week No. ____

My short-term goals are:

1. _____

2. _____

3. _____

How will I know when I have met these goals? _____

_____

_____

_____

Did I meet my goals last week? If I didn't, what could I do differently in the next week?

_____

_____

_____

Chart 17g

Short-Term Goals

Week No. 2

My short-term goals are:

1. *Go to the library and check out books.*

2. *Start reading a novel.*

3. *Get the class catalog from the community college.*

How will I know when I have met these goals? *I'll have checked out several books, started reading one, and looked through the community college catalogue.*

Did I meet my goals last week? If I didn't, what could I do differently in the next week?

Deep breathing exercises have helped me say no to shopping. But I feel bored. I need to develop other activities.

Chart 17h

Now you have a plan for changing your spending habits. Try to look at this as a long-term project. It took a while for your spending to get out of control. It will take a while for you to get it under control.

Shopping and Spending Tips

- Develop a family budget and stick to it.

- Make a list before shopping.

- Shop at stores where you can get in and out easily. Stay out of malls as much as possible.

- Ask yourself, "Why? Why am I shopping? Why am I making this purchase?" If your answer is that you are shopping to relieve anxiety, stress, tension, depression, or boredom, find another activity.

- Shop with a support person who is aware of your goals.

- Recognize advertising gimmicks. Make a game of it—see how many marketing techniques you can discover in catalogs, stores, and advertisements.

- Talk back to your automatic thoughts that encourage overspending. Complete an Alternative Thoughts worksheet before going shopping.

- Acknowledge your feelings. Would spending money *really* relieve your depression, anxiety, or boredom?

- Take regular breaks to relax when you must shop.

Excessive Spending and Shopping   193

- Discuss major purchases with your spouse or a friend, and then wait twenty-four hours before buying them.

- Leave your credit cards at home and carry only as much cash as you plan to spend.

- Always be prepared to engage in one of your alternative activities when the urge to shop or spend hits.

- If you find catalog, TV, or Internet shopping to be the most tempting, shop in stores only. Consider using the channel-blocking feature on your TV to block out the shopping channels and asking catalog merchants to stop sending you their catalogs.

- Don't shop when you're tired, hungry, anxious, depressed, lonely, or bored.

- If shopping is a leisure activity for you, check out the advice in chapter 18.

- Continue to keep a DSR for at least six months, or as long as you have a problem with excessive spending.

Habit Change Strategy

Print your favorite shopping-control tips on three-by-five-inch cards and put them in places you need reminders—in your wallet, by the phone, in your car, and on the TV, for example.

More Help

We've given you tools to help you change your spending and shopping habits. For some people, their problem with overspending is so severe that counseling is needed in addition. Therapists who are experienced in treating addictions and impulse-control disorders can help. If your overspending has led to serious debt problems, you may need more assistance. Credit counseling is available free or inexpensively through the National Foundation for Consumer Credit. To find an office near you, call 1-800-388-2227, or write to:

National Foundation for Consumer Credit
8701 Georgia Avenue, Suite 507
Silver Spring, MD 20910
www.nfcc.org

Debtors Anonymous, a twelve-step program for people with spending problems, may be helpful. Debtors Anonymous offers support groups and education on how to get out of debt, negotiate with creditors, and change spending habits. To find a group near you, call 1-212-642-8222 or write to:

Debtors Anonymous General Service Office
P.O. Box 400
Grand Central Station
New York, NY 10163-0400

Read chapters 11 and 12 now. You'll learn more about changing your shopping habits and developing healthy habits, including your competing response. You'll probably think of a few more habits that you would like to incorporate into your life. Focusing on the good habits will take your mind off the bad habits you are trying to eliminate. Habit changing just might become a habit!

You might be wondering how you are going to keep the changes you make. Will they end up being only short-term changes, or will you be free of your bad habits and keep the healthy ones for good? Chapter 12 will help you fight back against temporary lapses in your Habit Change efforts.

Do you know others who might like to change their habits? Chapter 20 can help you make habit changing a family affair or a group effort. You don't all have to be interested in changing the same type of habit, only in changing whatever habits each finds troublesome in his or her life.

18

Excessive Leisure Activities

Dost thou love life? Then do not squander time; for that's the stuff life is made of.
—Benjamin Franklin

Take care of the minutes, for the hours will take care of themselves.
—Lord Chesterfield

Are your leisure activities taking over your life? Do you spend hours watching TV, sitting in front of a computer, or playing video games? If not for the games, TV, or computer, what would you be doing with all that time? If you have a sense that you are really wasting this time, then you can work on using your time more effectively. That's really what this chapter is all about—getting control of your time. We're not here to condemn use of computers or playing video games. We are not going to tell you that these behaviors are good or bad. Our goal is to help you examine your use of technology, and your use of time, for negative effects. Of course, it's not the technology that's the problem. Any leisure activity can take over your life and eat up time. Playing checkers all day or spending hours on the golf course can also have negative effects on your life. The key question to ask is, Does this activity interfere with the rest of my life?

When you are assessing the problem, it's important to distinguish between a temporary infatuation with an activity and a long-term love affair. Many people spend days exploring the Internet or playing with their new computers when they first bring them home; others spend hours in front of the TV when they first get cable installed. The amount of information you can find on the Internet seems infinite and the wide range of cable channel choices can be tempting. Likewise, playing with a new video game or computer software program can take over a weekend. Enjoying and exploring a new activity is a normal and expected reaction. But when the lost hours continue to mount for weeks, a problem might be developing. When the time and energy invested in the leisure activity takes away from your doing other important things, it can begin to affect your relationships, your work, and your health.

Habit Change Strategy

Don't get concerned about spending too much time with a new toy, such as a computer or a video game when you first bring it home. Be concerned when you're still spending too much time with the toy weeks later.

What Are You Looking For?

Why do we get hooked on these activities? Why do we allow them to take over our lives? The most obvious answer is that the activity meets a need or desire. We've listed a few needs or desires that you might be seeking to fulfill. Check off the items that you can relate to. What alternative activities could meet those needs but in a healthier way? At the bottom, write in any needs and desires that aren't listed here.

- ❑ I need to escape from reality.
- ❑ I need to reduce stress.
- ❑ I want support and understanding and find it through Internet friends.
- ❑ I need to know things—I am on a quest for information.
- ❑ I enjoy gambling and can do it on the Net. (If gambling is a problem for you, see chapter 19.)
- ❑ I want to buy "stuff." (If excessive shopping and spending are problems for you, see chapter 17.)
- ❑ I need intimacy or love.
- ❑ I'm bored and need something to do.
- ❑ I need a sense of belonging.
- ❑ I need to feel important or needed, and I feel that way in the chat rooms.
- ❑ I need relief from anxiety or depression.
- ❑ _____
- ❑ _____
- ❑ _____

Habit Change Strategy

Think about the following questions every time you spend excessive time on a leisure activity: What am I really looking for? What need am I trying to fill?

Your Balanced Leisure Activity Plan

As with any habit, we can change our leisure-activity habits. We can learn to make better choices when it comes to how we spend our time. Do you have a problem with leisure activities? If you haven't worked through chapters 5 and 6, do so before completing the exercises in this chapter. It is important that you believe that you do indeed have leisure-activity habits that are destructive and in need of change, and that you are ready to commit to working on it.

In order to change them, you need to recognize the negative consequences of these habits. When the going gets rough—and it will—your Advantages and Disadvantages chart and Consequences chart will remind you of why you are trying to change.

After reading chapter 5, you kept a record of your habit. You discovered the emotions, automatic thoughts, triggers, and consequences associated with your leisure-activity habit. Look at the charts you completed and think about your problem activity as you answer the following questions. We've provided George's answers as an example.

What *feelings* do you typically experience before, during, and after you spend time on the problem activity?

Before: _____

During: _____

After: _____

What *automatic thoughts* do you often have before, during, and after you spend time on the problem activity?

Before: _____

During: _____

After: _____

What are the most frequent *emotional triggers* for your spending time on the problem activity?

_____

_____

What are the most frequent *situational triggers* for your spending time on the problem activity?

_____

_____

George:

What *feelings* do you often experience before, during, and after you spend time on the problem activity?

Before: *I usually feel bored. Sometimes I feel anxious, nervous, or worried.*

During: *I feel excited or calm. Sometimes I feel nothing—I'm kind of in a fog, dazed.*

After: *I feel less nervous and worried. A lot of the time I feel guilty and tired.*

What *automatic thoughts* do you often have before, during, and after you spend time on the problem activity?

Before: *I need to relax. Just a few minutes here. Gotta hurry so I can get on my computer.*

During: *Just a few more minutes. I don't really have anything important to do.*

After: *I know I spent too much time online. It's my time, though. I'm a real jerk.*

What are the most frequent *emotional triggers* for your spending time on the problem activity?

Feeling pressured at work, boredom at work or at home, worry, anxiety, anger with my wife or boss, disappointment with other people or with life in general.

What are the most frequent *situational triggers* for your spending time on the problem activity?

Arguing with my wife or kids, having a conflict with others—my friends or coworkers. Coming home from work and getting up in the morning, passing the computer.

In chapter 5, you learned about your habit by filling out Habit Records and Triggers and Consequences Records. In chapter 6, you discovered the advantages and disadvantages of keeping your leisure-activity habits and changing them. Since you've read this far, you are probably quite ready to change. The first step is to record the time spent on your leisure activities. First, make about thirty copies of the blank Leisure Activity Time Record (LATR). Then start recording every moment spent participating in your leisure activity. Underline the entries for sessions in which you think the time spent was excessive. How long should you keep an LATR? As long as it takes! Keep an LATR until you feel comfortable with the amount of time spent on leisure activities, but for at least six months. After you stop, check up on yourself at least every six months; keep an LATR for several weeks so you can assess yourself for relapse. You may want to continue keeping an LATR indefinitely.

We cannot overemphasize the importance of the Leisure Activity Time Record. Cherry had a problem with spending a few years ago. In typical fashion she bought not one but three books on the subject of overspending. She flipped through them and noted that record keeping was an important factor in spending reduction. So she kept a record of every penny she spent for several months. Seeing the patterns of her habit on paper made her want to change. The spending problem was significantly reduced. Just seeing where money goes each month can make *you* want to reduce your spending, too. And motivation to change brings about change. In the same way, seeing where your time is spent will motivate you to change, so you can make better use of your time in the future.

We've provided George's LATR as an example. George spent hours playing computer games on the Internet, visiting message boards and chat rooms, and "surfing the Net." On his LATR he underlined almost every session he spent on the computer, because he viewed the time spent as excessive. George had lost his job due to excessive Internet use at work. He knew it was a problem, but he just couldn't seem to control his time spent online. In addition to losing his job, George had lost contact with most of his local friends and had withdrawn from his family.

While you continue to keep track of your habit on your LATR, read chapters 7 through 10, then meet us back here. In chapter 7 you will be asked to develop a competing response—an activity that you will do whenever you're tempted to engage in your habit. What will you do with the time you once spent practicing your leisure activity? What will you do instead of watching TV, playing video games, or "surfing the Net?" Line up several activities to take the place of your habit. Be ready with an alternative activity, a competing response, when the urge hits. In chapter 8, you will learn relaxation techniques; choose your favorite technique and incorporate it into your balanced leisure activity plan. And in chapters 9 and 10 you will learn to recognize the automatic thoughts that contribute to your habit.

Leisure Activity Time Record

Date	Time	Notes	Date	Time	Notes

Chart 18a

		George's Leisure Activity Time Record			
Date	Time	Notes	Date	Time	Notes
1/1	8:00–11:30 A.M.	Played computer games with online friends	1/6	9:00–11:30 A.M.	Played computer games, surfed the Net
1/1	2–7:30 P.M.	Read e-mail, surfed the net	1/6	12:30–2:30 P.M.	Read message boards
1/2	8:30–11:30 A.M.	Played computer games	1/6	5:00–7:00 P.M.	Visited chat rooms, read e-mail
1/2	12:30–3:00 P.M.	Talked in chat room	1/6	11:00 P.M.–1:30 A.M.	Played computer games
1/2	6:00 P.M.–1:30 A.M.	Played computer games, read message boards	1/7	9:00–10:00 A.M.	Read e-mail
1/3	9:00–11:30 A.M.	Read e-mail, played computer games	1/7	5:00–10:00 P.M.	Played computer games, posted on message boards
1/3	6:00–10:00 P.M.	Played computer games, surfed the Net	1/8	7:30–8:00 A.M.	Read e-mail
1/3	12:00–1:00 A.M.	Talked in chat room	1/8	4:30–6:30 P.M.	Talked in chat room
1/4	7:30–8:30 A.M.	Read e-mail	1/8	10:00 P.M.–1:30 A.M.	Played computer games
1/4	5:30–9:30 P.M.	Played computer games	1/9	9:00–10:00 A.M.	Read e-mail
1/4	10:30–11:30 P.M.	Read message boards	1/9	5:00 P.M.–12:30 A.M.	Played computer games, read message boards
1/5	7:30–8:30 A.M.	Read e-mail	1/10	7:30–9:30 A.M.	Read e-mail
1/5	5:00–10:00 P.M.	Played computer games			
1/5	11:30 P.M.–12:30 A.M.	Read e-mail			

Chart 18b

Negative Consequences

At this point, let's take a closer look at the consequences of your excessive leisure activity. Perhaps you missed a few when you listed them in chapter 5. Below, check off the consequences that apply to your situation and add ones that aren't listed here.

- ❑ Feeling powerless to manage your time.

- ❑ Longer and longer periods of time lost to your leisure activity.

- ❑ Poor performance at work, or falling grades if you are in school.

- ❑ Reduced quality and quantity of time spent with family and friends.

❑ Neglect of necessary personal activities, such as paying bills, personal grooming, and household chores.

❑ Feeling restless, irritable, anxious, or depressed when you are not participating in the activity or when you are trying to resist the activity.

❑ Lying to loved ones about the amount of time lost to the leisure activity.

❑ Spending too much money on the leisure activity, or money problems as a result of the leisure-activity habit.

❑ Difficulty concentrating on other activities.

❑ Getting too little sleep.

❑ Loss of interest in activities you once enjoyed.

❑ Interference with achieving life goals and plans.

❑ _____

❑ _____

❑ _____

⚘ Habit Change Strategy

Make these negative consequences have a positive influence on your life by letting them increase your motivation and commitment.

Developing Your Balanced Leisure Activity Plan

Did you notice that the title of this section is *Your* Balanced Leisure Activity Plan? That's because it will be your plan. We aren't going to tell you what to change, or how to change. Although we are providing tools to help you with the planning, you will set your own goals and make your own plans for change. Review your Habit Records and Leisure Activity Time Records. What are your problem areas? When and where do you spend too much time on your activity? Do you think you should cut down or quit? You probably have a general goal in mind. Now, we'll break that goal down into smaller goals and help you make a step-by-step plan for achieving those goals. For a few pointers on making your plan, review chapter 15. Most of the principles discussed there will apply here.

Step 1: Develop Long-Term Goals

Choose a general achievement you would like to accomplish—a long-term goal. You may have more than one long-term goal. After keeping an LATR for a month, George thought he could cut down on Internet use, get involved in new activities, and improve his relationships. We've provided his long-term goals as an example. What are your long-term goals? How will you know when you have met your goals? Complete the Long-Term Goals worksheet.

✖️🦋 Habit Change Strategy

Make specific goals that are challenging, yet attainable. They don't have to be perfect though—you can always change them later.

Long-Term Goals

My long-term goals are:

1. _____

2. _____

3. _____

How will I know when I have met these goals?_____

_____

_____

Chart 18c

George's Long-Term Goals

My long-term goals are:

1. _Reduce computer use to two hours a day, no more than one hour at a time._

2. _Find other activities to replace computer use—at least three other activities._

3. _Repair relationships with my family and friends._

How will I know when I have met these goals? _I'll know I'm succeeding when I am participating in and enjoying three other activities and when my family and friends notice a difference in our relationships. My LATR will show few underlined computer-use times._

Chart 18d

Step 2: Make a Plan

Looking at these goals and imagining achieving them all at once can feel overwhelming. But you can break them into smaller parts, so that they don't seem so overwhelming. Now you will make plans for achieving your goals. An important part of your plan will be making short-term goals. Your major focus will be on meeting these short-term goals instead of the long-term ones. For example, when we first decided to write this book, the project seemed overwhelming. How would we ever get it written by the deadline? When we divided it into chapters and gave ourselves mini-deadlines to meet, it seemed much less daunting because we had a plan and goals for carrying out our plan.

We've provided a Balanced Leisure Activity Plan worksheet for you to complete. Make copies of the blank worksheet so you can make revisions if it needs adjustment later. Once you get started, you may find you need to adjust your plan, adding more ways to balance your time or eliminating ideas that don't work. At first, George thought he could reduce the time he spent with his computer, but the urge was too strong. He found that it worked better for him to eliminate computer use completely for the first few weeks, reassessing his plan once he felt he had gained control. We've included George's original plan as an example. As you create your plan for change, include some of the things we mentioned earlier. Use the ideas you've gathered in this book: stages of change, record keeping, competing response, rewards, relaxation, changing the way you think, triggers, and social support.

Habit Change Strategy

In your plan include something from every category—record keeping, competing response, relaxation, triggers, thoughts and feelings, social support, rewards—they are all important to your success.

Balanced Leisure Activity Plan

**Record
Keeping**

_____

_____

_____

**Competing
Response**

_____

_____

_____

Relaxation

_____

_____

_____

**Trigger
Management**

_____

_____

_____

**Thoughts
& Feelings**

_____

_____

_____

**Social
Support**

_____

_____

_____

Rewards

_____

_____

_____

Time Limits

_____

_____

_____

Chart 18e

George's Balanced Leisure Activity Plan

Record Keeping

I will keep an LATR and evaluate it each week. I'll try to honestly decide whether I used my time wisely. I'm going to try to have no underlined computer-use times—no sessions over one hour.

Competing Response

I will go for a walk with my wife every night during the time when I am most tempted to get online. Develop alternative activities—get more involved in church, read more books, and do jigsaw puzzles and play games with the kids. Spend more quality time with my family and friends.

Relaxation

I will learn and use the progressive muscle relaxation exercise daily.

Trigger Management

Seeing the computer in its usual place is a trigger. I'll move it to the family room. This way it will be out in the open and everyone will be able to see how much time I am spending online. Arriving home from work seems to be a trigger. I'll find something else to do as soon as I get home.

Thoughts & Feelings

I will recognize that I do have feelings and automatic thoughts. When I have the urge to get online, I will ask myself what those feelings and thoughts are and how can I better deal with them. I'll challenge the thought that there is no other way to cope. I can use an alternative thoughts worksheet to come up with more reasonable thoughts.

Social Support

I will talk to my wife about my use of the Internet and ask her to support my efforts to reduce my time spent online.

Rewards

My reward for reducing computer time will be to get a new book each week.

Time Limits

I will limit my time on the computer to two hours a day, no more than an hour at a time. I will stay off the computer until I have spent at least eight hours looking for a job each day.

Chart 18f

Step 3: Develop Short-Term Goals

What will you accomplish tomorrow and in the next few days? Assess your Balanced Leisure Activity Plan and your LATR, and set one to three short-term goals for the coming week. Make copies of the Short-Term Goals worksheet and at the beginning of each week set goals for the following week. Evaluate your work in the previous week and decide how you could improve. Your short-term goals should be based on behaviors you need to change, so that you can better meet your long-term goals. We've provided George's Short-Term Goals worksheet for his second week as an example.

Habit Change Strategy

Remember, goals should be specific, challenging, and attainable. Be a bit easy on yourself the first few weeks to help yourself build confidence, then get more challenging.

Short-Term Goals   Week No. ____

My short-term goals are:

1. _____

2. _____

3. _____

How will I know when I have met these goals? _____

_____

_____

_____

Did I meet my goals last week? If I didn't, what could I do differently in the next week?

_____

_____

_____

Chart 18g

George's Short-Term Goals   Week No. __2__

My short-term goals are:

1. *Start a jigsaw puzzle with the kids.*

2. *Go to church with my wife this week and go to the Men's Prayer Breakfast.*

3. *Move the computer to the family room.*

How will I know when I have met these goals? *I'll have started a jigsaw puzzle and moved the computer to the family room. I will have gone to church on Sunday and to the Men's Prayer Breakfast on Saturday morning.*

Did I meet my goals last week? If I didn't, what could I do differently in the next week?

The kids and I got a jigsaw puzzle out and started it. My wife and I went to church, but I didn't make it to the Men's Prayer Breakfast. We moved the computer to the family room. Next week, I'll find other ways to get involved in other activities.

Chart 18h

Now you have a plan for balancing your leisure activities. Try to look at this as a long-term project. It took a while for your habit to get out of control. It will take a while for you to get it under control.

⋈ Habit Change Strategy

Print your favorite tips for balancing your time on three-by-five-inch cards and put them in places you need reminders—in your wallet, by the computer, in your car, and on the TV, for example.

Tips for Balancing Your Leisure Activities

- Reassess your priorities at home, work, school, church, and so on. Work toward excellence in the areas most important to you.

- Be honest with your loved ones about your lost time. Ask them to support your efforts to change.

- Spend more quality time with your family and friends.

- If you plan to limit your problem activity, schedule time for it and stick to your schedule. Set a timer if needed.

- Take a break from your problem activity and consider stopping the activity altogether.

- If Internet use is a problem, but you can't avoid using the Internet, get on, do your work, then get off. Or budget a limited amount of online time.

- Develop alternative activities in order to meet your needs and desires.

- Explore your former activities and hobbies.

- Always be prepared to engage in one of your alternative activities when the urge to participate in the problem activity hits.

- Recognize triggers as a challenge to your balanced activity plan.

- If the problem activity involves the TV or computer, place the problem device out in the open in your home where everyone can see how much time you spend with it.

- Learn relaxation techniques and practice a relaxation exercise daily.

- Acknowledge your feelings. Would this activity really relieve your anxiety, stress, tension, depression, or boredom?

- Ask yourself, "Why? Why am I doing this?" If your answer is that you are doing the activity to relieve anxiety, stress, tension, depression, or boredom, try to find another activity that will accomplish the same thing.

- If loneliness is a problem for you, take steps to get more involved with other people—join a club or church, take a class, or reconnect with friends and family.

- Talk back to negative thoughts that encourage you to engage in your habit. Use one of the thought-changing forms from chapters 9 and 10, such as the Distorted Thought Record.

- When you are away from the computer or TV, keep your thoughts focused on the present activity, not on the habit.

- If you spend too much money on Internet shopping or gambling, read chapter 17 or 19.

- Consider joining a support group that focuses on addictions or coping with emotions.

- Get professional help from a mental health professional if the ideas here aren't working well enough.

- Continue to keep an LATR for at least six months, or as long as you have a problem with balancing your leisure activities.

- Don't rely on someone else to police your time. Police yourself. One of the best ways to do this is to keep records like the LATR.

Read chapters 11 and 12 now. You'll learn more about changing your negative habits and developing healthy habits, including your competing response. You'll probably think of a few more habits that you would like to incorporate into your life. Focusing on the good habits will take your mind off the bad habits you are trying to eliminate. Habit changing just might become a habit!

You might be wondering how you are going to keep the changes you make. Will they end up being only short-term changes, or will you be free of your bad habits and keep the healthy ones for good? Chapter 12 will help you fight back against temporary lapses in your Habit Change efforts.

Do you know others who might like to change their habits? Chapter 20 can help you make habit changing a family affair or a group effort. You don't all have to be interested in changing the same type of habit, only in changing whatever habits each of you finds troublesome in his or her life.

19

Problem Gambling

The roulette table pays nobody except him that keeps it. Nevertheless, a passion for gambling is common, though a passion for roulette tables is unknown.

—George Bernard Shaw

There are two times in a man's life when he should not speculate: when he can't afford it, and when he can.

—Mark Twain

Pathological gambling is listed in the *Diagnostic and Statistical Manual of Mental Disorders* (American Psychiatric Association 1994) the official diagnostic classification used in the United States, as an impulse control disorder. These disorders include a failure to resist an impulse, temptation, or drive to engage in a behavior that can be harmful to self or others.

You're Not Alone

Problem gambling is usually divided into three basic categories depending on the severity. These categories have been given various names by different sources. People with severe problems with gambling have been called "pathological," "probable pathological," and "compulsive" gamblers. People with moderate problems have been called "potential pathological," "problem," "at-risk," and "in-transition" gamblers. The third category is made up of people who do not have a gambling problem. They may or may not gamble, but if they do it is not causing them problems.

These labels tend to be ambiguous. There are no generally accepted definitions of these categories. If you examine yourself and find that gambling is causing problems with your finances, your relationships, your work, or any other important aspect of your life, then you have a problem. If you determine that you have a problem with gambling, the next step is to determine if you are ready to change. Chapter 6 discusses stages of change. Making a commitment to yourself is central to making the change.

If you suspect your problem is severe, you are feeling desperate, or you think that you might be suffering from another psychiatric disorder in addition to the gambling problem, you need to seek professional mental health care. People with problems with gambling can get very depressed, especially if they are losing a lot. If you are having suicidal thoughts, you need to seek help immediately. Most communities have a suicide hotline that can help—check the front section of your Yellow Pages for the telephone number. Your county mental health department can also give you guidance. More than thirty states have a council on problem gambling. The National Council on Problem Gambling (1-800-522-4700) can give you contact information the state council closest to you.

At least one form of gambling is legal in forty-eight of the fifty states in the United States. Legalized gambling now exists in more than ninety countries. Availability of gambling brings with it a higher incidence of problem gambling. One study showed that, in states that had legalized gambling for more than twenty years, 1.5 percent of adults were probable pathological gamblers, while .5 percent were probable pathological gamblers in states that had legalized gambling for fewer than ten years. Twenty years ago, 61 percent of people in the United States were gambling (Bujold, Ladouceur, Sylvain, and Boisvert 1994). Today that figure has risen to 80 percent. In the United States 1 to 2 percent of people have a problem with gambling. Another 1.5 to 3 percent have moderate gambling problems (Spunt, Dupont, Lesieur, Liberty, and Hunt 1994).

Researchers have found a 4 to 8 percent incidence of problem gambling in college students (Spunt, Dupont, Lesieur, Liberty, and Hunt 1998). Why do young people have a higher rate of problem gambling? Perhaps it is partly because they are more likely to engage in risk-taking behavior, and this makes them more vulnerable. Environment also plays an important role. Most teens and young adults have been exposed to legalized gambling their entire lives. Research indicates that pathological gamblers are more likely to have parents with gambling problems and/or alcohol or drug use problems.

Although women are catching up, surveys indicate that men are more likely to be pathological gamblers. One study reported that while men tend to be attracted to the thrill of winning, women turn to gambling to escape overwhelming personal problems. Researchers report that in some women, gambling gives them a sense of personal power (Spunt, et al. 1998).

Gambling is becoming more of a problem among seniors. This problem is sometimes further complicated by cognitive impairment due to medical conditions, such as stroke, Alzheimer's disease, or long-term alcohol use. For most seniors, however, problem gambling develops because of lifestyle changes, loneliness, isolation, and increased free time. Gambling is made quite available to senior adults in some regions with casinos doing things like providing free transportation. Gambling may start out as entertainment, but it often gets out of control. This is particularly devastating for an elderly person living on a fixed income, with limited resources and limited ability to recover those resources if they are lost.

Problem gambling tends to affect everyone in the gambler's life. It can have a devastating impact on the person's family. The consequences can include the family member spending more time away from home, telling lies, taking money meant for other things, and breaking trust. We recommend a very good book for families dealing with their loved one's gambling problem: *Don't Leave It to Chance: A Guide for Families of Problem Gamblers*, by Edward J. Federman, Charles E. Drebins, and Christopher Krebs (2000), is a helpful resource, whether the family member is seeking help or not.

Research has found that the incidence of pathological gambling is 4 to 10 times higher in people with alcoholism or drug addiction. Indeed, alcohol use and gambling often go together. The risk of having a gambling problem also goes up for people with other psychiatric disorders, such as depression, bipolar disorder (manic depression), attention deficit disorder (ADD), and schizophrenia. If you are suffering from one of these disorders, getting treatment of the disorder will improve your chances of escaping your gambling problem.

Treatment Options

Psychoanalytic therapy was one of the first treatments of pathological gambling. In this type of therapy pathological gambling is thought to be related to early losses and deprivation, or to childhood conflicts that caused an unconscious need to lose. Psychoanalytic therapy for a gambling problem would involve trying to gain insight into childhood conflicts and unconscious needs. Typically psychoanalytic therapy involves extended treatment. Little information is available on the effectiveness of psychoanalytic therapy.

Medication is sometimes used to treat pathological gambling. Usually this is suggested when another problem or diagnosis, such as depression, bipolar disorder, ADD, or schizophrenia, is involved. When the other psychiatric disorder is treated, the gambling problem may also improve. There is little research on using medication to treat pathological gambling as the primary problem. Medications that have been tried include Naltrexone, a drug sometimes used to reduce cravings in the treatment of alcohol or other drug-abuse disorders, anti-seizure medications that are also used to stabilize mood, and serotonin reuptake blocking drugs used to treat depression and obsessive-compulsive disorder. There is no general agreement as to which of these work well or which to try first. The usual recommendation is to try some type of talk therapy along with medications.

Is gambling an addiction? Is it a compulsion? Gambling and other problem behaviors people engage in excessively have some things in common with addictions, but there are also very important differences. In the same vein, there are important differences between behaviors that are done for pleasure and compulsions. This book is not the place for a debate about the question of addiction models or the difference between impulse disorders and compulsions. If you think of gambling as an addiction or compulsion, your viewpoint should not conflict with the approach we recommend here.

What about twelve-step programs? The "twelve-step" approach is at the center of Alcoholics Anonymous (AA). Members of AA complete twelve steps on a path to recovery. This model has been successful for many people with alcohol problems. The AA approach has inspired groups to adapt the twelve-step model to other problems thought of as addictions, including gambling. Because of the nature of anonymous organizations, it is impossible to know for sure how well this approach works. Our best guess is that it helps. We recommend that anyone with a gambling problem tries going to Gambler's Anonymous (GA) meetings. Some researchers have argued that just making the commitment to go to GA is important—if someone will go to GA then they are motivated enough to make the tough changes involved in stopping a problem habit.

The Habit Change Plan for Gambling

Behavior therapists view gambling as a learned behavior, begun and maintained by reinforcement. The early behavior therapists tried aversion therapy for problem gambling in the 1960s. Since then, behavior therapists have developed more sophisticated ideas and have included new techniques. Cognitive therapy involves working with beliefs and attitudes about gambling and other areas of life. The evolving schools of thought behind behavior therapy and cognitive therapy have common roots, and most modern therapists trained in these approaches would describe themselves as cognitive behavioral therapists. A cognitive model of problem gambling holds that the problem concerns distorted beliefs about gambling, probability, and luck. This is the approach we will use.

Not much reliable research has been done on treating gambling problems with cognitive behavioral approaches, but clinical experience and existing research support the idea that cognitive behavioral therapy is an effective treatment of gambling problems. It is interesting to note that the most successful treatments seem to involve the use of a self-help manual.

Do you have a problem with gambling? If you haven't worked through chapters 5 and 6, do so before completing the exercises in this chapter. It is important that you believe that you do indeed have a gambling problem that is destructive and in need of change, and for you to be ready to commit to working on it. In order to change your habit, you need to recognize the negative consequences of your gambling. When the going gets rough—and it will—your Habit Advantages and Disadvantages worksheet and Habit Consequences worksheet will remind you why you are trying to change.

After reading chapter 5, you kept a record of your habit. You discovered the emotions, automatic thoughts, triggers, and consequences associated with your gambling habit. Look at the worksheets you completed and think about your problem activity as you answer the following questions. We've provided Lucy's and Fred's answers as examples.

What *feelings* do you typically experience before, during, and after spending time gambling?

Before: _____

During: _____

After: _____

What *automatic thoughts* do you often have before, during, and after spending time gambling?

Before: _____

During: _____

After: _____

What are the most frequent *emotional triggers* for your gambling habit?

_____

_____

What are the most frequent *situational triggers* for your gambling habit?

_____

_____

Lucy:

What *feelings* do you typically experience before, during, and after spending time gambling?

Before: *Boredom, worry, then excitement, indecision, anticipation, fleeting guilt.*

During: *Excitement, fleeting guilt, power, exhilaration, then anxiety, hope, tension.*

After: *Exhaustion, guilt, depression, shame, anger with self, stress, tension.*

What *automatic thoughts* do you often have before, during, and after spending time gambling?

Before: *I shouldn't go, but I want to. I'm bored. Maybe I'll win. I deserve some fun.*

During: *I feel lucky; I know I'll win. I should stop; I don't want to stop. I can win it back.*

After: *Why did I go? Why didn't I stop? I'm a terrible person. Who can I borrow from?*

What are the most frequent *emotional triggers* for your gambling habit?
When I'm bored. Also when I'm anxious or worried. When I'm tense and want to get away from it all and have fun.

What are the most frequent *situational triggers* for your gambling habit?
When I don't have anything planned and want to have fun. When friends invite me out to go play bingo or video poker. When I get off work and pass by a casino.

Fred:

What *feelings* do you typically experience before, during, and after spending time gambling?

Before: *Excitement, anticipation, power.*

During: *Excitement, enjoying myself, power, exhilarated, then angry, depressed if losing.*

After: *If won, happy, excited, if lose, depressed and angry with whoever I see.*

What *automatic thoughts* do you often have before, during, and after spending time gambling?

Before: *I deserve to have some fun. Besides, I know what I'm doing. I'm ready to win.*

During: *I am due for a win. I know my sports and I know who's most likely to win.*

After: *I know I'll win next time. I learn more with every loss. Next time I'll win.*

What are the most frequent *emotional triggers* for your gambling habit?
Boredom. Worry about bills—I think that maybe I can win enough to catch up with bills. Angry with my wife for complaining about my gambling.

What are the most frequent *situational triggers* for your gambling habit?
Invitation to play cards with my friends. Big sports games. Talking about the games with my friends. Weekends.

In chapter 5, you learned about your habit by filling out Habit Records and Triggers and Consequences Records. In chapter 6, you discovered the advantages and disadvantages of keeping and changing your habit. At the end of chapter 6, you made a commitment to change. You are taking the first step toward change by continuing to record your participation in your habit, using the Habit Records and Triggers and Consequences Records. How long should you continue to fill out these records? As long as it takes! Keep them until you have significantly changed your habit, for at least six months. After you stop keeping these records, check up on yourself regularly every six months: keep Habit Records and Triggers and Consequences Records for several weeks so that you can assess yourself for relapse. You may even want to continue keeping records indefinitely. We cannot overemphasize the importance of keeping the Habit Record. Cherry had a problem with spending a few years ago. In typical fashion she bought not one but three books on the subject of overspending. She flipped through them and noted that record keeping was an important factor in spending reduction. So she kept a record of every penny she spent for several months. Seeing the patterns of her habit made her want to change. The spending problem was significantly reduced. Just seeing where your money goes each month can make *you* want to change your habit, too. And motivation to change brings about change. In the same way, seeing the money and time spent gambling will motivate you to change.

While you continue to keep a Habit Record, read chapters 7 through 10, then meet back here. In those chapters you will be asked to develop a competing response and deal with some of the thoughts that are getting in the way of changing. What will you do with the time you once spent gambling? You will need to fill the void. In chapter 7 you will line up several activities to take the place of your gambling. Be ready with an alternative activity when the first urge hits.

In chapter 8, you will learn relaxation techniques. Choose your favorite technique and begin to practice it daily. Chapters 9 and 10 will help you recognize the automatic thoughts that contribute to your habit. Pay special attention to these chapters. Then return to this page and continue working through the rest of chapter 19. We will expand on the idea of refuting faulty thoughts and beliefs, as they relate to problem gambling.

Faulty Beliefs about Gambling

You probably don't realize that you have irrational beliefs about gambling. In the following pages, we will help you recognize some of your faulty beliefs and thoughts. In chapters 9 and 10 we focused on automatic thoughts. We'll apply the information in those chapters to helping you learn to catch your automatic thoughts when you are gambling or thinking about gambling. We will also look at your automatic thoughts at other times when you are at high risk for giving in to the urge to gamble. Then you will be better prepared to deal with these thoughts, test their validity, and develop alternatives.

A cognitive behavioral approach to problem gambling involves many of the elements that are found in the treatment of other habit problems in this book. It is important to understand the habit, look at the thoughts that are related to gambling, and evaluate them. You will identify high-risk situations and develop new ways to deal with them. And you'll develop competing responses—new ways of dealing with your impulses to gamble.

People with gambling problems have false beliefs about cause and effect. The house wins! That's how the thousands of lights are kept lit in the casinos, and that's how states raise money through lotteries. Most gamblers don't seem to accept this fact. Instead of recognizing that games are determined by chance, they rely on an illusion of personal control by their skills, actions, luck, or superstitions.

Statisticians talk of the *gambler's fallacy*, a belief that one event changes the probability of another. For example, if you flip a coin and get heads five times in a row, a person who believed the gambler's fallacy would say that on the next flip it is more likely to be tails. In fact, with each coin flip there is the same chance of its being heads or tails. Beliefs like these lead to continued gambling. After all, you can't keep losing, right? Understanding and changing these beliefs can make the problem more manageable. If these beliefs about gambling sound like yours, don't feel bad, because you're not alone. The reward of the occasional win and the way we experience gambling maintain these beliefs. Let's take a look at several types of faulty beliefs about gambling.

1. I'm on a winning streak!

What is fascinating about the gambler's fallacy is that it seems to work only one way. When people are betting on an outcome, they will believe that the past outcome affects the next. This theory, however, is always interpreted in favor of the gambler. When a gambler flips a coin several times, he or she will likely believe that a long series of heads means that the odds of getting tails is improved so he needs to bet on tails. The same gambler will likely also believe in streaks of luck. He may think, "I am winning, so I have to keep playing as long as my luck holds." Since the outcome of each bet is separate and independent, the run of luck is simply an illusion. The odds of winning the next bet are the same as the last one. Actual odds are determined by the game, not by what the outcome was last time. Every time I flip a coin, I am facing a 50 percent chance of getting heads. It doesn't matter how many times I've gotten heads.

2. I'm due for a win!

Beliefs about odds get reversed when it comes to a losing streak. Gamblers tend to believe that it can't go on indefinitely. You may believe that losing somehow will make the next bet more likely to be a winner. This belief leads to what is known as "chasing the losses." Gamblers believe that only by continuing to gamble will they be able to recover their losses. They often seem to believe in a form of entitlement—that they deserve to win since they have lost so much. It makes more sense to think of the money lost as the cost of the entertainment—or the cost of the habit. Gamblers distort their sense of time when they believe the win is about to happen. Even after hours of playing, they might still be thinking, "I can't quit now—I am close to a big win." Gamblers also remember their wins much more clearly than they remember their losses simply because wins are less common, or because of selective memory.

3. It's entertainment!

Gambling is an expensive form of entertainment. The casinos know this. They bring in expensive attractions and offer cut-rate food and lodging in order to attract people. But these hotel and restaurant prices only seem low. Casino owners know that the real money comes not from hotel and restaurant business but from gamblers. They know that you will lose money when you gamble. Keep this fact in mind when you think of gambling as entertainment—losing money is an unavoidable part of gambling. Over time, you'll find that gambling is really a costly form of entertainment.

4. Gambling as a way to earn money?

Important to keeping a gambling lifestyle going are the beliefs that you can win in the long run and that it is a reasonable way to earn money. It is clear, however, that the house always wins in the long run. Realize that corporations could not keep those fancy casinos going if they didn't make a great profit from gambling. Why do states start lotteries and legalize gambling? Because they know they will make money as a result. State lotteries and similar forms of gambling are sometimes called "a tax for people who are bad at math." State-run gambling, such as lotteries, often publish the percentage of their total that goes to winners and the percentage that goes into the state treasury. These figures leave no doubt that the house wins.

Do people *ever* hit it big? Of course they do. People also get struck by lightning, and you are much more likely to be hit by lightning than to win big in a lottery. It is simply not possible to make a reasonable living from gambling.

5. Superstition

Gamblers are a superstitious group. They may believe that any of a number of things can affect their chances of winning. A *talismanic superstition* is a belief that possession of a particular object affects chances of winning. "Lucky" shirts, hats, cups, jewelry, particular colors, special numbers, and certain dates—these are all examples of this type of superstition.

A *behavioral superstition* involves the idea that performing some special behavior or ritual changes the chances of winning. These behaviors can include blowing on dice, getting certain bingo cards, sitting in particular chairs, playing at certain gambling machines, buying a lottery ticket at a particular store, and giving verbal encouragement to the chosen horse or to the dealer in a card game. Another form of behavioral superstitions is called "chasing winnings." Gamblers sometimes believe that they have to keep going until they win. They believe that if they stop, they will be quitting before the big win that is bound to be coming soon and they will miss out. Gamblers often believe that their state of mind has some influence on the outcome—that they will win if they are enthusiastic, say a prayer, or believe that a big win is about to happen.

6. Overestimation of skill

Another form of distorted belief in problem gambling is an overestimation of skill or exaggerated self-confidence. Many problem gamblers believe that there is a method to winning consistently and that they can find it. Strangely enough, this belief seems to get stronger when the gambler is losing. He or she may see brief periods of winning as proof of this idea. The gambler's belief in his or her skill, or exaggerated self-confidence, also leads to efforts to find a "system," learn more about the game of choice, or find other ways to make the belief that there is a way to control the outcome of the game come true.

The gambler may believe he is learning from his losses, that all his or her losing will lead to learning how to win consistently in the future. When gamblers win, they tell themselves that they made the right decision, but when they lose they tell themselves they should have known, and will know next time.

Since gamblers lose more often than they win, they need to find an explanation for this fact, and they work hard to find ways to make sense of their losses. When they win, gamblers tend to think their superior skill earned them the prize, even with types of gambling where no skill is involved, slot machines, for example. When they lose, however, gamblers talk about flukes or outside influences as explanations, not attributing the losses to any faults in their skills.

Changing Faulty Beliefs about Gambling

Let's try an exercise to help you examine your beliefs about gambling. The Gambling Thoughts Record is similar to the Distorted Thoughts Record in chapter 10. In the left-hand column, write your thoughts about gambling that are facilitating or permission-giving thoughts. Indicate by number what kind of faulty belief each thought is, using the numbered list of faulty beliefs in the preceding pages. Examples might include thoughts that gambling will help you make money (4), that you can't keep losing like you have been (2), that you are really good at gambling (6), or that you have a system that will help you win (6). In the right-hand column write a more reasonable statement or belief about gambling. Make at least six copies and complete Gambling Thoughts Records until you run out of gambling thoughts. Do this every week until you have your gambling problem under control, but for at least six weeks.

Gambling Thoughts Record

Distorted Gambling Thought	#	Reasonable Gambling Thought

Chart 19a

Lucy's Gambling Thoughts Record

Distorted Gambling Thought	#	Reasonable Gambling Thought
This is my lucky day. I got a refund on my taxes and that is definitely lucky. The rest of the day will probably be lucky too.	5	This could be a lucky day for me, but there is no guarantee. I was expecting to get my tax refund money, so receiving my refund doesn't make this particular day a lucky one. Even if that is lucky, it doesn't make the rest of the day lucky.
This bingo card has three sevens on it. That is lucky. I can't lose.	5	Is there really a rule that sevens are lucky? I have won and lost using cards with sevens on them.
I had to borrow to pay bills this month. I've lost so many times lately, I've just gotta win today.	2	Whether I've lost or won in the recent past, I still have the same chances of winning or losing today.
BINGO! I love to say that. I have more now than I came with. I should stop now. No, I could win more. I'm on a winning streak.	1	I could choose to stop now. It would probably be a good idea to stop. I could win more, but there is no guarantee. I still have the same chances of winning or losing.
So I'm losing now. I still have what I came with. Even if I lose a bit more it would be OK. It's entertainment. How else could I have fun for so long on so little?	3	I've lost what I won, but I still have what I came with. I could choose to stop now. This is gambling; it is not really entertainment. It's not really fun to be on this roller coaster of emotions.
I've been losing, but I know I'm bound to start winning again. I can't keep losing all day. This is my lucky day.	5, 2	I still have the same chances of winning or losing. Past winning or losing has nothing to do with chance. I could keep losing all day, or I could win. The idea that certain days are lucky is a superstition.
I've really blown it. I'll have to borrow more money to buy groceries. Surely I'll win next time. These losing streaks happen and they can't last forever.	2	I gambled and lost. I will need to try to borrow to buy groceries. I could win next time, or I could lose. A losing streak could last forever. Most people do lose at gambling over time.

Chart 19b

Fred's Gambling Thoughts Record

Distorted Gambling Thought	#	Reasonable Gambling Thought
I know I'll win this weekend. I know the teams and I know who's going to win.	6	I might win this weekend. I know the teams, their weaknesses and strengths. But the casinos know the teams too. I might know the teams better than them, but then they might know more.
If I got good enough at sports betting I could quit my job and support my family on my winnings. I could make a living doing something I enjoy.	4	If I got good enough at sports betting I could quit my job and support my family on my winnings. That's a big IF! I don't like my job. I could look for a career that earns sure money and that I would enjoy. Gambling isn't sure money.
I've found a system at the tables. Well, I don't have it figured out yet, but every time I play, I get closer.	6	Wins and losses have to do with chance. Sometimes I win, sometimes I lose.
I've gotta win. I have my lucky hat on.	5	I sometimes win when I wear this hat. I could win this time, or I could lose.
I've been on a winning streak lately. I just keep on winning. I think my system is working.	1, 6	I have been winning lately. I could keep winning, or I could lose. The chances of winning or losing stay the same.
I've been losing all night. I can't keep losing—I'm due for a win.	2	The chances of winning or losing are the same now as they were when I started. I could win, or I could keep losing.
I'm going to keep playing until I win. I can feel it in the air. The big win is coming and I'm going to be here for it.	2	Winning doesn't float in the air. It isn't destined to happen. It's chance.
Well, I didn't win tonight, but I did have fun. I might not be able to make a living gambling just now, but maybe someday. Meanwhile, I'll enjoy myself.	3, 4	I don't have enough money to pay the bills now, and my wife and kids will be disappointed in me. The price of this entertainment is quite high.

Chart 19c

Developing Your Gambling Cessation Plan

Did you notice that the title of this section is Developing *Your* Gambling Cessation Plan? That's because it will be your plan. Now you are ready to put what you have learned into action. You've discovered that gambling is interfering with your life. You've learned some ways to make changes in your life and ways to challenge the negative thoughts and beliefs that have kept you from changing. Your main goal will be to stop gambling, but how will you get there? First, you will need to break that goal down into smaller goals and develop a step-by-step plan for achieving those goals. For a few pointers on making your plan, look over chapter 15. Most of the principles discussed there will apply here.

Step 1: Develop Long-Term Goals

Complete cessation of gambling will be one of your goals. Just cutting down is not recommended. List a couple of other goals on the worksheet that follows. What will you change that will most help you stop gambling? What are your long-term goals? How will you know when you have met your goals? We've provided Lucy's and Fred's long-term goals as examples. Complete the Long-Term Goals worksheet.

✗ℬ Habit Change Strategy

Make specific goals that are challenging, yet attainable. They don't have to be perfect though—you can always change them later.

Long-Term Goals

My long-term goals are:

1. _____

2. _____

3. _____

How will I know when I have met these goals?_____

_____

_____

Chart 19d

Lucy's Long-Term Goals

My long-term goals are:

1. _Stop gambling, get involved with Gamblers Anonymous._

2. _Get caught up on my bills and get out of debt._

3. _Enjoy other activities—chess and daily walking._

How will I know when I have met those goals? _I will know I've met these goals when I'm no longer gambling, I'm regularly attending Gamblers Anonymous meetings, I'm enjoying other activities, and I'm out of debt._

Chart 19e

Fred's Long-Term Goals

My long-term goals are:

1. *Stop gambling. Join Gamblers Anonymous. Get bill payments caught up.*

2. *Enjoy other activities—model trains with the kids, crossword puzzles.*

3. *Reconnect with friends and family, strengthen these relationships.*

How will I know when I have met these goals? *I will know I've met these goals when I'm no longer gambling, my bills are caught up, I'm regularly attending GA, I'm enjoying other activities, and when I have better relationships with family and friends.*

Chart 19f

2: Make a Plan

Looking at these goals and imagining achieving them all at once can feel overwhelming. But you can break them into smaller parts, so that they don't seem so overwhelming. Now you will make plans for achieving your goals. An important part of your plan will be making short-term goals. Your major focus will be on meeting these short-term goals instead of the long-term ones. For example, when we first decided to write this book, the project seemed overwhelming. How would we ever get it written by the deadline? When we divided it into chapters and gave ourselves mini-deadlines to meet, it seemed much less daunting because we had a plan and goals for carrying out our plan.

We've provided a Gambling Cessation Plan worksheet for you to complete. Make copies of the blank worksheet so you can make revisions if it needs adjustment later. As you complete your plan for change, include some of the things we mentioned earlier. Use the ideas you've learned from this book: record keeping, competing responses, relaxation, triggers, changing the way you think and deal with feelings, social support, and rewards.

Gambling Cessation Plan

Record
Keeping

_____

_____

_____

Competing
Response

_____

_____

_____

Relaxation

_____

_____

_____

Trigger
Management

_____

_____

_____

Thoughts
& Feelings

_____

_____

_____

Social
Support

_____

_____

_____

Rewards

_____

_____

_____

Chart 19g

Lucy's Gambling Cessation Plan

Record Keeping

Keep Habit Records and Triggers and Consequences Records for at least six months and evaluate them each week. I'll try for no gambling.

Competing Response

I like playing chess. I've joined a chess club and will hone my skills. When I'm home alone and have nothing to do, I'll play chess on the computer. I'm going to a financial counselor and will dedicate some time to setting up a budget. I will get a second job. I need exercise too so I'll start walking daily.

Relaxation

I'll practice meditation and abdominal breathing daily.

Trigger Management

I'll tell my friends and everyone who will listen that I no longer gamble and ask them not to invite me out gambling anymore. I'll also ask them not to talk about gambling with me since I would then feel more tempted to go gamble. I'll stay out of the casinos. I can eat and go to movies elsewhere, so there's no reason to go to the casinos. I will go straight home from work, so I won't be tempted to stop and gamble on my way home. Then I could go back out for errands if I needed to.

Thoughts & Feelings

When I'm bored or worried, I'll call a nongambling friend, or I'll call my sister. I'll complete Gambling Thoughts Records and Distorted Thoughts Records every week and challenge unreasonable gambling thoughts.

Social Support

My sister helped me recognize I had a gambling problem. She will serve as a support person. I'll join Gamblers Anonymous. I'll keep going to the financial counselor. Learning to handle my money better will help me look at money more reasonably and stay away from gambling.

Rewards

Every week that I don't gamble I'll go out to lunch with my sister. Every month I'll treat myself to a new item of clothing.

Chart 19h

Fred's Gambling Cessation Plan

Record Keeping

Keep Habit Records and Triggers and Consequences Records for at least six months and evaluate them each week. My goal is to not gamble at all.

Competing Response

I need to come up with a new form of entertainment. I'll get the model trains out of the attic and set them up. The kids will enjoy that too. I used to enjoy crossword puzzles, so I'll start doing them again. I'm going to contact some old friends who don't gamble and get involved with them again.

Relaxation

Learn the progressive muscle relaxation exercise and use it daily.

Trigger Management

Weekends are big triggers for my gambling habit. I'll plan my weekends so I'll have plenty to do. I have plenty to do around the house and can plan things to do with my wife, children, and friends. I'm going to tell my gambling friends about my resolve to stop gambling and ask them not to talk about sports around me. Worry about bills is a big trigger. I'll get a second job so I can get caught up on my bills.

Thoughts & Feelings

I'll recognize when I am bored and stressed and I'll handle it in different ways. I'll remind myself that gambling only increases my worries. Every week I'll fill out Gambling Thoughts Records and Distorted Thoughts Records and challenge unreasonable gambling beliefs.

Social Support

My wife and children have suffered the most from my gambling. I'll discuss my goals and struggles with them and ask them to support my efforts to stop gambling. I'll join Gamblers Anonymous. Some of my nongambling friends will be glad to help me with support.

Rewards

Each week that I can go without gambling I'll buy myself a crossword puzzle book. Every month I'll take my children out to look at model trains and purchase something to add to our trains. I'll keep it small at first, until I can get caught up on my bills.

Chart 19i

◯◯ Habit Change Strategy

Include something from every category in your plan. Record keeping, competing response, relaxation, triggers, thoughts and feelings, social support, rewards—they are all important for your success.

Step 3: Develop Short-Term Goals

What will you accomplish tomorrow and in the next few days? Assess your Gambling Cessation Plan and make one to three short-term goals for the coming week. Make copies of the blank Short-Term Goals worksheet and at the beginning of each week set goals for the following week. Evaluate the previous week and decide how you could improve. Your short-term goals should be based on behaviors you need to change, so that you can better meet your long-term goals. We've provided Lucy's and Fred's Short-Term Goals worksheets, both for their second week, as examples.

◯◯ Habit Change Strategy

Remember, goals should be specific, challenging, and attainable. Be a bit easy on yourself the first few weeks to help yourself build confidence, then get more challenging.

Short-Term Goals   Week No. _____

My short-term goals are:

1. _____

2. _____

3. _____

How will I know when I have met these goals? _____

_____

_____

_____

Did I meet my goals last week? If I didn't, what could I do differently in the next week?

_____

_____

_____

Chart 19j

Lucy's Short-Term Goals

Week No. __2__

My short-term goals are:

1. _Attend at least one Gamblers Anonymous meeting._

2. _Keep appointment with financial counselor._

3. _Attend a chess club meeting and take a walk at least four days this week._

How will I know when I have met these goals? _I will have attended at least one Gamblers Anonymous meeting. I will have seen the financial counselor—no canceling this week. And I will have walked four days and attended the chess club meeting._

Did I meet my goals last week? If I didn't, what could I do differently in the next week?

I looked up GA in the phone book and picked out meeting times and places. I really need the support. I kept my appointment with the financial counselor and attended a chess club meeting. I only walked twice. Next week I'll walk at least four days.

Chart 19k

Fred's Short-Term Goals

Week No. __2__

My short-term goals are:

1. _Attend at least one Gamblers Anonymous meeting._

2. _Get model trains out and set them up._

3. _Look for a second job—put in at least two applications._

How will I know when I have met these goals? _I will have attended a Gamblers Anonymous meeting. I will have the model trains set up and hopefully will have played with them with the kids. I will have applied for at least two jobs._

Did I meet my goals last week? If I didn't, what could I do differently in the next week?

I attended two GA meetings, got the model trains out, and put in one job application. Next week, I'll step up my job search and put in at least three applications.

Chart 19l

Now you have a plan for stopping your gambling. Try to look at this as a long-term project. Even when you aren't gambling, the thoughts and feelings will be with you for some time. Read chapter 11 now. You'll learn more about quitting your gambling habit and developing healthy habits, including your competing response. You'll probably think of a few more habits that you would like to incorporate into your life. Focusing on the good habits will take your mind off the bad habits you are trying to eliminate. Habit changing just might become a habit!

You might be wondering how you are going to keep the changes you make. Will they end up being only short-term changes, or will you be free of your bad habits and keep the healthy ones for good? Read chapter 12 to help yourself fight back against temporary lapses in your Habit Change efforts.

Do you know others who might like to change their habits? Chapter 20 can help you make habit changing a family affair or a group effort. You don't all have to be interested in changing the same type of habit, only in changing whatever habits each of you finds troublesome in his or her life.

Part IV

Further Help

20

Family and Group
Habit Change

Alone we can do so little; together we can do so much.
—Helen Keller

You can't push anyone up the ladder unless he is willing to climb himself.
—Andrew Carnegie

Change is difficult, and even more so if tackled alone. For some people, habit change can be more easily tackled as a family or group. No, we don't mean everyone ganging up on Dad with his computer games, Mom with her gambling problem, or Junior with his wild spending. Everyone doesn't have to be working on the same habit.

Let's face it, we all have habits that we could change. The consequences of habits, and the results of changing them can range from moderate to extreme, but changing even little habits can have significant positive results. Families and groups working together with similar goals generate tremendous support and encouragement. It is unlikely that an entire family will have exactly the same habits in need of change. And that isn't even necessary to make good use of this program. Each family member can work on the habits he or she has decided to change.

Habit Change Strategy

The entire group doesn't have to have one habit in common, or even one type of habit. You only need to have *habit change* in common.

The Group Habit Change Program

Any group can work together to change individual habits. Each group member will simultaneously be working as an individual and as part of a group. Each will follow the Habit Change Program designed for his or her habit. The group should meet regularly, weekly if possible, to share progress and encourage each other. A group could also form as an Internet club, using e-mail or a Web site to communicate with each other. For example, Dr. Claiborn acts as an adviser to e-mail groups of people trying to help themselves with problems such as hoarding and skin picking.

Step 1: Preparation

Read chapters 1 to 6, and the first part of chapter 7, of *The Habit Change Workbook* at home, one or two chapters each week. It is important for all participants to write out their own answers and fill in the worksheets for themselves. Each week, the group should meet and discuss the chapters read that week. Even at this early stage in the process, encourage each other to make weekly goals. It is a good idea to track individual progress on a chart, showing each person's success at meeting his or her goals. The goals need to be stated in measurable terms so that you can all see your progress.

We have provided a Weekly Habit Change Success Chart for your use. Make enough copies of the blank chart for everyone in the group. Every week, write in an attainable but challenging goal, then rate success on a scale of one to ten. To make it more fun, you could use colorful stickers or stars instead of or in addition to ratings.

Weekly Habit Change Success Chart

Name: _____ Date: _____ to _____

Week	Goal	Rate
Week 1		
Week 2		
Week 3		
Week 4		
Week 5		
Week 6		
Week 7		
Week 8		
Week 9		
Week 10		
Week 11		
Week 12		

Chart 20a

Step 2: Action

When everyone has a good understanding of chapters 1 to 6 and the first part of chapter 7, each group member needs to begin work on the chapter for his or her particular habit. If some members have difficulty understanding the concepts in the book, paraphrasing the material and discussing the ideas in the group will help. Group members may want to review the other chapters in order to be more familiar with the habits others are working on. Continue to make individual goals each week. You may also want to make goals as a group. If some group members are lagging behind, keep in mind that they may still be in the early stages of change. Encourage them as they move from the contemplation stage to the action stage. Remember, goals should be appropriate for each person's stage of change. In the contemplation stage, getting information may be a reasonable goal.

Step 3: Support

Continue to meet regularly, weekly if possible. Discuss your struggles with habit change and be open to the comments and suggestions of others. Try to make meetings fun and uplifting. Think of ideas for inexpensive rewards that can be given to group members when they meet their weekly goals.

Step 4: Maintenance

Even after everyone in the group has worked through *The Habit Change Workbook*, continue to meet regularly. At this point you may want to meet biweekly or monthly. Some members may decide they want to work on other habits, while others will continue to work on maintaining their habit changes. In order to prevent relapses, ask for help—contact a helpful member of the group if you are having trouble maintaining your gains.

⋘ Habit Change Strategy

Don't stop meeting together too soon. Support and encouragement will be helpful in the maintenance stage also.

Children

The Habit Change Program can be an effective tool for helping children change habits. Read *The Habit Change Workbook* before working with the child. Explain the principles in words appropriate for the child's age. Help the child see the disadvantages and consequences of keeping the habit and the advantages of changing. Be sure to also acknowledge the advantages of keeping the habit, which will make it clear to the child that you understand that changing is hard or scary. Make the process fun, not threatening. Help the child choose an enjoyable competing response if possible.

Encourage the child to give input and work collaboratively on the change. Don't prescribe work for the child. He or she probably receives enough directions and commands, and you have probably told him or her to stop the habit plenty of times. Instead of nagging or dictating, aim to empower the child. Empowerment is especially important for children. By using our approach to habit change, you are giving them the tools to help them change their own habits and empowering them to shape their own lives.

Put great effort into developing rewards for making progress, even minimal progress at first. A star or sticker chart works well for young children—or older "children," like Cherry! A sticker is given for milestones in the child's habit change journey, such as a day without thumb sucking. Try to arrange the system so that a reward such as a sticker can be given at least once a day. At the end of the week a tangible reward can be given. There's no need to break the bank here—make the rewards affordable. You don't want to get to the middle of the program and find you can no longer afford your reward system. We've included a Daily Habit Change Success Chart, with spaces for recording daily goals and successes. Up to four stickers or stars can be awarded each day.

It is important to get input from the child about what rewards would be effective for him or her. We often presume we know what is important to a child. However, you may be surprised at what the child chooses. It may be something as inexpensive as time spent playing a game with Mom or Dad. Help the child learn ways to reward himself or herself also. When Cherry's son was a teenager, he rewarded himself for getting school projects done. The rewards he had received from his parents when he was a child had taught him the value of using rewards as incentives. Communication is especially important with children changing habits. Avoid criticizing, and heap on the praise, even for small efforts and progress.

The rest of this chapter will offer additional helpful advice, suitable for both adults and children.

Daily Habit Change Success Chart

Name: _____   Date: _____ to _____

Day	Goal	1	2	3	4
Sunday					
Monday					
Tuesday					
Wednesday					
Thursday					
Friday					
Saturday					

Chart 20b

How Family Members Can Help

You need your family's support as you change your habits. If other family members are also making changes, they need your support. But wait a minute—let's use what we've learned about examining our automatic thoughts here. Do you really *need* support? What if your family doesn't want to give you support? What if they like you just the way you are? In this context, *need* probably isn't the best word. You *want* support. Making changes is usually easier if done with the support of family and friends. If your family can't provide support, seek it from friends or a support group.

The Habit Change Program offers several areas where support can be helpful:

- **Managing triggers.** Certain situations probably trigger your habit. Family members may be willing to help you arrange your home environment in order to remove or reduce the effects of some of these triggers. This task takes a bit of negotiating and compromise. For example, getting rid of *unhealthy* snacks is good for the entire family, but you can't expect *all* snack foods to be removed. Don't depend on your family to help you make changes. Remember, *you* are making changes and *you* are responsible for the changes.

- **Using your competing response.** You may want to involve family and friends in your competing response. If going for walks is one of your competing responses, ask family members to come along. If reading is one of your competing responses, perhaps someone will join you in reading a novel and discuss it with you. Don't depend on it, though. Change is still your responsibility, with or without help. When the urges hit, be ready with competing responses you can do with others and competing responses you can do alone. Don't depend on family members to take a walk with you every time your urge hits.

- **Using rewards.** Rewards can take on special meaning when others are involved. Dinner for two may be more enjoyable than dinner alone. Shopping for a special outfit is often more fun when someone else comes along. Make rewards be a time of celebration with those you love.

- **Preventing relapse.** Sometimes habits come sneaking back into our lives. What could be your warning signs? Discuss these signs with family and friends. Ask them to remind you of your goals when they see the warning signs. No judgment, no punishment—just a gentle reminder, then praise when you get back on track. Read more about relapse prevention in chapter 12.

- **Communication.** Talk to your family members about your changes. Listen to their feelings. They'll probably be glad to see you making positive changes, but they may also feel grief over the loss of the old you. Some may also have negative feelings about their own habits. Be aware of the temptation to proselytize. No one is more annoying to a person thinking about trying to change than a person who has overcome the same habit and preaches about it. This process is about changing *your* habits, not the habits of those around you. Let them go through their own stages of change. Your pushing may even backfire and result in an even stronger determination to keep their habits.

You may want to consider making amends if your habit has caused harm to others. Saying, "I'm sorry" won't completely erase the harm, but it can be a first step toward healing relationships. It can ease your guilt and the anger or hurt they feel. And don't forget to forgive yourself—look toward the future, not back to the past.

❀ Habit Change Strategy

Family support is important, but not absolutely necessary. Without it, you can still change. And your efforts to change may encourage your family members to be more supportive.

What If Your Loved One Doesn't Want to Change?

Does a family member or friend have a habit that drives you crazy? Is it just an irritating quirk or is it quite disrupting to your lives? Why does it bother you? What are the negative consequences of the habit? What is the advantage of changing? Try to answer these questions before speaking to your loved one about the habit. Reading chapters 1 through 6 will help you better understand habits and answer these questions. Armed with this information, you'll be ready to speak to your family member or friend about the habit. Choose an appropriate time and place; it's not good to talk about excessive TV-watching during the person's favorite program, for example. Choose a time when you are both relaxed and in good moods. Express yourself with an attitude of love and concern, not anger or bitterness.

Tell your loved one how the habit affects you. Often, we don't realize the extent to which our behavior affects others. Then ask how the habit affects your loved one's own life. He or she may not have realized there was a problem—or he or she may have recognized the problem but didn't know how to change. If the person is willing to consider changing, offer to help work through *The Habit Change Workbook* and act as a support person. Make it clear that you want to help, but only as much as he or she wishes.

What if your family member still doesn't want to consider changing? Then you are the one with a problem. You need to make a decision. Will you stay connected with that person and tolerate the habit? Or distance yourself from a relationship that may have a negative effect on your life? Whatever you decide never allow yourself or other loved ones to be in danger because of the person's habit. People can and do change. There is help and hope. Gently, keep demonstrating how the habit is affecting your relationship. Example is a great motivator. Set a good example by changing a habit of your own, even if it's only a minor problem habit. Seeing you work through the Habit Change Program might encourage your loved one to tackle his or her own habit.

Resources

For knowledge, too, is itself power.

—Francis Bacon

Now this is not the end. It is not even the beginning of the end. But it is, perhaps, the end of the beginning.

—Sir Winston Churchill

Helpful Books about Change

Behavioral Perspective

Azrin, Nathan, and R. Gregory Nunn. 1977. *Habit Control in a Day.* New York: Simon & Schuster.

Birkedahl, Nonie. 1990. *The Habit Control Workbook.* Oakland, Calif.: New Harbinger Publications, Inc.

LeVert, Suzanne, and Gary McClain. 1998. *The Complete Idiot's Guide to Breaking Bad Habits.* New York: Alpha Books.

Cognitive Perspective

Burns, David D. 1993. *Ten Days to Self-Esteem.* New York: William Morrow and Co.

———. 1999. *The Feeling Good Handbook.* New York: Plume.

———. 1999b. *Feeling Good: The New Mood Therapy.* New York: Avon.

Daley, Dennis C. 1998. *Kicking Addictive Habits Once and for All: A Relapse-Prevention Guide.* San Francisco: Jossey-Bass Publishers.

Ellis, Albert. 1994. *How to Stubbornly Refuse to Make Yourself Miserable about Anything, Yes, Anything!* New York: Carol Publishing Group.

Greenberger, Dennis, and Christine Padesky. 1995. *Mind Over Mood: Change How You Feel by Changing the Way You Think.* New York: Guilford Press.

Harvath, A. Thomas. 1998. *Sex, Drugs, Gambling, and Chocolate: A Workbook for Overcoming Addictions.* Atascadero, Calif.: Impact Publishers, Inc.

Knaus, William J. 1994. *Change Your Life Now: Powerful Techniques for Positive Change.* New York: John Wiley and Sons, Inc.

McKay, Matthew, Martha Davis, and Patrick Fanning. 1997. *Thoughts and Feelings: Taking Control of Your Moods and Your Life.* Oakland, Calif.: New Harbinger Publications, Inc.

Prochaska, James O., John C. Norcross, and Carlo C. DiClemente. 1994. *Changing for Good: A Revolutionary Six-Stage Program for Overcoming Bad Habits and Moving Your Life Positively Forward.* New York: Avon Books.

Motivational Perspective

Gabor, Don. 1998. *Big Things Happen When You Do the Little Things Right.* Rocklin, Calif.: Prima Publishing.

Simon, Sidney R. 1998. *Getting Unstuck: Breaking Through Your Barriers to Change.* New York: Warner Books.

Spiritual Perspective

Gregory, Susan. 1994. *Out of the Rat Race: A Practical Guide to Taking Control of Your Time and Money so You Can Enjoy Life More.* Ann Arbor, Mich.: Vine Books.

Jantz, Gregory L. 1998. *Hidden Dangers of the Internet: Using It without Abusing It.* Wheaton, Ill.: Harold Shaw Publishers.

O'Connor, Karen. 1992. *When Spending Takes the Place of Feeling.* Nashville: Thomas Nelson Publishers.

Tirabassi, Becky. 1999. *Change Your Life, Achieve a Healthy Body, Heal Relationships, and Connect with God.* New York: G. P. Putnam's Sons.

Relaxation

Benson, Herbert, and Miriam Z. Klipper. 2000. *The Relaxation Response.* New York: William Morrow and Co.

Davis, Martha, Elizabeth Robbins Eshelman, and Matthew McKay. 2000. *The Relaxation and Stress Reduction Workbook*, 5th ed. Oakland, Calif.: New Harbinger Publications, Inc.

McKay, Matthew, and Patrick Fanning. 1997. *The Daily Relaxer.* Oakland, Calif.: New Harbinger Publications, Inc.

Specific Habits

Benson, Herbert, and Eileen M. Stuart. 1992. *The Wellness Book: The Comprehensive Guide to Maintaining Health and Treating Stress-Related Illness.* New York: Fireside.

Bookspan, Jolie. 1998. *Health and Fitness in Plain English.* New York: Kensington Books.

Burns, David D. 1999. *Intimate Connections.* New York: New American Library.

Catalano, Ellen Mohr, and Nina Sonenberg. 1993. *Consuming Passions: Help for Compulsive Shoppers.* Oakland, Calif.: New Harbinger Publications, Inc.

Coleman, Sally, and Nancy Hull-Mast. 1992. *Can't Buy Me Love: Freedom from Compulsive Spending and Money Obsession.* Minneapolis, Minn.: Fairview Press.

Federman, Edward, Charles Drebing, and Christopher Krebs. 2000. *Don't Leave It to Chance: A Guide for Families of Problem Gamblers.* Oakland, Calif.: New Harbinger Publications, Inc.

Greenfield, David N. 1999. *Virtual Addiction: Help for Netheads, Cyberfreaks, and Those Who Love Them.* Oakland, Calif.: New Harbinger Publications, Inc.

Hauri, Peter, Shirley Linde, and Philip Westbrook. 1996. *No More Sleepless Nights: A Proven Program to Conquer Insomnia*. New York: John Wiley and Sons.

Hauri, Peter, Murray Jarman, and Shirley Linde. 2001. *No More Sleepless Nights Workbook: Tracking Your Progress Toward a Great Night's Sleep*. New York: John Wiley and Sons.

Roberts, Susan. 1995. *Living Without Procrastination: How to Stop Postponing Your Life*. Oakland, Calif.: New Harbinger Publications, Inc.

Wallace, Patricia. 1999. *The Psychology of the Internet*. Cambridge, U.K.: Cambridge University Press.

Walsleben, Joyce, and Rita Baron-Faust. 2000. *A Woman's Guide to Sleep: Guaranteed Solutions for a Good Night's Rest*. New York: Crown Publishers.

Young, Kimberly S. 1998. *Caught in the Net: How to Recognize the Signs of Internet Addiction—and a Winning Strategy for Recovery*. New York: John Wiley and Sons.

Trichotillomania and Skin Picking

Keuthen, Nancy J., Dan J. Stein, and Gary A. Christenson. 2001. *Help for Hair Pullers*. Oakland, Calif.: New Harbinger Publications, Inc.

Penzel, Fred. 2000. *Obsessive Compulsive Disorders: A Complete Guide to Getting Well and Staying Well*. New York: Oxford University Press.

Stein, Dan, Gary Christenson, and Eric Hollander, eds. 1999. *Trichotillomania*. Washington, D.C.: American Psychiatric Press.

Obsessive Compulsive Disorder

Baer, Lee. 2000. *Getting Control: Overcoming Your Obsessions and Compulsions*. New York: Plume.

———. 2001. *The Imp of the Mind: Exploring the Silent Epidemic of Obsessive Bad Thoughts*. New York: E. P. Dutton.

Ciarrocchi, Joseph W. 1995. *The Doubting Disease: Help for Scrupulosity and Religious Compulsions*. Mahwah, N.J.: Paulist Press.

Foa, Edna B. and Reid Wilson. 1991. *Stop Obsessing! How to Overcome Your Obsessions and Compulsions*. New York: Bantam Books.

Hyman, Bruce M., and Cherry Pedrick. 1999. *The OCD Workbook: Your Guide to Breaking Free from Obsessive-Compulsive Disorder*. Oakland, Calif.: New Harbinger Publications, Inc.

Osborn, Ian. 1998. *Tormenting Thoughts and Secret Rituals: The Hidden Epidemic of Obsessive-Compulsive Disorder*. New York: Pantheon Books.

Penzel, Fred. 2000. *Obsessive Compulsive Disorders: A Complete Guide to Getting Well and Staying Well*. New York: Oxford University Press.

Steketee, Gail, and Kerin White. 1990. *When Once Is Not Enough: Help for Obsessive Compulsives*. Oakland, Calif.: New Harbinger Publications, Inc.

Schwartz, Jeffrey, and Beverly Beyette. 1996. *Brain Lock: Free Yourself from Obsessive-Compulsive Behavior*. New York: ReganBooks.

Body Dysmporphic Disorder

Pope, Harrison G. Jr., Katharine A. Phillips, and Roberto Olivardia. 2000. *The Adonis Complex: The Secret Crisis of Male Body Obsession*. New York: The Free Press, a division of Simon & Schuster, Inc.

Phillips, Katharine A. 1996. *The Broken Mirror: Understanding and Treating Body Dysmorphic Disorder*. New York: Oxford University Press.

Addictions

Fanning, Patrick, and John T. O'Neill. 1996. *The Addiction Workbook: A Step-by-Step Guide to Quitting Alcohol and Drugs.* Oakland, Calif.: New Harbinger Publications, Inc.

Organizations of Interest

Albert Ellis Institute, 45 East 65th Street, New York, NY 10021. Internet: http://www.rebt.org

Al-Anon Family Groups, Inc., 1600 Corporate Landing Parkway, Virginia Beach, VA 23456. (804) 563-1600, (800) 344-2666. Internet: http://www.al-anon.org

Alcoholics Anonymous, General Services Offices, 475 Riverside Drive, New York, NY 10115. (212) 870-3400. Internet: http://www.alcoholic-anonymous.org

American Foundation for Suicide Prevention, 120 Wall Street, Twenty-second Floor, New York, NY 10005. (212) 363-3500. Internet: http://www.afsp.org

American Heart Association, National Center, 7272 Greenville Avenue, Dallas, TX 75231-4596. (800) 242-8721, (214) 373-6300. Internet: http://www.amhart.org

American Lung Association, 1740 Broadway, New York, NY 10019. Internet: http://www.lungusa.org

Anorexia Nervosa and Related Eating Disorders, Inc., P. O. Box 5102, Eugene, OR 97405. (541) 344-1144. Internet: http://www.anred.com

Anxiety Disorders Association of America, Department A, 6000 Executive Blvd., Suite 513, Rockville, MD 20852. (301) 231-9350. Internet: http://www.adaa.org

Association for the Advancement of Behavior Therapy, 305 Seventh Avenue, New York, NY 10001-6008. (212) 647-1890. Internet: http://server.psych.vt.edu/aabt/

The Center for Internet Studies, Virtual Addiction.com. Internet: http://www.virtual-addiction.com

Debtors Anonymous General Service Office, P. O. Box 400, Grand Central Station, New York, NY 10163-0400.

Gam-Anon International Service Office, Inc., P. O. Box 157, Whitestone, NY 11357. (718) 352-1671. Internet: http://www.gam-anon.org (support for families of people with gambling problems)

Gamblers Anonymous, International Service Office, P. O. Box 17173, Los Angeles, CA 90017. (213) 386-3789. Internet: http://www.gamblersanonymous.org/

Internet Anonymous. Internet: http://members.aol.com/lainmacn/addicts/

Internet Junkies Anonymous (IJA). Internet: http://www.cyberramp.net/~bam/links/ ol.html

National Alliance for the Mentally Ill, 200 North Glebe Road, Suite 1015, Arlington, VA 22203-3754. (800) 950-NAMI (800-950-6264)

National Anxiety Foundation, 3135 Custer Drive, Lexington, KY 40517-4001. (606) 272-7166. Internet: http://lexington-on-line.com/naf.ocd.2.html

National Association of Anorexia Nervosa and Associated Disorders, Box 7, Highland Park, IL 60035. (847) 831-3438. Internet: http://www.healthtouch.com

National Depressive and Manic-Depressive Association, 730 North Franklin, #501, Chicago, IL 60610. (800) 82N-DMDA

National Foundation for Consumer Credit, 8611 Second Avenue #100, Silver Spring, MD 20910. www.nfcc.org

National Foundation for Depressive Illness, P. O. Box 2257, New York, NY 10116. (800) 248-4344

National Council on Problem Gambling, 208 G Street, NE, Second floor, Washington, DC, 20002. (202) 547-9204. Nationwide Help Line: (800) 522-4700

National Institute of Mental Health, 9000 Rockville Pike, Building 10, Room 30-41, Bethesda, MD 20892. (301) 496-3421. Information services: Panic and other anxiety disorders: (800) 647-2642. Depression: (800) 421-4211

National Mental Health Association, 1201 Prince Street, Alexandria, VA 22314-2971. (703) 684-7722

National Mental Health Consumers' Self-Help Clearinghouse, 1211 Chestnut Street, Philadelphia, PA 19107. (800) 553-4539

Obsessive-Compulsive Foundation, Inc. P. O. Box 70, Milford, CT 06460-0070. (203) 878-5669. Internet: http://www.ocfoundation.org

The President's Council on Physical Fitness and Sports, 400 Sixteenth Avenue NW, Washington, DC 20036

Trichotillomania Learning Center, 1215 Mission Street, Suite 2, Santa Cruz, CA 95050. (408) 457-1004. Internet: http://www.trich.org/

References

American Psychiatric Association. 1994. *Diagnostic and Statistical Manual of Mental Disorders* (DSM-IV). 4th ed. Washington, D.C.: American Psychiatric Association.

Azrin, N. H., and G. R. Nunn. 1977. *Habit Control in a Day: Simple, Effective, and Professionally Tested Techniques for Eliminating the Physical Habits that May Be Keeping You from Leading a Normal Life.* New York: Simon and Schuster.

———. 1973. Habit-reversal: A method of eliminating nervous habits and tics. *Behavior Research and Therapy.* 11:619–628.

Baker, R. C., and D. S. Kirschenbaum. 1998. Weight control during the holidays: Highly consistent self-monitoring as a potentially useful coping mechanism. *Health Psychology.* 17(4): 367–70.

Beck, J. S. 1995. *Cognitive Therapy: Basics and Beyond.* New York: Guilford Press.

Bujold, A., R. Ladouceur, C. Sylvain, and J. M. Boisvert. 1994. Treatment of pathological gamblers: An experimental study. *Journal of Behavior Therapy and Experimental Psychiatry.* 25(4): 275–83.

Burns, D. D. 1999. *The Feeling Good Handbook.* New York: Plume.

Christenson, G., and C. Mansueto. 1999. Trichotillomania: Description, characteristics, and phenomenology. In *Trichotillomania,* edited by D. Stein, G. Christenson, and E. Hollander. Washington, D.C.: American Psychiatric Press, Inc.

Fanning, P., and J. T. O'Neill. 1996. *The Addiction Workbook: A Step-by-Step Guide to Quitting Alcohol and Drugs.* Oakland, Calif.: New Harbinger Publications, Inc.

Federman, E., C. Drebing, and C. Krebs. 2000. *Don't Leave It to Chance: A Guide for Families of Problem Gamblers.* Oakland, Calif.: New Harbinger Publications, Inc.

Frankel, M. S., and M. Merbaum. 1982. Effects of therapist contact and a self-control manual on nail biting reduction. *Behavior Therapy.* 13:125–29.

Hansen, D. J., A. C. Tishelman, R. P. Hawkins, and K. J. Doepke. 1990. Habits with potential as disorders: Prevalence, severity, and other characteristics among college students. *Behavior Modification.* 14:66-80.

Idzikowski, C. 1999. *The Insomnia Book.* New York: Penguin Studio.

Marlat, G. A. 1985. Relapse prevention: Theoretical rationale and overview of the model. In *Relapse Prevention,* edited by G. A. Marlat and J. Gordon. New York: Guilford Press.

Miltenberger, R. G., W. R. Fuqua, and D. W. Woods. 1998. Applying behavior analysis to clinical problems: Review and analysis of habit reversal. *Journal of Applied Behavior Analysis.* 31:447–469.

Morin, C. M., C. Colecchi, J. Stone, R. Sood, and D. Brink. 1999. Behavioral and pharmacological therapies for late-life insomnia: A randomized controlled trial. *Journal of the American Medical Association.* 281(11) (March 17):991–99.

Morin C. M., P. J. Hauri, C. A. Espie, A. J. Spielman, D. J. Buysse, and R. R. Bootzin. 1999. Nonpharmacologic treatment of chronic insomnia, an American Academy of Sleep Medicine review. *Sleep.* 8(December 15, 22):1134–56.

Penzel, F. 2000. *Obsessive-Compulsive Disorders: A Complete Guide to Getting Well and Staying Well.* New York: Oxford University Press.

Prochaska, J. O., J. C. Norcross, and C. C. DiClemente. 1994. *Changing for Good, A Revolutionary Six Stage Program for Overcoming Bad Habits and Moving Your Life Positively Forward.* New York: Avon.

Prochaska, J. O., C. C. DiClemente, and J. C. Norcross. 1992. In search of how people change: Applications to addictive behaviors. *American Psychologist.* 47:1102–14

Reeve, E. 1999. Hair pulling in children and adolescents. In *Trichotillomania,* edited by D. Stein, G. Christenson, and E. Hollander. Washington, D.C.: American Psychiatric Press, Inc.

Spunt, B., I. Dupont, H. Lesieur, H. J. Liberty, and D. Hunt. 1998. Pathological gambling and substance misuse: A review of the literature. *Substance Use and Misuse.* 33(13):2535–2560.

Stein, D., R. Sullivan, B. van Heerden, S. Seedat, and D. Niehaus. 1998. Neurobiology of trichotillomania. *CNS Spectrums.* (October):47–55.

Stein, D., G. Christenson, and E. Hollander. *Trichotillomania.* Washington, D.C.: American Psychiatric Press, Inc.

Warmbrodt. L., E. Hardy, and S. Chrisman. 1996. Understanding trichotillomania. *Journal of Psychosocial Nursing.* 34(12):11–15

Wilhelm, S., N. Keuthen, T. Deckersbach, I. Engelhard, A. Forker, L. Baer, R. O'Sullivan, and M. Jenike. 1999. Self-injurious skin picking: Clinical characteristics and comorbidity. *Journal of Clinical Psychiatry.* July:454–59.

Woods, D., and R. G. Miltenberger. 1996. Are persons with nervous habits nervous? A preliminary examination of habit function in a nonreferred population. *Journal of Applied Behavior Analysis.* 29:259–61.

Woods, D., R. G. Miltenberger, and A. D. Flach. 1996. Habits, tics, and stuttering: Prevalence and relation to anxiety and somatic awareness. *Behavior Modification.* 2:216–25

James M. Claiborn, Ph.D., ABPP, is a licensed psychologist in private practice in New Hampshire, where he specializes in cognitive behavioral therapy. He is a Diplomate of the American Board of Professional Psychology in Counseling Psychology, a Fellow of the Academy of Counseling Psychology, a Founding Fellow of the Academy of Cognitive Therapy, and a member of the Scientific Advisory Board of the Obsessive Compulsive Foundation. He is also a member of the American Psychological Association and the Association for the Advancement of Behavior Therapy.

Cherry Pedrick is a registered nurse and freelance writer in North Las Vegas, Nevada. In 1994 she was diagnosed with OCD, which began an intensive search for knowledge, effective treatment, and management of compulsive behaviors. She is also coauthor of *The OCD Workbook: Your Guide to Breaking Free from Obsessive-Compulsive Disorder*.

Some Other
New Harbinger Titles

The Anxiety & Phobia Workbook, 3rd edition, Item PHO3 $19.95

Beyond Anxiety & Phobia, Item BYAP $19.95

The Self-Nourishment Companion, Item SNC $10.95

The Healing Sorrow Workbook, Item HSW $17.95

The Daily Relaxer, Item DALY $12.95

Stop Controlling Me!, Item SCM $13.95

Lift Your Mood Now, Item LYMN $12.95

An End to Panic, 2nd edition, Item END2 $19.95

Serenity to Go, Item STG $12.95

The Depression Workbook, Item DEP $19.95

The OCD Workbook, Item OCD $18.95

The Anger Control Workbook, Item ACWB $17.95

Flying without Fear, Item FLY $14.95

The Shyness & Social Anxiety Workbook, Item SHYW $15.95

The Relaxation & Stress Reduction Workbook, 5th edition, Item RS5 $19.95

Energy Tapping, Item ETAP $14.95

Stop Walking on Eggshells, Item WOE $14.95

Angry All the Time, Item ALL 12.95

Living without Procrastination, Item $12.95

Hypnosis for Change, 3rd edition, Item HYP3 $16.95

Don't Take it Personally, Item DOTA $15.95

Toxic Coworkers, Item TOXC $13.95

Letting Go of Anger, Item LET $13.95

Call **toll free, 1-800-748-6273,** or log on to our online bookstore at **www.newharbinger.com** to order. Have your Visa or Mastercard number ready. Or send a check for the titles you want to New Harbinger Publications, Inc., 5674 Shattuck Ave., Oakland, CA 94609. Include $4.50 for the first book and 75¢ for each additional book, to cover shipping and handling. (California residents please include appropriate sales tax.) Allow two to five weeks for delivery.

Prices subject to change without notice.